Praise for *Empire of the Owls*

"The Old South died hard, after a gigantic struggle unsurpassed in American history in high principle, valour, and sacrifice. Even worse, perhaps, the Old South has been buried under an avalanche of libels. It is very seldom allowed to speak for itself, especially in recent decades. Mr. Traywick has allowed the South, and especially Virginia, to speak for itself, in a variety of voices and in a very original and persuasive way. Not to be missed by anyone looking for a different perspective on the War for Southern Independence."

— CLYDE N. WILSON, PH. D.
Emeritus Distinguished Professor of History,
University of South Carolina

*

"For years, I have known several things about Bo Traywick. He has strong opinions, he doesn't mince words, and he does meticulous research. Here he has shared that research with us, letting the words from history speak for themselves to support the thesis that he lays out in his introduction. I often tell people to go to the primary sources. Traywick takes us there in *Empire of the Owls*."

— HON. S. WAITE RAWLS, III
President and CEO, Museum of the
Confederacy

*

"This splendid book does what nearly all modern histories of the Civil War era fail to deliver by providing an objective and fair accounting of what actually took place in that consequential time in American history. We take a walk through the past to view America and the South as it existed from 1859 through 1865 and the subsequent Reconstruction era. The tale is told in a straightforward chronology as the gentle agricultural Southern people are swept up economically, politically and militarily by the larger imperialistic industrialized North bent on establishing political and economic hegemony over the South. We meet the leading figures of the day such as Lincoln, Lee, Davis, Grant, and civilian leaders such as W. E. B. DuBois and Booker T. Washington. And we are told the story by people who actually lived, fought, and wrote during the time, their analysis unfiltered by today's politics and culture which predetermines how all modern accounts of the war are spun. I always have preferred firsthand narratives to secondary historical analysis delivered by progressive historians who interpret for modern readers what they should think and feel. *Empire of the Owls* demonstrates that the South is not evil. The Confederacy is shown to actually have a *raison d'etre* and proud Virginians such as Mr. Traywick can vividly recall and relate what the South stood for and stands for today.

"Mr. Traywick's skillful editing of the voices of the past explodes the Yankee version of American history, carefully and clearly analyzing the systematic and cruel destruction of the South. From John Brown's raid, the great battles, slavery and emancipation, and finally Appomattox, the end result of this tragic fight was a foregone conclusion. Might and money triumphs over right. The South refused to go quietly into the night, preferring to retain their liberty, economy, honor and way of life, and their brave fight against the North will be forever remembered. This book goes a long way in helping us understand what really happened."

— HON. BRAGDON BOWLING
Former Commander, Virginia Division, Sons of
Confederate Veterans
Former Commander of the Army of
Northern Virginia of the SCV
Former President, Richmond Civil War Roundtable

*

"H. V. Traywick's *Empire of the Owls*, is characteristically Bo – iconoclastic, judging truth according to where his research takes him, and forthright in his expression. For some, because this book rejects established perceptions, they will immediately reject this book. For others, and I believe for many, it will be warmly received as the struggles of the South during and after the Civil War are placed before us in the voices of those who lived during the period. A well-edited volume does what a contemporary writer's running narrative would find difficult to accomplish.

"By bringing together carefully introduced and edited texts drawn from diverse sources, Traywick has enabled the unique but often silenced voice of the South to be heard and appreciated. The writer has broad interests coupled with eclectic knowledge, and he draws upon all of his resources to set contextually each quoted passage. Letting individuals of the period speak for themselves is crucially important, for it both challenges long held perceptions and serves to redeem those often falsely castigated.

"This volume is neither an attempt to return to a neo-orthodox statement of the conflict fought valiantly but lost by the South, nor is it an attempt to sanctify the South, its leaders, or its aspirations. The *Empire of the Owls* is simply an attempt to permit real life individuals to interpret the history as they lived it – this could not be a more simple task, nor could it be a more difficult task!"

— FRANK E. EAKIN, JR. PH. D.
Marcus M. and Carole M. Weinstein and Gilbert M. and Fannie S. Rosenthal
Professor of Jewish and Christian Studies
University of Richmond

*

EMPIRE OF THE OWLS

Reflections on the North's War against

Southern Secession

Collated and edited by
H. V. Traywick, Jr.

[signature] Dec 4, 2013

If the Union were to undertake to enforce by arms
the allegiance of the confederate States by military means,
it would be in a position very analogous to that of England
at the time of the War of Independence.
- Alexis de Tocqueville
from Democracy in America (1)

FRONT COVER
Richmond, Virginia, April 1865 - Library of Congress

First Printing

Copyright © 2013

Author - H. V. Traywick, Jr.

Publisher
Wayne Dementi
Dementi Milestone Publishing, Inc.
Manakin-Sabot, VA 23103
www.dementimilestonepublishing.com

Cataloging-in-publication data for this book is available from The Library of Congress.

ISBN: 978-0-9889099-4-6

Graphic design by:
Dianne Dementi

Printed in U.S.A.

RIGHT *General Robert E. Lee in 1863* (altered to three-quarter image) – Courtesy of the Virginia Historical Society

RIGHT *Map of the Virginia Campaign* - Courtesy of Virginia Historical Society

RIGHT *The Army of Northern Virginia Crossing the Potomac September 1862* - Courtesy of Library of Congress

Previous to Antietam

To the Knight of Melrose

and

to His Lady

TABLE OF CONTENTS

FOREWORD

By Dr. H. Jackson Darst

This is an unusual and marvelous book. Since the War there has been an endless stream of volumes about the Cause and conflict. Some have been personal recollections of participants, but most are secondary accounts – such as Douglas Southall Freeman's monumental works. This volume places the reader in the center of activities through the use, in large part, of selected accounts by contemporary writers.

Early on, the reading is in the neighborhood of Patrick Henry's plantation, Red Hill, where the happy and pleasant life of old Virginia still prevails, but at the same time Henry's patriotic sons and their neighbors are prepared to defend Virginia against the invaders. Four years later, we stand beside General Lee at Appomattox and hear him say he would "rather die a thousand deaths" than surrender the ragged, barefoot, starving army to the industrial might and enormous horde of the enemy.

The motivation for this project, which has taken thirty years to complete, is in Captain Traywick's youth. "Bo," as he is known to his friends, was reared in a city where the fortifications erected to protect against the enemy were still conspicuous. Around the dinner table and elsewhere, he was exposed to the stories of the War and its tragic aftermath told by the children and grandchildren of the men in gray.

I can easily identify with Bo's experience. It was my good fortune to know two Confederate veterans, both over ninety and close kin, one of whom was the son of the author of the Virginia Ordinance of Secession. We stood in awe of these old soldiers, and the entire community held them in honor and respect. A battle had taken place a few miles away, and our town was burned. These events were recounted by the children of the veterans – my great-aunts, uncles, and grandmother.

Those who heard family accounts of our efforts to maintain the Constitution as it was understood by our Revolutionary fore-bears are fast disappearing. Where are those who should be listening? Scattered like the wind to places where there are no familiar landmarks or older members of their families. Then there is ignorance and lack of interest. For many, the Lost Cause is indeed lost!

Further, we are in an age when history is being rewritten to conform to political correctness. These modifications range from Mr. Jefferson's personal life to the motives, sacrifices and losses which our fathers experienced in their struggle for old Virginia. By providing intimate and vivid accounts, this book should kindle in this and future generations an interest in our glorious Cause, and correct the current distorted pages of history.

> Dr. H. Jackson Darst
> Historian, Educator, Farmer, Conserva-
> tionist, Registrar for Virginia's Society of
> Colonial Wars, and Registrar, Society of the
> Cincinnati in the State of Virginia.

EDITOR'S NOTE

Over forty years ago I left Virginia to serve a tour of duty in Vietnam. By the time I returned, I felt that everything I had ever believed in had been shot all to hell, so I wiped the slate clean, caught a freight train, and set out in search of the Truth. After wandering far - body and soul - on land and on the sea, I found myself one balmy, drizzly November day in the late 70's back home in Virginia. The crows cawing over the broom straw and the dark pines brought back memories of my boyhood when I walked the woods and fields with my dog and my gun, and I remember having on that day a sense of being in continuity with something eternal.

I was riding up Route 30 in a blue Ford pickup truck with Dalton Brownley and Eugene "Dilly-Dally" Norman. We were the survey crew for G. T. Wilson, Land Surveyor, whose office was above the post office in the town of West Point. As it was too wet to do survey work in the field that day, we were on the way to King William Courthouse to do some deed research.

The old brick courthouse buildings, surrounded by woods and fields, were set back off the road in a grove of trees. The hamlet itself was lost in time, with the peacefulness disturbed only by a passing car or an occasional log truck heading down for the paper mill at West Point. A little sign out on the road read:

King William Courthouse
Oldest courthouse
in continuous use
in the United States

One could almost expect to see Patrick Henry coming down here on a blooded horse from neighboring Hanover County to argue a case.

In front of the courthouse was an ancient moss-covered brick wall of colonial-era vintage enclosing a square, in the center of which stood a Confederate monument beneath the bare branches of the trees. At the foot of the monument, a lone, wet, and bedraggled rooster was pecking for worms that had come up with the misty rain. I stopped for a moment and read the names and the units carved into the granite. Marse Robert's men. I looked up at the soldier, who stood there atop the pedestal, hands resting on the muzzle of his musket, gazing across the land he had fought for, a land little changed at this particular spot even now, except for the telephone poles and the cars over there on the tar road. I remarked to myself how young he looked for someone who had fought in a war over a hundred years ago, but of course that was just a trick of the mind, for I was remembering the news reports on the radio when the last old soldiers were passing away back in the 50's.

Standing there, I remembered sitting at the dinner table as a boy listening to the family's stories about the War. I remembered hearing about how Uncle Beaufort had been killed before Richmond, and how after the war had stormed away northward his father drove a wagon up from South Carolina to get his boy and bring him back home. And I remembered hearing about how Grandpa Traywick had lost four brothers in that war, and how he himself had been captured up in the Valley and sent to Point Lookout when he was nineteen years old, and how they put him in a long wagon train full of other prisoners of war and galloped the teams all night down the Valley Pike to Winchester for fear of Mosby's men. I remembered the story of how Grandma Pearl, as a little girl, had "refugeed" out of West Virginia with her family back to Bedford in the dead of winter because of all the bushwhackers and barn burners out there in the border country. And I remembered hearing how one night she slipped out of bed and crept to the top of the stairs and heard her fifteen-year-old brother - home on leave - downstairs in the parlor sitting on the sofa with his mother, crying because he didn't want to go back, and how his mother told him that he had to go so he wouldn't be shot as a deserter. I remembered hearing the story about one of my grandmother's elderly cousins, who - as a young child - was at home with her family at Curdsville the night before the surrender, when Grant and Meade and some staff officers - bivouacked nearby - were in the parlor listening to her mother playing the piano. And I remembered hearing how she toddled over to General Grant with a switch in her hand and began switching him on the boots, saying "Look, Papa! I can whip the Yankees!" until her father gently stopped her. And I remembered hearing how, after the war, Grandpa Crute told his people that they were free to go, but that he needed help on the place there at Melrose and they needed work and some place to live, and that they could stay on if they wanted to, and how they and Grandpa worked out some arrangement and all of them stayed. I had not forgotten these things, but they had been buried under another war and another revolution.

Some had gone to Vietnam while others had gone to Woodstock. The three of us had gone to war. Dalton had come home and thrown his uniform into the creek. I had come home and hit the road. Eugene had just come home. Dalton once said that countries make mistakes sometimes, just like people do. This remark eventually led me to discover that nations and "Great Men" (as well as Missus O'Leary's cow or the random act of an idiot,) may "change the course of history," but no one can direct the tide of evolution; men and nations can only hope to navigate that tide the best they can using their skill, wisdom, and experience. History itself is merely the chronicle - the "log book" - of the voyage (1).

If Dalton was right, then I suppose his observation would apply to me as well. I don't know what that says about my navigational skills up to that point. It was the dawning of the Age of Aquarius, and Tradition once again was under assault from all quarters. I had found myself being swept along by that tide and sometimes engaged in things that were not very well calculated to improve my chances for salvation. That was the least of it; among other things - in order to conform to the revolutionary herd - I had at one point repudiated my heritage.

Although I was later to realize that the Truth lies before us, and that it is only the murk of our perception that prevents us from seeing it clearly, I felt at that point in my life that I had not been faring very well in my quest. As the rooster pecked worms at the base of the monument I looked up at the soldier. Perhaps I could learn something from him. He had been through far worse things than anything I had experienced, but as his Traditions had come crashing down all around him in a bloody cataclysm I suspected that he had carried himself with a little more dignity and self-respect than I had done. He had certainly not denied his heritage and sold his birthright for a mess of pottage.

And as I stood there thinking these things, looking up at the soldier standing like a stone wall against the low-scudding clouds, the cock crowed. That was the beginning of this manuscript.

* * *

… but when I met
Merlin, and ask'd him if these things were truth…
He laugh'd as is his wont, and answer'd me
In riddling triplets of old time, and said:
    Rain, rain, and sun! a rainbow in the sky!
A young man will be wiser by and by;
An old man's wit may wander ere he die.
    Rain, rain, and sun! a rainbow on the lea!
And truth is this to me, and that to thee;
And truth or clothed or naked let it be.

Rain, sun, and rain! and the free blossom blows:
Sun, rain, and sun! and where is he who knows?
From the great deep to the great deep he goes.

- Tennyson, *Idylls of the King* (2)

H. V. Traywick, Jr.
Richmond, Virginia
March 2013

* * *

INTRODUCTION

In the middle of the nineteenth century steam power replaced muscle power as the prime mover of civilization, and the Industrial Revolution roared across the world (1). A new World-Cycle, the Machine Age, was born. But in the Southern United States men took up arms against the imperatives of the machine, and their Lost Cause marked the end of the Age of Agriculture – the Age that had given rise to all of the ancient civilizations.

By the editing of contemporary diaries, letters, essays, newspaper editorials, memoirs, histories and official records, and the collation of them into a narrative form, this work offers a contemporaneous portrait of the old Republic, the Old South, the storm-tossed Confederacy, and the revolution that swept it all away.

In *Book I*, the reader will see through the eyes of a Northern visitor to Virginia the bustling tobacco market in Lynchburg before the War. The son of the Governor of Virginia then shows the excitement in Richmond generated by John Brown's raid on Harper's Ferry. A portrait of radical Abolitionism will be rendered to the reader, along with the economics of emancipation. Alexis de Tocqueville shows how the Northern States abolished slavery without freeing any of their slaves, and why the South was unable to rid herself of that ancient institution. A noted economist of the time shows how the institution of slavery would not expand into the territories for economic reasons, and that the question merely agitated the political relations between the North and the South - eventually driving the South to secession for self-preservation at the election of Abraham Lincoln to the Presidency. The reader is next shown why the North could not afford to let the Southern States go in peace; how Lincoln provoked the South into firing the first shot;

and how he then inaugurated total war against the Southern States in order to "save the Union" for Northern interests.

In *Book II*, the reader will see the South's preparations for war, visit a tobacco plantation in Charlotte County when the boys go off to war, and hear the ground shake from the cannon fire from the first battle of Manassas – one hundred miles away. A year later, the lovely Connie Cary takes us into a hospital in Richmond during the Battle of Seven Pines, and shows us the carnage from the battle raging at the gates of the Confederate capitol. We will ride with "Jeb" Stuart's cavaliers around McClellan's entire army, and then be given - by a wounded artillery officer who was present nearby - a portrait of General Lee and General Jackson conferring on tactics during the Seven Days' Battles around the Chickahominy swamps. At Second Manassas we will stand in line with Jackson's "Foot Cavalry" behind the abandoned railroad cut, gripping a musket and waiting for the next Union assault, and see Jackson riding along his thin lines giving reassurance to his men: "Only two more hours, men, and Longstreet will be here. Can you stand it? You must hold on for two more hours…." Then the reader is carried along on the Maryland Campaign, where a woman of Shepherdstown recalls the ragged, hungry soldiers of Lee's army, their battles at South Mountain, Harper's Ferry, and Sharpsburg, and the wagon-loads of the wounded coming back into town with "de blood runnin' out dem dat deep!" as her house servant reports it.

In *Book III*, upon the army's withdrawal into Virginia, the reader will share the jolly cavalry camp with "Jeb" Stuart at the Dandridge plantation, "The Bower," before moving eastward with the army to Fredericksburg. There we will see the Mississippi sharpshooters keeping the Union Engineers from effecting a crossing of the river, and watch the Union guns bombard the town while Confederate artillerymen ferry refugees across a frozen creek on their artillery horses, and see little girls among the refugees trudging along holding up the dresses of their doll babies to keep them out of the snow and slush. At Chancellorsville, the reader will be escorted on Jackson's famous flank march by one of his staff officers, hear the wild "Rebel Yell" as his men roll up Hooker's flank, and help carry the mortally wounded General from the field after he is mistakenly shot by his own men in the twilight jungle of The Wilderness. We will march again northward two months later and fight the Battle of Gettysburg, where a correspondent from a Richmond newspaper gives us a picture of the thunderous artillery battle on the third day. Then we watch as Pickett's and Pettigrew's men march in dressed ranks across a half mile of open ground up the slopes of Cemetery Hill under a solid sheet of enemy fire, and see Pickett's Division make it over the stone wall - in the *beau geste* of the Lost Cause - before being obliterated. And the next day, with the rain pouring in torrents and the wind whipping up a gale, we will ride in agony on the bare planks of a wagon back to Virginia in a wagon train seventeen miles long that is filled with nothing but the wounded. A summer visit to a cotton plantation in King William County with Connie Cary will give us a respite from the war before the storm breaks again in 1864.

Book IV presents us with Grant's Wilderness Campaign and his "two-for-one" strategy of attrition inaugurated against the Army of Northern Virginia. "Jeb" Stuart will be killed saving Richmond from Sheridan's cavalry, and all that is light and gay will go out of the Confederacy. The siege of Petersburg will begin and the son of the commander who saved the city before Lee's army got there will tell of the Battle of the Crater and the slaughter of US Colored Troops. Then, with Sherman's Army burning and pillaging its way through Georgia and up through the Carolinas to join Grant's army, Lee detaches Jubal Early and the Second Corps to meet a Union threat to his communications in the Valley. Early's Adjutant takes us along as Early wins a victory at Lynchburg and marches down the Valley, crosses the Potomac, and threatens the very gates of the Northern capitol. In his subsequent Valley campaign, Early and his little army keep troops away from Lee's front before Petersburg and Richmond for nearly three months, until Sheridan defeats Early at Winchester and Fisher's Hill and sends him back up the Valley. With reinforcements sent from Richmond, Early again advances down the Valley to attack Sheridan at Cedar Creek. Along the way, a gunner in the Horse Artillery shows the reader the ruins of the burned Valley that Sheridan's cavalry has left in its wake. Captain Jed Hotchkiss, Jackson's old Topographical Engineer, tells of Early's masterful flank march around Sheridan's left on Cedar Creek, routing the Union army in the morning, only to suffer a heartbreaking defeat with Sheridan's counterattack that evening. Confederate prisoners of war take us into the Union prison camp at Point Lookout, which has a higher rate of mortality than the Confederate prison camp at Andersonville. Here we will see starvation in the midst of plenty, and go on daily burial details to carry away the bodies of prisoners who had frozen to death the night before. Back at Richmond, we will see short rations in the city, and see starvation in the cold, muddy trenches before Petersburg as the Confederacy dwindles in size to southern Virginia, northern North Carolina, and remote and scattered pockets of the Deep South and Texas. Then an officer in Richmond tells us the news of the lines being broken at Five Forks and of Petersburg's evacuation, and shows us the fall of Richmond in all of its horrific splendor.

In *Book V* the last courier to carry a dispatch from the Army of Northern Virginia takes us on Lee's retreat. Col. Marshall, of Lee's staff, describes their last meal in the Confederacy - a thin corn meal gruel heated in a shaving cup while the starving horses gnaw bark from the trees in the twilight dawn. Then the way is blocked at Appomattox Court House and Marse Robert issues General Order Number 9 to his men, giving them the terms of the Surrender and bidding them Farewell.

Notwithstanding Lincoln's stirring rhetoric in his Gettysburg Address, government "of the people, by the people, and for the people" did not "perish from the earth" when the Southern States withdrew from the Union. It perished when they were driven back into it at the point of the bayonet. Then a Northern-dictated Reconstruction solidified the North's political control of the Federal government while increasing its power at the expense of the States. And to put the victor's oft-trumpeted moral narrative concerning "government of the people, etc." into further perspective, it is worth remembering that while the North – for its own political advantage - gave Southern black men the vote in 1867, it in many cases continued to deny it to blacks in the North until 1870. This is not to mention the disfranchised Southern white men during Reconstruction, much less the never-franchised Northern women throughout the nineteenth century.

Morality may condition but it seldom determines the cause of war. If one delves deeply enough, one will more than likely find that at base wars are waged over the control of resources. This war was no different. The industrializing North, with her sectional majority, had been able to pass high protective tariffs to protect the emerging Northern economy from free-trade England and her well-established industries. But the tariff had the opposite effect on the South. It not only deprived the South of free-trade with England and her better-quality manufactured goods, it exploited the South through the unequal terms of trade it created, paving the way for her to become an economic colony of the neo-colonialist North - of the sort that, say, Massachusetts and her Boston-based United Fruit Company would create in later years with their banana plantations and "Banana Republics" in Central America. As the Argentine economist Raul Prebisch would argue in a rebuttal to the "Modernity Theory" put forth as an explanation for the Third World's stalled economy, the concentration of exports in primary commodities has a structural tendency to deteriorate the terms of trade, because, over time, the price of the primary commodities exported rises more slowly than the cost of the manufactured commodities imported (2). This, according to his "Dependency Theory," is what happened to the "Banana Republics" in the twentieth century; and with the agrarian South's economy based likewise on primary commodities traded against Northern manufactures, the same might be said of the economic relationship developing between the South and the North in the years before the War.

Southern statesmen, with their insistence on maintaining the States' rights and a strict interpretation of the Constitution, were a constant stumbling block to Northern politicians who wanted to twist the Constitution and concentrate power into the hands of the Federal Government in order to facilitate their industrial ambitions with tariffs, national banks, transcontinental railroads, and the like. John Randolph considered tariffs to be merely bounties paid by agriculturalists to the manufacturers in order to subsidize manufacturers for doing – if worthwhile - what they would do for their own sakes without it. "It eventuates in this," he argued, "whether you, as a planter, will consent to be taxed in order to hire another man to go to work in a shoemaker's shop, or to set up a spinning jenny. For my part, I will not agree to it, even though they should by way of return agree to be taxed to help us to plant tobacco; much less will I agree to pay all and receive nothing for it…." Randolph also argued at every turn against the incorporation of a national bank: "Connected as it is to be with the Government, whenever it goes into operation, a scene will be exhibited on the great theatre of the United States at which I shudder…. However great the evil of their conduct may be, who is to bell the cat? Who is to take the bull by the horns? You might as well attack Gibraltar with a pocket pistol as to attempt to punish them…. The true secret is, the banks are creditors as well as debtors; and, if we were merely debtors to them for the paper in our pockets, they would soon … go to jail (figuratively speaking) for having issued more paper than they were able to pay when presented to them. A man has their note for $50.00, perhaps, in his pocket, for which he wants fifty Spanish milled dollars; but they have his note for five thousand in their possession and laugh at his demand…. If I must have a master, let him be one with epaulets, something that I can fear and respect, something that I can look up to, but not a master with a quill behind his ear….” (3)

Shortly before his death, Thomas Jefferson wrote: “I see, as you do, and with the deepest affliction, the rapid strides with which the federal branch of our government is advancing towards the usurpation of all rights reserved to the States, and the consolidation in itself of all powers, foreign and domestic; and that, too, by constructions which, if legitimate, leave no limits to their power…. Under the power to regulate commerce, they assume indefinitely that also over agriculture and manufactures, and call it regulation to take the earnings of one of these branches of industry, and that too the most depressed, and put them into the pockets of the other, the most flourishing of all. Under the authority to establish post roads, they claim that of cutting down mountains for the construction of roads, of digging canals, and aided by a little sophistry on the words ‘general welfare,’ a right to do, not only the acts to effect that which are specifically enumerated and permitted, but whatsoever they shall think, or will pretend will be for the general welfare. And what is our resource for the preservation of the Constitution? Reason and argument? You might as well reason and argue with the marble columns encircling them…. We must have patience and longer endurance, then, with our brethren while under delusion; give them time for reflection and experience of consequences … and separate from our companions only when the sole alternatives left are the dissolution of our Union with them, or submission to a government without limitation of powers. Between these two evils, when we must make a choice, there can be no hesitation….” (4)

With the North’s growing industrialization came growing populations and a growing sectional majority. The issue of slavery in the Territories was agitated by Northern demagogues to whip up the votes of this sectional majority, turn them to their party's political advantage, and use this power to press their centralizing agenda over the Constitutional objections of the Southern stumbling block. This, however, threatened not only to impoverish the South, but to threaten her very existence - and to wreck the Union. Thomas Prentice Kettell, a noted economist, wrote in 1860: "The Emperor of the French has said that 'France is the only nation that goes to war for an idea.' With more truth may it be said that 'the United States is the only nation that goes to destruction for an idea.' This appears to be the settled policy of a party at the North…. We are told that there is no intention of destroying the institutions of the States – that the design is only to exclude the institution from territory where it would have been long since had nature permitted. There is here, then, nothing practical – a mere pretense of agitating the popular mind and engendering animosities…. The agitation has at the North no one practical application whatever; while at the South it has in the background servile insurrection, bloodshed, and annihilation of person and property, involving ultimately the ruin of the North…. The South views the matter in the spirit of Patrick Henry: 'The object is now, indeed, small, but the shadow is large enough to darken all this fair land….'" (5) This came to fruition in 1860 when the strictly sectional Northern party won the Presidential election and precipitated the secession of the Cotton States.

With this inconvenient development the North lost not only the source of cotton for her mills, she lost a large part of her tariff revenues and a large part of the markets for her manufactures. In addition, she lost control of the mouth of the Mississippi River, the commercial artery that drained her heartland. This would never do, so the North blockaded the Southern coast with her navy, marched her armies from the Potomac to the Rio Grande, drove the Southern States back into the Union as conquered provinces, and pinned them down with bayonets until she could - once and for all - transform the Federated Union created by the Revolutionary Fathers into a centralized industrial Empire.

With the triumph of the Industrial Revolution and the inauguration of the Machine Age came also the Age of Reason and the knell of Faith. But as the revolutionaries of this new world order attempted to turn the Great Chain of Being upside down with their machines, traditionalists reminded them that there is no new thing under the sun. As the technological foundation of civilization shifted and the social and political structure shifted with it in order to organize and direct it, the basic class dichotomy remained the same. The landed aristocracy was merely supplanted by an industrial and financial oligarchy, while slaves and serfs were replaced by mechanization and a more efficient free labor system. The basic class antagonisms remained also, but with slave insurrections and peasant uprisings being supplanted by labor strife, ghetto riots, and terrorism (6).

Who will count the gains and the losses? Unlike the relatively static structure of self-sufficient agrarian estates, where a stable labor force is necessary in order to ensure that the crops will not be lost over the season or over the years, industrial economies require a fluid labor force and an ever-expanding market for their goods, or they stagnate and die in the midst of plenty. As economic and social instability are inherent in the dynamic complexities of industrialization, political power centralizes and government control increases in order to contain these instabilities. With an ever-expanding bureaucracy effecting this containment, the public servant soon becomes the master, evolving into a vast and complex machine with an increasing appetite for stifling free enterprise with taxes and regulations; for undermining civil society as a threat to government's hegemony; and for atomizing the citizenry and leveling it into servitude or dependency – all of which are advanced symptoms of the stagnating bureaucratic totalitarianism that marks the point of diminishing returns in the metabolic aging process of the industrialized State (7).

Adapt or die is the law of evolution. Those that don't adapt either become subjugated to those that do, or they perish. Resting upon an economic foundation of muscle power and staple-crop agriculture, and shackled to her large population of African slaves, the Old South was unable to adapt successfully to the new Machine Age - but she refused subjugation to an alien rule, and she refused to worship an alien god. The Old South died hard. That story is told in these pages. But this work also warns that mortality – Nemesis of men, nations, and empires – stalks alike the vanquished and the victor.

ACKNOWLEDGEMENTS

Many generous people have contributed time, research, friendship, advice, encouragement, and material resources to my efforts to bring this work to fruition, and they have added greatly to the quality of the outcome. To all I extend my heartfelt thanks, and I cheerfully give them credit for the good things. The mistakes are all my own.

First and foremost, I would like to thank Wayne Dementi, of Dementi Milestone Publishing, for agreeing to publish this work and bring my efforts to fruition. It is a great privilege to have such a friend, and a great pleasure to work with him on this project.

Next, I would like to thank my uncle, Dick Neher, for taking the time to read my manuscript and offer his encouragement - and for offering a most valued suggestion, which I took to heart. The book is better for it. In addition, I particularly wish to thank him for his generous offer of material support for this project.

I owe an enormous debt of thanks to Dr. H. Jackson Darst for reading my manuscript and for writing the beautiful Foreword to go with it. He is the true voice and embodiment of all that was best in Old Virginia and her gentlemen, and he nobly carries on the tradition.

I also owe an enormous debt to the following distinguished gentlemen who so kindly took their time to review my manuscript and offer their endorsement: The Hon. S. Waite Rawls, III, President and CEO of the Museum of the Confederacy; Dr. Clyde Wilson, Emeritus Distinguished Professor of History, University of South Carolina; The Hon. Bragdon Bowling, past Commander,

Virginia Division, Sons of Confederate Veterans, past Commander, Army of Northern Virginia of SCV, and past President, Richmond Civil Way Roundtable; and Dr. Frank E. Eakin, Jr., Markus M. and Carole M. Weinstein and Gilbert M. and Fannie S. Rosenthal Professor of Jewish and Christian Studies, University of Richmond.

Special thanks go to my friend and philosophical sparring partner, Dr. Alma Dell Smith, of Boston University. Her expertise in the field of Psychology has put me at a natural disadvantage, but - like the mule at the Kentucky Derby - I have "benefitted from the association," and her intelligent counter-arguments have challenged me to articulate my thesis with care.

I wish also to thank my friend David A. Bovenizer, IV, Esq. – Traditionalst, former scholarly editor, and a true gentleman of the Old School – for his personal interest, help, encouragement and guidance in directing me on the path towards both publication and the Perennial Philosophy.

I particularly wish to thank my sister, Robin Traywick Williams – herself a published author – for introducing me to both Wayne Dementi and David Bovenizer, and for offering her support throughout in my creative efforts and advice in my negotiation of the author's path. She has smoothed the way for me considerably.

As always in everything, I thank my brother Cris for his never-flagging moral support. He is a man you can ride the river with.

My special thanks go to the professional staffs of the Library of Virginia, of Boatwright Memorial Library at the University of Richmond, of the Library of Congress, and of the Virginia Historical Society. Without their patient assistance, and without the extensive resources of these libraries, this work would have been impossible.

I would like to thank all of my professors in the Master of Liberal Arts program at the University of Richmond for going the extra mile in offering me Directed Studies when necessary in order that I might fit my course of study around a demanding employment schedule that kept me away much of the time. Particularly accommodating in this regard were Professors Frank Eakin, John Gordon, Robert Kenzer, and Yuchel Yanikdag. This wonderful program gave me a solid and objective foundation upon which to build this work.

Thanks go to Dr. Allen Stokes, Jr. and Mr. Henry Fulmer of the South Caroliniana Library in Columbia for permission to use excerpts from Chancellor Henry William Desaussure's pamphlet of 1822 entitled "A Series of Numbers Addressed to the Public on the Subject of the Slaves and Free People of Colour." I also thank my cousin (and good deer hunting companion) Dr. Jim Gettys, of Columbia, for locating the pamphlet for me.

I wish to thank Ms. Judy Bolton, Head of Public Services at the Louisiana State University Library Special Collections for allowing me to publish from their microfilm files the editorial entitled "The Difference" from the January 21, 1861, issue of the New Orleans *Daily Crescent*.

I also owe thanks to Ms. Erica Bossier, Permissions Coordinator at Louisiana State University Press, for permission to quote an excerpt from Andrew Nelson Lytle's essay "The Hind Tit," found in *I'll Take My Stand: Essays by Twelve Southerners*, published by LSU Press. As I wrestled with edits, she exhibited a monumental patience with my changing requests, for which I am most appreciative.

Thanks go also to Ms. Elizabeth Clementson, Permissions Coordinator at W. W. Norton, for permission to quote an excerpt from Jose Ortega y Gasset's *The Revolt of the Masses*, an excerpt that illustrates a critical point in my work on the growth of Statism.

For providing me with the image of General Lee in 1863, and the map of the Virginia Campaign, I extend my thanks to Mr. Jamison D. Davis, Visual Resources Manager of the Virginia Historical Society, Richmond.

Last but not least, I thank the Knight of Melrose for teaching me how to ride, to shoot straight, and to speak the Truth. And I thank his Lady for coming home from Fort Benning, Georgia in 1945, to see to it that I would be born on Virginia soil - most particularly on the good red clay of Southside, home of Patrick Henry, John Randolph of Roanoke, and Generals "Jeb" Stuart and Jubal Early, CSA.

BOOK I

SPRING (1861)

I have a rendezvous with Death
At some disputed barricade.
When Spring comes back with rustling shade
And apple-blossoms fill the air ....
                    - Alan Seeger, "Rendezvous" (1)

RIGHT Henry A. Wise - Courtesy of the Library of Congress

The Land of Dreams

J. Alexander Patten, a Northern visitor to Virginia in 1859, from his description of a Lynchburg tobacco market: (1)

Those who sing the songs of Virginia, have long been familiar with "Lynchburg Town," and those who indulge in the finer kinds of manufactured tobacco, know that it comes rather from Lynchburg than Richmond. Hence, although away off – considerably more than a hundred miles – from the seaboard, Lynchburg has a renown that is universal. The South Side Railroad, with its connections to Richmond, Petersburg, and City Point, has its terminus here, connecting again with the Virginia and Tennessee, which forms a portion of the near route to New Orleans. A branch road to Alexandria is soon to go into operation, which will very much shorten the distance to Baltimore and the cities of the North. Cotton has already been received over the Virginia and Tennessee road, giving promise that large quantities of this great staple will eventually seek this course of transportation to market.

Lynchburg is located on a series of hills, running back from James River. Each of the long, parallel streets is on an elevation, getting higher and higher, until the loftiest hill is reached. Then, you look down upon the river, canal, and a most picturesque grouping of buildings. It seems as if some day a great land-slide might sweep everything, from the rookeries to the stately mansions, in chaos to the bottom. Indeed, from the way many of the buildings are secured by walls, some such idea seems to have pervaded the minds of those constructing them. One dwelling may serve as a description of many. It was a large double brick edifice, elevated not less than ten feet above the street. Along the whole front was a covered piazza or porch, of wood, resting on a stone wall, built up from the street, and, evidently, mainly intended to keep the hill from giving way under the weight of the building. This was extended beyond the house some forty or fifty feet, facing even with the surface of the garden, and overhung at the top by a profusion of blooming vines. The entrance was by some clumsy wooden steps, rising between the side foundation-walls of the building and an outer wall, still necessary to keep the hill in its place. Reaching a level, paved landing, you can step upon the porch, or ascend to another story, by another pair of break-neck steps. Out from the wall the street is paved with cobble-stones.

On almost any of the lower streets this untasteful and inconvenient arrangement is to be found. Altogether, there is such a curious adaptation of buildings to locations; such walls, such overhanging porches and gardens, that the stranger cannot but be profoundly impressed with the ingenuity and perseverance thus evinced by the inhabitants.

Main street is a long, straight thoroughfare, lined with stores, and active with business. Great wagons, drawn by four and six horses and sometimes by both horses and oxen, make their way slowly along, loaded with tobacco, and wheat from the neighboring counties. These wagons are curiosities. To very heavy wheels, necessary for the rough road, is added a high, cumbrous body, over which a cover is drawn in bad weather. The driver is mounted on one of the horses, and thus pursues his tedious way, coming to town with some produce, and homeward with sup-plies. One individual is said to drive an ox, a mule, and a horse. A yoke of oxen and a team of horses are frequently seen. Some of the teams, however, are fine, noble horses, and as the driver goes along, he cracks his huge whip, not so much to increase the speed, as to draw attention to his animals. Very many of the wagoners are white men from the mountain districts. They have coarse, tow-colored hair, high cheek-bones, sunken eyes, and whiskey breaths. They are clad in home-spun – few of them can read or write. In their manners, they are very near to the swine upon which they feed so greedily; their language is merely a dialect, and quite inferior to the vulgarisms of the negro; they are utterly corrupted with brutish vices and are completely deadened to the influences of any noble virtue. With the forms of men, they seem to belong to some lower order of brutes.

A colored individual may be noticed at one of the corners of Main street, with a long tin horn. This he applies to his lips, and discourses "sweet sounds" for tobacco buyers. It is a notice that there is a "beck" or public sale of the article at some neighboring warehouse. Immediately, a procession of gentlemen is seen hastening from other warehouses, eager for a chance at the new lots. The tobacco is generally sent by the planter to his commission merchant, who employs a crier at the day of sale. The crier receives ten cents per hogshead, the factor one dollar, and sometimes two and a half per cent. In the warehouse, the tobacco is inspected, weighed, the hogsheads broken and duly arranged for examination. Some of the tobacco is sent in loose, but it commands a better price when prized and duly arranged for examination. The warehouses are large buildings, with room for several hundred hogsheads, and yards adjoining, convenient for unloading the wagons and feeding the horses. The whole air is redolent with tobacco, and every man about seems an inveterate chewer of the weed. The crowd at the sales is made up of the buyers, planters, warehouse-men, commission merchants, and idlers. Some are in conversation, some bidding, some smelling, some leaning on the piles of tobacco, some sprawling over the emptied hogsheads, and all – black and white, bond and free – chewing.

The crier is a person with a stout stick, good lungs, and a glib tongue. He mounts first one pile and then another, accumulating many dimes in the course of a day. His thought, from morning to night, is tobacco; it makes him eloquent, and it makes him daily heard. Every lot is *the* lot, and every bidder is frowned at, persuaded, coaxed, and implored to buy, until the gentleman seems to conclude that he has given ten cents worth of breath.

The commission merchant hops from pile to pile, after the noisy crier. The tongues of the two run races, and if there is any shrewd exaggeration on the part of the one, the other comes gallantly to endorse it; and thus they reciprocate favors of this kind profitably, and from hour to hour. Now the crier makes a noise to please the commission merchant, and the commission merchant to tickle the planter, who looks daggers at him if he does not keep up the excitement; but the cool coons who do the purchasing are but little moved by it. They pull the bundles from the top and the bottom, they lift the leaves, they examine, smell, and chew, as attentive to their own interests – guided by experience and judgment – as they are deaf to the eloquence of the crier, and the pleading of the commission man. The stick is shaken over their heads – there is wit, there are tones of anger, and there are tones of satisfaction as the bids come brisker. The commission merchant pulls his hat down and pushes it back, he drags at his pants, and he plunges into his pockets; he holds the tobacco aloft, and he dashes it down; he taps his friends on their shoulders, and begs them not to think of losing such bargains; he smiles cheerfully to encourage the planter, and grows morose as the prospect of obtaining a high price becomes "small by degrees and beautifully less." Thus go the "hogsheads," and the "loose," the "manufacturing," and the "shipping." Thus do the manufacturers glean out the fine qualities for the choice brands of chewing; and thus is selected the heavy, coarser article which is destined for the foreign market.

All leaf-tobacco is disposed of at these public sales, and there is quite a number of warehouses. When the "breaks are heavy," as it is called, the tin-horn is sounding continually, filling the street with a wild, but not unpleasant sort of music. The yards and streets will then be crowded with wagons, and the greatest excitement exists among the buyers. And another class of very interested people will be the planters themselves, who, to some extent, attend the sales of their crops. The length of time required in the growing and preparation of this crop, its continued liability to injury, and the care which must be bestowed upon it, together with the fact, that, after all, it is an extremely profitable product, always saleable for the ready money-vendors, the final disposition of it is a matter of much importance to the grower.

Tobacco is the idol of the Lynchburgs. In it are their fortunes, and in it are beggars' graves. If there are movements in the firmament, the only concern is to know how they will affect the tobacco crops and market. If the earth is shaken by wars and trodden by pestilence, they care nothing, should the idolized staple come regularly to their town. They take the planter by the hand, they press him to their bosoms, and inquire, with almost tearful solicitude, how the crop stands the wet – the drought – the heat – the cold – how it ripens – has he cut yet – has he manufacturing or shipping? They talk about the last crop; they grow wise over the prospects of the market; they are full of calculations as to the tobacco still growing in the fields. A merchant may be in the port or whiskey lines, but he knows that he will not sell much of either, if any undue misfortune should befall the tobacco people; another may be in the dry-goods way, and yet, if this crop fails, he may hang up his yardstick. Consequently, these interests, and all other interests, are linked with the ups and downs of the weed itself. It is hardly possible to buy a Bible or a tea-kettle, without either falling into a discussion on the crop, or at least being affectionately invited to partake of a reviving quid. The article of "cut tobacco," used out of the southern country, is laughed at here, and nobody is anybody unless he carries a plug as broad as his hand. With this he scents his pockets and his person, and having it, he drips the juice from the corners of his mouth, and, at convenient intervals, spouts out a spray like a fountain.

You can hardly turn into a street without seeing tobacco-factories. They are often old, tottering buildings; but sometimes substantial structures of brick. Here, too, the air is strongly impregnated with the aroma of tobacco, made more delicate as the article passes the process of manufacturing. Out in the streets, and in the yards, are long, shallow boxes, containing thousands of the newly made "rolls" – called, after prizing, "plugs" – undergoing the drying necessary before being prized. There are shops for preparing the various kinds of boxes in which it is finally packed. In the factory which we visited, the hogsheads were taken to the second story for "sorting," and all the other successive stages, until ready to be "stemmed" and "rolled." These operations were performed in some cramped-up rooms on the second and third floors. On either side were high, double tables; and as fast as the leaves were separated from the stems, by workpeople standing on one side, they were tossed over to others facing them, and busy making the rolls. The operatives are all slaves – male and female, adults and children. Their nimble fingers do not stop, although, upon your entrance, every eye wanders to your face, and the younger frequently indulge in a broad grin. The tobacco was prized on the lower floor. In this operation, it is placed in enormously thick iron chambers, closed with hinges. Upon each of these comes a screw, turned by an iron lever, which requires four men to lift and a dozen to work it. The bar is no quicker in its place, than the whole gang lay hold of it; and first by short jerks, and then by more powerful efforts – in which they exert every muscle – the screw is turned tighter and tighter. Then four of them pull it out, trot back with it, thrust it into the socket, and in a moment the measured jerks begin again. With all this tremendous power, the tobacco sometimes requires to be prized a second time. After this operation, it is packed in the stout but tasteful boxes in which it is sent over the world.

The superintendent, not only of this but two other factories, was an intelligent slave. He was a man some forty years of age, large-framed, and seemingly of an amiable disposition. He could read and write; and, we were informed, wrote letters of business for his master. He was not only perfectly familiar with the qualities of tobacco, and all the details regarding its manufacture, but he gave a clear and interesting account of the whole operation. Withal, we did not see that he ever forgot that he was a slave. He spoke, with some pride, of the factories owned by "master"; and applied the same term to the gentleman who escorted us. His politeness seemed to be a study. A humility was expressed as well in his tone as in his manners. He spoke to the other negroes as if he expected or intended to be obeyed; but he was neither rude, nor unnecessarily severe. With the women, his directions were more in the form of suggestions than of commands.

Of course, there is a very large negro population in Lynchburg. During the day, not much is seen of them; but early in the evening, they are unpleasantly numerous. The sidewalks, at the best, are narrow and uneven; and the pleasures of a walk are not increased by the crowds of blacks, who intercept your way. They are generally polite, but sometimes run the risk of a kick for the satisfaction of a little insolence. They hang about the corners, they perch on the fences and walls; and, when not asleep on the steps of the porches, keep up a continual whistling. All along the streets, come the notes of this boy-beloved music. From the dark corners, where some chap is getting himself to sleep; from groups, where they have made wagers as to harmony and wind; from the kitchens, and away down to the river bank. Moreover the Lynchburg blacks have genius, as well as lips; and whistle in a manner well calculated to "soothe the savage breast." It is the tunes of the plantations where they were born, and hope to die; of the factories, where the song lightens their labor; and each is given with an accuracy, and even sweetness, which the instrument cannot always achieve. The negroes stand with their backs to the palings and walls, their hands in their pockets, and braced by their extended legs, whistle away the evening hours. Other gangs pass, whistling their loudest and best, which incites the first to displays of their fullest capacity; and thus the concert goes on. At an early hour, however, the whistling is hushed; and the streets are deserted by the negroes for their blankets in outbuildings and garrets, from which the earliest dawn will call them.

At the Norval House lives "Ned" – undoubtedly related to the person of the same name who "died long ago." We saw a model porter down at the rail-road, who said that he was Ned; and after that, we had Ned to light us to our chamber; Ned, to bring us our boots; Ned, to wait at the dinner table; Ned, to run our errands; Ned, to receive quarters, and Ned, to bow to the ground as he bade us farewell. Ned was everywhere, Ned did everything, and what is more, Ned did it well. Ned is a tall, yellow fellow, as straight as an arrow, and as supple as an eel. He certainly never sleeps, and he never sits. His whole life is devoted to the traveling public, and especially that portion allured by his politeness to the Norval House. When the stage rushes to the cars, Ned's face carries a smile as serene as a saint's; and when it rumbles back, loaded with travelers, he hangs on to the door, conversing like a gentleman. He hands out the males, he is delicate with the females. He takes the babies; he lugs baskets, he gathers up shawls and umbrellas; he backs in at the front door; he bows at the foot of the stairs; he lingers at the parlor; he brushes the gentlemen; he sympathizes with exhausted mothers, and caresses squalling infants. But Ned is an example of politeness when you reward him. His hand closes over the coin, his countenance is lighted with the beams of a celestial smile, he places his closed fist upon his heart, and he bows his graceful and grateful thanks. Friend of the weary traveler – man of many accomplishments – thou yellow-hued Chesterfield, may your own journey end "where good darkies go."

There are so many kitchens, stables, and other outbuildings in and about Lynchburg, that the good people are continually apprehensive of fire. Such a calamity happened in July last. As the thermometer ranged something over ninety, and we had witnessed fires rather larger than any likely to occur in Lynchburg, we did not propose to go. But business seemed pretty much suspended, and most of the population – white and black – repaired to the hill where the fire raged. We, accordingly, took our way thither. We found four frame buildings in flames, and the people in a frantic state of excitement. The only means of obtaining water was in pails, from a reservoir not far off, and in this way they expected to check the devouring demon. That wily scoundrel, Richard III., on a certain occasion very much desired a horse; but the cry of the Lynchburgers was for buckets. (In Virginia, all vessels of this kind are singularly called "buckets.") Buckets they demanded of the

housekeepers and the shopkeepers; buckets! they cried, rushing down the hills, and buckets was their demand as they came
perspiring back. New buckets and old buckets, those with hoops
and those without; those with holes in the bottom and those
with no handles. Everything that day of any description went for
a bucket; and every public-spirited citizen ran home to gather all
that belonged to him. They formed water lines, and began the
battle. Old gentlemen threw water, looking for the object through
their spectacles, and young gentlemen threw water around at the
fire, but ducking the old gentlemen. Tall fellows ran up ladders
and got in the way of other tall fellows, while some youthful but
ambitious workers lost half of the water in hauling it up, and then
proudly tossed many of the most venerable buckets from the roofs
to the ground. There were ladies in full fashion, and influential
citizens on horseback; there were ancient Virginians with pipes in
their mouths and sadness in their hearts; and there were juvenile
negroes, who danced and stood on their heads for very joy at
such a frolic. After wasting as much water as they could, smash-
ing up most of the pails, and each man had worked himself up to
the standard of a hero, the fire had burnt itself out, and the labors
were happily suspended.

Near us was an old negro woman. On her head was a kind
of sun-bonnet, and her sleeves were rolled up very nearly to her
shoulders. She had a loud voice, knew everybody, and was overwhelmed at the scene before her. "King of Israel," she exclaimed,
"dis am thy judgment. Oh, golly! oh, golly!" Another aged negress
approached, and desired to talk with this one. "You, Aunt Chloe,"
said the first, angrily, "la, sakes now, ain't you ashamed to open
you mouf, when de King of Israel am in de elements. Get along,
get along wid ye." "La, Aunt Dinah," was all the second seemed
to dare say. "I doesn't want dese yer niggers speaking to me,"
continued Aunt Dinah, for the edification of the crowd of blacks
standing about her. "Dis am a day of wrath – de Lord Jesus am
aggravated at sinners. Oh, golly, child'en, oh golly." The old woman raised the corner of her apron to wipe the big tears which now
started from her eyes. Presently she burst through the crowd with

uplifted hands, exclaiming, "Great King of Israel! g- r- e- a -t King of I-s-r-a-e-l!"…..

…..for then she seem'd to stand
On some vast plain before a setting sun,
And from the sun there swiftly made at her
A ghastly something, and its shadow flew
Before it, till it touched her, and she turn'd –
When lo! her own, that broadening from her feet,
And blackening, swallow'd all the land, and in it
Far cities burnt…..

- Tennyson, *Idylls of the King* (2)

BOOK I - CHAPTER TWO

A Fire-bell in the Night

John S. Wise, son of Virginia's Gov. Henry A. Wise, from *The End of an Era*: (1)

The attack of John Brown upon Harper's Ferry came upon Virginia like a clap of thunder out of a clear sky.

In the afternoon of October 17, 1859, I was passing along Main Street in Richmond, when I observed a crowd of people gathering about the bulletin board of a newspaper. In those days, news did not travel so rapidly as now; besides which, the telegraph lines at the place from which the news came were cut.

The first report read:

"There is trouble of some sort at Harper's Ferry. A party of workmen have seized the Government Armory."

Soon another message flashed: "The men at Harper's Ferry are not workmen. They are Kansas border ruffians, who have attacked and captured the place, fired upon and killed several unarmed citizens, and captured Colonel Washington and other prominent citizens of the neighborhood. We cannot understand their plans or ascertain their numbers."

By this time an immense throng had assembled, agape with wonder.

Naturally reflecting that the particulars of an outbreak like this would first reach the governor, I darted homeward. I found my father in the library, roused from his afternoon siesta, in the act of reading the telegrams which he had just received. They were simply to the effect that the arsenal and government property at Harper's Ferry were in possession of a band of rioters, without describing their character. I promptly and breathlessly told what I had seen on the bulletin boards, and, while I was hurriedly delivering my news, other messengers arrived with telegrams to the same effect as those posted in the streets. The governor was by this time fully aroused. He was prompt in action. His first move was to seize the Virginia code, take a reference, and indite a telegram addressed to Colonel John Thomas Gibson, of Charlestown, commandant of the militia regiment within whose territory the invasion had occurred, directing him to order out, for the defense of the State, the militia under his command, and immediately report what he had done.

Within ten minutes after the receipt of the telegram, these instructions were on the way. Similar instructions were flashed to Colonel Robert W. Baylor, of the Third Regiment of Militia Cavalry.

The military system of the State was utterly inefficient, having nothing but skeleton organization. The telegrams continued to come rapidly, describing a condition of excitement amounting to a panic in the neighborhood of Harper's Ferry. The numbers of the attacking force were exaggerated, until some reports placed them as high as a thousand. The ramifications of the conspiracy were of course unknown.

I was promptly dispatched to summon the Secretary of the Commonwealth, the Adjutant-General, and the colonel and adjutant of the First Regiment. I found almost immediately all but the adjutant, for whom I searched long. At last this young gentleman was discovered, all unconscious of impending trouble, playing dominoes in a German restaurant, and regaling himself with the then comparatively new drink of "lager." Hurrying back with my last capture, we found the others assembled, and instantly the adjutant received instructions to order out the First Virginia Regiment at eight o'clock P.M., armed and equipped, and provided with three days' rations, at the Washington depot.

In those days, the track ran down the center of the street, and the depot was in the most popular portion of the city. News of the disturbance having gone abroad, it was an easy task to assemble the regiment; and, by the time appointed, all Richmond was on hand to learn the true meaning of the outbreak, and witness the departure of the troops. Company after company marched through the streets to the rendezvous. The governor transferred his headquarters to the depot, where he and his staff awaited the last telegrams which might arrive before his departure. Telegrams were sent to the President and to the governor of Maryland for authority to pass through the District of Columbia and Maryland with armed troops, that route being the quickest to Harper's Ferry. The dingy old depot, generally so dark and gloomy at this hour of the night, was brilliantly illuminated. The train of cars, which was to transfer the troops, stood in the middle of the street. The regiment was formed as the companies arrived, and was resting in the badly lighted street, awaiting final orders.

The masses of the populace swarming about the soldiers presented every variety of excitement, interest, and curiosity.

As for me, my "manishness" (there is no other word expressive of it) was such that, forgetting what an insignificant chit I was, I actually attempted to accompany the troops.

Transported by enthusiasm, I rushed home, donned a little blue jacket with brass buttons and a navy cap, selected a Virginia rifle nearly half as tall again as myself, rigged myself with a powder-horn and bullets, and, availing myself of the darkness, crept into the line of K Company. The file-closers and officers knew me, and indulged me to the extent of not interfering with me, never doubting the matter would adjust itself. Other small boys, who got a sight of me standing there, were variously affected. Some were green with envy, while others ridiculed me with pleasant suggestions concerning what would happen when father caught me.

In time, the order to embark was received. I came to "attention" with the others, went through the orders, marched into the car, and took my seat. It really looked as if the plan was to succeed. Alas and alas for these hopes! One incautious utterance had thwarted all my plans. When I went home to caparison myself for war, the household had been too much occupied to observe my preparations. I succeeded in donning my improvised uniform, secured my arms, and had almost reached the outer door of the basement, when I encountered Lucy, one of the slave chamber-maids.

"Hi! Mars' John. Whar is you gwine?" exclaimed Lucy, surprised.

"To Harper's Ferry," was the proud reply, and off I sped.

"I declar', I b'leeve that boy thinks hisself a man, sho' 'nuff," said Lucy, as she glided into the house. It was not long before she told Eliza, the housekeeper, who in turn hurried to my invalid mother with the news. She summoned Jim, the butler, and sent him to father with the information....

"What!" exclaimed the governor, on hearing Jim's report of my escapade, "is that young rascal really trying to go? Hunt him up, Jim! Capture him! Take away his arms, and march him home in front of you!" Laughing heartily, he resumed his work, well knowing that Jim understood his orders and would execute them....

I was sitting in a car, enjoying the sense of being my country's defender starting for the wars, when I recognized a well-known voice in the adjoining car, inquiring, "Gentlemen, is any ov you seed anythin' ov de Gov'ner's little boy about here? I'm a-lookin' fur him under orders to take him home."

I shoved my long squirrel-rifle under the seats and followed it, amid the laughter of those about me. I heard the dread footsteps approach, and the inquiry repeated. No voice responded; but, by the silence and the tittering, I knew I was betrayed. A great, shiny black face, with immense whites to the eyes, peeped almost into my own, and, with a broad grin, said, "Well, I declar'! Here you is at las'! Cum out, Mars' John." But John did not come. Jim, after coaxing a little, seized a leg, and, as he drew me forth, clinging to my long rifle, he exclaimed, "Well, 'fore de Lord! how much gun has dat boy got, anyhow?" and the soldiers went wild with laughter.

In full possession of the gun, and pushing me before him, Jim marched his prisoner home. Once or twice I made a show of resistance, but it was in vain. "Here, you boy! You better mind how you cut yo' shines. You must er lost yo' senses. Yo' father told me to take you home. I gwine do it, too, you understand? Ef you don't mind, I'll take you straight to him, and you know and I know dat if I do, he'll tare you up alive fur botherin' him with yo' foolishiss, busy ez he is." I realized that it was even so, and, sadly crestfallen, was delivered into my mother's chamber, where, after a lecture upon the folly of my course, I was kept until the Harper's Ferry expedition was fairly on its way.

What I learned of events at Harper's Ferry was derived from the testimony of others. The First Virginia Regiment reached Washington: but, on arrival there, the Richmond troops returned, in consequence of the news of the capture of all the insurgents at Harper's Ferry by the United States Marines.

This mad effort, so quickly and so terribly ended, was in itself utterly insignificant. John Brown, its leader, was the character of murderous monomaniac found at the head of every such desperate venture. He has often been described as a Puritan in faith and in type. It is not the province of this writer to inquire into the correctness of this classification. He was an uncompromising, bloodthirsty fanatic. Born in the year 1800, he lived for fifty-six years without any sort of prominence. He was never successful in business ventures, had farmed, raised sheep, experimented in grape culture, made wine, and engaged in growing and buying wool. At one time in his life, and up to a period not long before his death, he was regarded as an infidel by his associates, although at the time of his death, he declared himself a true believer. In October, 1855, he appeared in Kansas, and at once became prominent as a leader of armed bands of free-soilers. On his way to the defense of Lawrence, in 1856, he heard of the destruction which had taken place there, and turned back. He resolved to avenge the acts of the pro-slavery horde. He reckoned up that five free-soil men had been killed, and resolved that their blood should be expiated by an equal number of victims.

"Without the shedding of blood, there is no remission of sins," was a favorite text with Brown. He called for volunteers to go on a secret expedition, and held a sort of Druidical conclave before starting out. Four sons, a son-in-law, and two others accompanied him. He had a strange power of imbuing his dupes with his own fanaticism. When he avowed his purpose to massacre the pro-slavery men living on Pottawatomie Creek, one of his followers demurred. Brown said, "I have no choice. It has been decreed by Almighty God that I should make an example of these men."

On Saturday night, May 24, 1856, John Brown and his band visited house after house upon Pottawatomie Creek, and, calling man after man from his bed, murdered five in cold blood. They first visited the house of Doyle, and compelled a father and two sons to go with them. The next morning, the father and one son were found dead in the road about two hundred yards from the house. The father was "shot in the forehead and stabbed in the breast. The son's head was cut open, and there was a hole in his jaw as though made by a knife." The other son was found dead about a hundred and fifty yards away in the grass, "his fingers cut off and his arms cut off, his head cut open, and a hole in his breast."

Then they went to Wilkinson's, reaching there after midnight. They forced open the door and ordered him to go with them. His wife was sick and helpless, and begged them not to take him away. Her prayer was of no avail. The next day Wilkinson was found dead, "a gash in his head and side."

Their next victim was William Sherman. When found in the morning, his "skull was split open in two places, and some brains were washed out. A large hole was cut in his breast, and his left hand was cut off, except a little piece of skin on one side." The execution was done with short cutlasses brought from Ohio by Brown.

"It was said that on the next morning, when the old man raised his hands to Heaven to ask a blessing, they were still stained with the dry blood of his victims." (See Rhodes's *History of the United States*, vol. ii. p. 162, etc.) In his life by Sanborn is a picture of him made about this time. It represents him clean-shaven, and is, no doubt, the best picture extant by which to study the physiognomy of a man capable of these things.

The tidings of these executions caused a cry of horror to go up, even in bloody Kansas. The squatters on Pottawatomie Creek, without distinction of party, met together and denounced the outrage and its perpetrators. The free-state men everywhere disavowed such methods. The governor sent a military force to the Pottawatomie to discover the assassins. The border ruffians took the field to avenge the massacre. One Pate, feeling sure "Old Brown," as he was called, was the author of the outrage, went in search of him. Brown met him, gave battle, and captured Pate and his command.

Kansas was in a state of civil war; the governor ordered all armed companies to disperse; and Colonel Sumner, with fifty United States dragoons, forced Brown to release his prisoners, but, although a United States marshal was with him, made no arrests.

This gives an insight into the character of John Brown, "the martyr." Drunk with blood, inflamed by the death of one of his sons in these border feuds, impelled to further deeds of violence, no doubt, by the immunity secured from those committed in Kansas, John Brown began, as early as the fall of 1857, in far-away Kansas, to formulate his plans for an outbreak in Virginia. His confederate Cook, in his confession, has left the whole story.

Inducing Cook and eight or ten others, over whom he seems to have possessed complete mastery, to join him, they started east to attend a military school, as it was said, in Ashtabula County, Ohio. The party united at Tabor, Iowa; there, in the autumn of 1857, he revealed to this choice band that his ultimate destination was the State of Virginia. His companions demurred at first, but his strong will prevailed. They shipped eastward two hundred Sharp's rifles that had been sent to Tabor for his Kansas enterprises the year previous. In May, 1858, Brown held a convention in Chatham, Canada, in a negro church, with a negro preacher for president, and adopted a constitution, which, without naming any territory to which it was to apply, said; "We, the citizens of the United States, and the oppressed people, who, etc., do ordain and establish for ourselves the following provisional constitution and ordinances." This constitution, drawn up by John Brown, and adopted by himself and half a dozen whites, and as many more negroes in Canada, provided for legislative, executive, and judicial branches of his government. It also provided for treaties of peace, for a commander-in-chief, for communism of property, for capturing and confiscating property, for the treatment of prisoners, and for many absurd things besides. After providing for the slaughter or the robbery of nearly everybody in the United States who did not join the organization, or voluntarily free their slaves and agree to keep the peace, it culminated in a declaration:

"Art. 46. The foregoing articles shall not be construed so as in any way to encourage the overthrow of any state government of the United States, and look to no dissolution of the Union, but simply to amend and repeal, and our flag shall be the same as our fathers fought under in the Revolution."

No one can read the absurd jargon and believe that it was the product of the same brain. Yet the last declaration of the document is no more inconsistent with the facts than were the repeated declarations of Brown, after he had killed a number of people at Harper's Ferry, that he proposed no violence. Nor was it a whit more absurd than the pretended loyalty to State and country of those who applauded his career of murder and robbery, and treason both state and national.

From May, 1858, to October, 1859, Brown pursued his plans. He rented a farm near Harper's Ferry, and there collected his arms and ammunition, without exciting suspicion. Delays occurred from lack of funds, etc. An anonymous letter was sent to the Secretary of War, in the spring of 1859, revealing his plans and purposes, but it seems to have made no impression, although the Secretary of War was a Southern man.

Shortly before Brown made his demonstration, his cohorts, to the number of twenty, black and white, assembled at his farmhouse, and Sunday night, October 16, 1859, they descended upon Harper's Ferry. About 10:30 P.M., they seized and captured the watchman upon the railroad bridge across the Potomac, and proceeded with him to the United States armory, of which they took possession. Brown then sent forth a party, headed by his lieutenant, Cook, to capture Colonel Lewis Washington and Mr. Allstadt, leading citizens, who were to be held as hostages. These gentlemen were compelled to leave their beds, and accompany the invaders. Their slaves, to the number of thirty, were also compelled, against their will, to join the party. Colonel Washington was a grand-nephew of George Washington, and a member of the staff of the governor of Virginia.

A sword of Frederick the Great, which had been presented to George Washington, was "appropriated" for use by John Brown. At this point we are introduced to the word selected by Brown as descriptive of his taking other people's property. He did not call it stealing, or robbery, or violent seizure. He invariably referred to it as "appropriating," and he pronounced the word in a peculiar way, - putting the whole emphasis upon the second syllable, as if it were a-*prop*-riating. It was a favorite and oft-repeated word with him. Here also we see, in his appropriating the sword of Frederick the Great to be worn by himself, that overshadowing egotism which was one of his most prominent characteristics, - the inordinate vanity of lunacy.

It was an ill omen for his venture that the first person killed by his band in the early morning was an inoffensive colored man, a porter at the railroad station, who, being ordered to stop and seeking to escape, was shot as he ran away. The next victim was a citizen killed standing in his own door. The next, a graduate of West Point, who, having heard of the trouble at the Ferry, was shot from the armory as he rode into town on horseback armed with a gun. It is impossible to describe the consternation which these scenes produced among the citizens of Harper's Ferry.

When the marines had completed their lawful and proper work the following morning, John Brown lay on the grass desperately wounded. His entire party was killed, wounded, or captured, and the dead bodies of two of his sons were beside him. It was a ghastly ending of a horrid venture....

Item in the *Daily Richmond Enquirer*, 3 December 1859: (2)

'TIS DONE

Virginia has vindicated her outraged laws, by the execution of John Brown, the leader of the Harper's Ferry Raid.

We allude to this execution not for the purpose of exultation; we hope we are incapable of entertaining any such feeling; "we vex not his ghost," but in recording the event, we desire the abolition world to know that their offers of bribe, their profers of political preferment, their threats of vengeance, their entreaties for mercy, have all proved to no avail.

If the execution of a criminal makes that felon a martyr, Virginia is prepared to incur all the consequences of that martyrdom; if from his grave comes the bloody results to the South, so often threatened; if from his blood springs the armed assassins of abolition revenge, we have only to say, Virginia will meet those results with ropes, for which South Carolina grows the cotton, and

Kentucky the hemp.

We hope conservatism may now rally to the cause of the Union, and exhibit some of that influence so often boasted, as still potent at the North. Conservatism has given place to fanaticism quite long enough; it is high time to assert its pretended supremacy, or acknowledge its real impotency. We hope the gallows of John Brown may as effectually rally the conservatives, as it assuredly will the fanatics.

BOOK I – CHAPTER THREE

The Knell of the Union

William Drayton, a South Carolinian, from *The South Vindicated from the Treason and Fanaticism of the Northern Abolitionists*: (1)

But a few years have elapsed since the commencement of the abolition movement. It originated in a few heated and disturbed minds, and was urged in the face of every obstacle. Wm. Lloyd Garrison, Lundy, and some others, who conceived themselves the chosen instruments of accomplishing abolition, proclaimed their peculiar doctrines with an ardour, which, if it did not excite respect, at least attracted attention. Garrison, the most talented and rabid of the corps, soon became notorious.... The Colonization Society had, by agitating the subject, prepared the country for the coming of this second Peter the Hermit....

George Fitzhugh, from *Cannibals All! or Slaves Without Masters*: (2)

Mr. Garrison... heads the extreme wing of the Socialist, Infidel, Woman's-Right, Agrarian and Abolition party, who are called Garrisonians. He edits the *Liberator*, which is conducted with an ability worthy of a better cause. He and his followers seem to admit that the Bible and the Constitution recognize and guarantee Slavery, and therefore denounce both, and propose disunion and no priests or churches as measures to attain abolition. Mr. Garrison usually presides at their meetings, and we infer, in part, [over] their principles and doctrines, from the materials that compose those meetings. A Wise-Woman will rise and utter a philippic against Marriage, the Bible, and the Constitution – and will be followed by negro Remond, who "spits upon Washington," and complains of the invidious distinction of calling whites Anglo-Saxons, and negroes Africans. And now, Phillips arises,

Armed with hell-flames and fury,

And gently begins, in tones more dulcet, and with action more graceful than Belial, to

Pour the sweet milk of concord into hell!
Uproar the universal peace –
Destroy all unity on earth.

Then Mr. Parker will edify the meeting by stirring up to bloody deeds in Kansas or in Boston – in which, as becomes his cloth, he takes no part – and ends by denouncing things in general, and the churches and parsons in particular. And, probably, the whole will conclude with a general indulgence and remission of sins, from Mr. Andrews, who assumes, for the nonce, the character of Father Confessor, and assures the tender conscience that it is right and incumbent to take the oath to sustain the Constitution with deliberate purpose of violating it, because such oaths are taken under moral duress. These Garrisonians are as intellectual men as any in the nation. They lead the Black Republican party, and control the politicians. Yet are they deadly enemies of Northern as well as of Southern institutions.

Now, gentlemen, all of you are philosophers, and most zealous philanthropists, and have for years been roaring, at the top of your voice, to the Oi Polloi rats, that the old crazy edifice of society, in which they live, is no longer fit for human dwelling, and is imminently dangerous. The rats have taken you at your word, and are rushing headlong, with the haste and panic of a *sauve qui peut*, into every hole that promises shelter – into "any port in a storm." Some join the Rappists and Shakers; thousands find a temporary shelter in Mr. Greeley's Fourierite Phalansteries; many more follow Mr. Andrews to Trialville, to villages in the far west, or to Modern Times; and a select few to the saloons of Free Love; and hundreds of thousands find shelter with Brigham Young, in Utah; whilst others, still more frightened, go to consult the Spiritual Telegraph, that raps hourly at the doors of heaven and of hell, or quietly put on their ascension robes to accompany Parson Miller in his upward flight. But the greater number are waiting (very impatiently) for Mr. Andrews to establish his New and Better World, or for Mr. Garrison and Mr. Goodell to inaugurate their Millennium....

William J. Grayson, from *The Hireling and the Slave, Chicora, and Other Poems*: (3)

The Levite tribes of Christian love that show
No care nor pity for a neighbor's woe;
Who meet, each distant evil to deplore,
But not to clothe or feed their country's poor;
They waste no thought on common wants or pains,
On misery hid in filthy courts and lanes,
On alms that ask no witnesses but Heaven,
By pious hands to secret suffering given;
Theirs the bright sunshine of the public eye,
The pomp and circumstance of charity,
The crowded meeting, the repeated cheer,
The sweet applause of prelate, prince, or peer,
The long report of pious trophies won
Beyond the rising or the setting sun,
The mutual smile, the self-complacent air,
The labored speech and Pharisaic prayer,

Thanksgivings for their purer hearts and hands,
Scorn for the publicans of other lands,
And soft addresses – Sutherland's delight,
That gentle dames at pious parties write –
These are the cheats that vanity prepares,
The charmed deceits of her seductive fairs,
When Exeter expands her portals wide,
And England's saintly coteries decide
The proper nostrum for each evil known
In every land on earth, except their own,
But never heed the sufferings, wants, or sins
At home, where all true charity begins….

The tear of sympathy forever flows,
Though not for Saxon or for Celtic woes;
Vainly the starving white, at every door,
Craves help or pity for the hireling poor;
But that the distant black may softlier fare,
Eat, sleep, and play, exempt from toil and care,
All England's meek philanthropists unite
With frantic eagerness, harangue and write;
By purchased tools diffuse distrust and hate,
Sow factious strife in each dependent state,
Cheat with delusive lies the public mind,
Invent the cruelties they fail to find,
Slander, in a pious garb, with prayer and hymn,
And blast a people's fortune for a whim.

Cursed by these factious arts, that take the guise
Of charity to cheat the good and wise,
The bright Antilles, with each closing year,
See harvests fail, and fortunes disappear;
The cane no more its golden treasure yields;
Unsightly weeds deform the fertile fields;
The negro freeman, thrifty while a slave,
Loosed from restraint, becomes a drone or knave;
Each effort to improve his nature foils,

Begs, steals, or sleeps and starves, but never toils;
For savage sloth mistakes the freedom won,
And ends the mere barbarian he begun.

Then, with a face of self-complacent smiles,
Pleased with the ruin of these hapless isles,
And charmed with this cheap way of gaining heaven
By alms at cost of other countries given –
Like Nathan's host, who hospitably gave
His guest a neighbor's lamb his own to save –
Clarkson's meek school beholds with eager eyes,
In other climes, new fields of glory rise,
And heedless still of home, its care bestows,
In other lands, on other Negro woes....

Wendell Phillips, from an Abolitionist speech, November 1, 1859: (4)

I said that the lesson of the hour was insurrection. I ought not to apply that word to John Brown of Osawatomie, for there was no insurrection in his case. It is a great mistake to call him an insurgent. This principle that I have endeavored so briefly to open to you, of absolute right and wrong, states what? Just this: "Commonwealth of Virginia!" There is no such thing. Lawless, brutal force is no basis of a government, in the true sense of that word.... No civil society, no government, can exist except on the basis of the willing submission of all its citizens, and by the performance of the duty of rendering equal justice between man and man.

Whatever calls itself a government, and refuses that duty, or has not that asset, is no government. It is only a pirate ship. Virginia, the Commonwealth of Virginia! She is only a chronic insurrection. I mean exactly what I say. I am weighing my words now. She is a pirate ship, and John Brown sails the sea a Lord

High Admiral of the Almighty, with his commission to sink every pirate he meets on God's ocean of the nineteenth century....

> And they, sweet soul, that most impute a crime
> Are pronest to it, and impute themselves....
>   - Tennyson, Idylls of the King (5)

From "The Slave-Trade in New York", in the *Continental Monthly*, January 1862: (6)

The number of persons engaged in the slave-trade, and the amount of capital embarked in it, exceed our powers of calculation. The city of New York has been until of late the principal port of the world for this infamous commerce; although the cities of Portland and Boston are only second to her in that distinction....

William J. Grayson, from *The Hireling and the Slave, Chicora, and Other Poems*: (7)

> They drag the Negro from his native shore,
> Make him a slave, and then his fate deplore;
> Sell him in distant countries, and when sold,
> Revile the buyers, but retain the gold:
> Dext'rous to win, in time, by various ways,
> Substantial profit and alluring praise,
> By turns they grow rapacious and humane,
> And seize alike the honor and the gain:
> Had Joseph's brethren known this modern art,
> And played with skill the philanthropic part,
> How had bold Judah raved in freedom's cause,
> How Levi cursed the foul Egyptian laws,

And Issachar, in speech or long report,
Brayed at the masters found in Pharaoh's court,
And taught the king himself the sin to hold
Enslaved the brother they had lately sold,
Proving that sins of traffic never lie
On knaves who sell, but on the dupes that buy.

Such now the maxims of the purer school
Of ethic lore, where sons of slavers rule;
No more allowed the Negro to enslave,
They damn the master, and for freedom rave,
Strange modes of morals and of faith unfold,
Make newer gospels supersede the old,
Prove that ungodly Paul connived at sin,
And holier rites, like Mormon's priest, begin;
There, chief and teacher, Gerrit Smith appears,
There Tappan mourns, like Niobe, all tears,
Carnage and fire mad Garrison invokes,
And Hale, with better temper, smirks and jokes;
There Giddings, with the Negro mania bit,
Mouths, and mistakes his ribaldry for wit....

There supple Sumner, with the Negro cause,
Plays the sly game for office and applause;
What boots it if the Negro sink or swim?
He wins the Senate – 'tis enough for him.
What though he blast the fortunes of the state
With fierce dissension and enduring hate?
He makes his speech, his rhetoric displays,
Trims the neat trope, and points the sparkling phrase
With well-turned period, fosters civil strife,
And barters for a phrase a nation's life....

George Fitzhugh, from his *Cannibals All! or*
Slaves Without Masters: (8)

More than a year since, we made a short trip to the North, and whilst there only associated with distinguished Abolitionists. We have corresponded much with them, before and since, and read many of their books, lectures, essays and speeches. We have neither seen nor heard any denial by them of the failure of their own social system; but, on the contrary, found that they all concurred in the necessity of radical social changes. 'Tis true, in conversation, they will say, "Our system of society is bad, but yours of the South is worse; the cause of social science is advancing, and we are ready to institute a system better than either." We could give many private anecdotes, and quote thousands of authorities, to prove that such is the exact state of opinion with the multitudinous "-isms" of the North. The correctness of our statement will not be denied. If it is, any one may satisfy himself of its truth by reading any Abolition or Infidel paper at the North for a single month. *The Liberator*, of Boston, their ablest paper, gives continually the fullest expose of their opinions, and of their wholesale destructiveness of purpose.

The neglect of the North to take issue with us, ... our own observations of the working of Northern society, the alarming increase of Socialism, as evinced by its control of many Northern State Legislatures, and its majority in the lower house of Congress, are all new proofs of the truth of our doctrine. The character of that majority in Congress is displayed in full relief, by the single fact, which we saw stated in a Northern Abolition paper, that "there are a hundred Spiritual Rappers in Congress." A Northern member of Congress made a similar remark to us a few days since. 'Tis but a copy of the Hiss Legislature of Massachusetts, or the Praise-God-Barebones Parliament of England.

Further study, too, of Western European Society, which has been engaged in continual revolution for twenty years, has satisfied us that Free Society everywhere begets "-isms", and that "-isms" soon beget bloody revolutions. Until our trip to the North, we did not justly appreciate the passage which we are about to quote from Mr. Carlyle's *Latter-Day Pamphlets*. Now it seems to us as if Boston, New Haven, or Western New York, had sat for the picture:

"To rectify the relation that exists between two men, is there no method, then, but that of ending it? The old relation has become unsuitable, obsolete, perhaps unjust; and the remedy is, abolish it; let there henceforth be no relation at all. From the 'sacrament of marriage' downwards, human beings used to be manifoldly related one to another, and each to all; and there was no relation among human beings, just or unjust, that had not its grievances and its difficulties, its necessities on both sides to bear and forbear. But henceforth, be it known, we have changed all that by favor of Heaven; the 'voluntary principle' has come up, which will itself do the business for us; and now let a new sacrament, that of DIVORCE, which we call emancipation, and spout of on our platforms, be universally the order of the day! Have men considered whither all this is tending, and what it certainly enough betokens? Cut every human relation that has any where grown uneasy sheer asunder; reduce whatsoever was compulsory to voluntary, whatsoever was permanent among us to the condition of the nomadic; in other words, LOOSEN BY ASSIDUOUS WEDGES, in every joint, the whole fabric of social existence, stone from stone, till at last, (all lie quite loose enough,) it can, as we already see in most countries, be overset by sudden outburst of revolutionary rage; and lying as mere mountains of anarchic rubbish, solicit you to sing Fraternity, &c. over it, and rejoice in the now remarkable era of human progress we have arrived at...."

BOOK I - CHAPTER FOUR

The Hell-broth

John Randolph of Roanoke, a planter of Charlotte County, Virginia, statesman and orator, from a letter appearing in the Richmond *Enquirer*, April 1, 1815: (1)

The very bonds, not only of union between these states, but of society itself are loosened, and we seem 'approaching towards that awful dissolution, the issue of which it is not given to human foresight to scan.' In the virtue, the moderation, the fortitude of the People is (under God) our last resource. Let them ever bear in mind that from their present institutions there is no transition but to military despotism; and that there is none more easy. Anarchy is the chrysalis state of despotism; and to that state have the measures of this government long tended, amidst professions, such as we have heard in France and seen the effects of, of Liberty, Equality, Fraternity....

Chancellor Henry William Desaussure, a South Carolinian, from "A Series of Numbers Addressed to the Public, on the Subject of the Slaves and Free People of Colour....", (1822): (2)

When the French Convention in its madness emancipated the slaves of St. Domingo, and its orators pronounced the dreadful dogma, let the earth and its inhabitants perish, rather than a principle, (the principle of universal freedom,) it little imagined that this decree would produce the extermination of the whites, the utter destruction of that fine colony, and the ruin of the best commerce which France enjoyed; - yet such were the fruits – and such would be the case in the southern states, in the struggle and civil wars which would inevitably follow, if the blacks were emancipated; unless the whites, feeling that their existence depended on it, put forth their strength vigorously, and subdued them promptly....

The wise and the good should then interpose, and prevent fools from casting about firebrands, which may light up a conflagration, that could not be extinguished without torrents of blood....

Thomas R. Dew, from his *Review of the Debates in the Virginia Legislature of 1831 and 1832*: (3)

In looking to the texture of the population of our country, there is nothing so well calculated to arrest the attention of the observer, as the existence of Negro Slavery throughout a large portion of the confederacy. A race of people differing from us in colour and in habits, and vastly inferior in the scale of civilization, have been increasing and spreading, "growing with our growth and strengthening with our strength," until they have become intertwined and intertwisted with every fibre of society. Go through our Southern country, and every where you see the negro slave by the side of the white man; you find him alike in the mansion of the rich, the cabin of the poor, the workshop of the mechanic, and the field of the planter. Upon the contemplation of a population framed like this, a curious and interesting question readily suggests itself to the inquiring mind: - Can these two distinct races of people now living together as master and servant, be ever separated? Can the black be sent back to his African home, or will the day ever arrive when he can be liberated from his thralldom, and mount upwards in the scale of civilization and rights, to an equal-

ity with the white? This is a question of truly momentous character; it involves the whole frame work of society....

Well then does it behoove even the wisest statesman to
approach this august subject with the utmost circumspection and
diffidence; its wanton agitation even is pregnant with mischief;
but rash and hasty action threatens, in our opinion, the whole
Southern country with irremediable ruin. The evil of *yesterday's*
growth, may be extirpated *to-day*, and the vigour of society may
heal the wound; but that which is the growth of *ages*, may require *ages* to remove....

Without further preliminary, then, we shall advance to
the discussion of the question of abolition... and, as the subject
of slavery has been considered in every point of view, and pronounced, in the *abstract* at least, as entirely contrary to the law
of nature, we propose taking in the first place, a hasty view of the
origin of slavery, and point out the influence which it has exerted
on the progress of civilization, and to this purpose it will be necessary to look back to other ages – cast a glance at nations differing
from us in civilization and manners, and see whether it is possible
to mount to the source of slavery....

*Both thy bondmen, and thy bondmaids, which thou shalt
have, shall be of the heathen that are round about you; of
them shall ye buy bondmen and bondmaids. Moreover of the
children of the strangers that do sojourn among you, of them
shall ye buy, and of their families that are with you, which
they begat in your land: and they shall be your possession.
And ye shall take them as an inheritance for your children
after you, to inherit them for a possession; they shall be your
bondmen for ever....*
                    - Leviticus 25: 44-46.

Thomas R. Dew, from his *Review of the Debates in the Virginia Legislature of 1831 and 1832*: (4)

Slavery was established and sanctioned by Divine Authority, among even the elect of Heaven – the favored children of Israel. Abraham, the founder of this interesting nation, and chosen servant of the Lord, was the owner of *hundreds* of slaves – that magnificent shrine, the Temple of Solomon, was raised by the hands of slaves. Egypt's venerable and enduring piles were reared by similar hands. Slavery existed in Assyria and Babylon. The ten tribes of Israel were carried off in bondage to the former by Shalmanezar, and the two tribes of Judah were subsequently carried in triumph by Nebuchadnezzar to beautify and adorn the latter. Ancient Phoenicia and Carthage had slaves – the Greeks and Trojans at the siege of Troy, had slaves – Athens, and Sparta, and Thebes, indeed the whole Grecian and Roman worlds, had more slaves than freemen. And in those ages which succeeded the extinction of the Roman Empire in the West, "*Servi* or slaves," says Dr. Robertson, "seem to have been the most numerous class." Even in this day of civilization, and the regeneration of governments, slavery is far from being confined to our hemisphere alone. The Serf and Labour rents prevalent throughout the whole of Eastern Europe and a portion of Western Asia; and the Ryot rents throughout the extensive and over populated countries of the East, and over the dominions of the Porte in Europe, Asia and Africa, but too conclusively mark the existence of slavery over these boundless regions. And when we turn to the vast continent of Africa, we find slavery in all its most horrid forms, existing throughout its whole extent – the slaves being at least three times more numerous than the freemen....

It is said slavery is wrong, in the *abstract* at least, and contrary to the spirit of Christianity. To this we answer as before, that any question must be determined by its circumstances, and if, as really is the case, we cannot get rid of slavery without producing a greater injury to both the masters and slaves, there is no rule of conscience or revealed law of God which *can* condemn us. The physician will not order the spreading cancer to be extirpated, although it will eventually cause the death of his patient, because he would thereby hasten the fatal issue. So, if slavery had commenced even contrary to the laws of God and man, and the sin of its introduction rested upon our heads, and it was even carrying forward the nation by slow degrees to final ruin – yet, if it were *certain* that an attempt to remove it would only hasten and heighten the final catastrophe – that it was, in fact, a "vulnus immedicabile" on the body politic which no legislation could safely remove, then we would not only not be found to attempt the extirpation, but we would stand guilty of a high offence in the sight of both God and man if we should rashly make the effort. But the original sin of introduction rests not on our heads....

Chancellor Henry William Desaussure, from "A Series of Numbers Addressed to the Public, on the Subject of the Slaves and Free People of Colour...." (1822): (5)

We state then, that the importation and slavery of the blacks was imposed upon us by the British Government, which refused to listen to the petitions of the Colonies against such importations.

That slavery, when the blacks were reduced to that state in this country, was universally considered lawful; and the scriptures no where prohibit slavery. Every power which now denounces it, encouraged and practised it, and particularly Great Britain, France, Spain, and Portugal. Northern capital and shipping were also employed in the trade.

That the slaves cost an enormous sum of money, and are as much the property of their holders, as any other property, of

any other owners – and that they cannot be justly or lawfully deprived of this property, but by their own consent, and at a fair and
full price.

That the price of 1,500,000 slaves would amount to so
enormous a sum of money, as to preclude all hope of the government of the United States being able to pay it, or to provide for
the payment of the usual interest of it. And that if it be attempted
to make a gradual reduction by annual purchases, the natural annual increase would exceed the annual number and amount which
they could purchase.

That if it were possible for the government to purchase
and pay for the slaves, they could not be transferred to Africa,
but at an enormous and overwhelming expense: and experience
shows that such a body of people could not be transported across
the ocean without great sufferings, miseries and destruction on
the passage, and probably utter annihilation on their arrival in
Africa. And that locating them on any part of the North American
continent, would not remove the difficulty in any degree....

Are the blacks now prepared, or could their descendants
be prepared for the enjoyment of liberty or political rights? The
answer founded on experience must be in the negative.... The
body of them would either be the blind and violent instruments
of some of their own cunning and base leaders, or of profligate
white demagogues who would condescend to use so coarse an
instrument to gain power; or they would be a dead, inert mass,
mere hewers of wood and drawers of water. They would either be
mischievously active, or uselessly inactive....

Alexis de Tocqueville, a French observer of America during the 1830's, from his two-volume classic, *Democracy in America*: (6)

But if the relative position of the two races which inhabit the United States is such as I have described, it may be asked why the Americans abolished slavery in the North of the Union ...? The answer is easily given. It is not for the good of the negroes, but for that of the whites, that measures are taken to abolish slavery in the United States....

The free workman is paid, but he does his work quicker than the slave; and rapidity of execution is one of the great elements of economy. The white sells his services, but they are only purchased at the times at which they may be useful; the black can claim no remuneration for his toil, but the expense of his maintenance is perpetual; he must be supported in his old age as well as in the prime of manhood, in his profitless infancy as well as in the productive years of youth. Payment must equally be made in order to obtain the services of either class of men: the free workman receives his wages in money, the slave in education, in food, in care, and in clothing. The money which a master spends in the maintenance of his slaves goes gradually and in detail, so that it is scarcely perceived; the salary of the free workman is paid in a round sum, which appears only to enrich the individual who receives it, but in the end the slave has cost more than the free servant, and his labor is less productive....

As soon as a competition was set on foot between the free labourer and the slave, the inferiority of the latter became manifest, and slavery was attacked in its fundamental principle, which is the interest of the master.

As slavery recedes, the black population follows its retrograde course, and returns with it towards those tropical regions from which it originally came. However singular this fact may at first appear to be, it may readily be explained. Although the Americans abolish the principle of slavery, they do not set their slaves free. To illustrate this remark, I will quote the example of the State of New York. In 1788 the State of New York prohibited the sale of slaves within its limits, which was an indirect method of prohibiting the importation of blacks. Thenceforward the number of negroes could only increase according to the ratio of the natural increase of population. But eight years later, a more decisive measure was taken, and it was enacted that all children born of slave parents after the 4th of July, 1799 should be free. No increase could then take place, and although slaves still existed, slavery might be said to be abolished.

From the time at which a Northern State prohibited the importation of slaves, no slaves were brought from the South to be sold in its markets. On the other hand, as the sale of slaves was forbidden in that State, an owner was no longer able to get rid of his slave (who thus became a burdensome possession) otherwise than by transporting him to the South. But when a Northern state declared that the son of the slave should be born free, the slave lost a large portion of his market value, since his posterity was no longer included in the bargain, and the owner had then a strong interest in transporting him to the South. Thus the same law prevents the slaves of the South from coming to the Northern States, and drives those of the North to the South.

The want of free hands is felt in a State in proportion as the number of slaves decreases. But in proportion as labour is performed by free hands, slave labor becomes less productive; and the slave is then a useless or onerous possession, whom it is important to export to those Southern States where the same competition is not to be feared. Thus the abolition of slavery does not set the slave free, but it merely transfers him from one master to another, and from the North to the South.

The emancipated negroes, and those born after the abolition of slavery, do not, indeed, migrate from the North to the South; but their situation with regard to the Europeans is not unlike that of the aborigines of America; they remain half civilized, and deprived of their rights in the midst of a population that is far superior to them in wealth and in knowledge; where they are exposed to the tyranny of the laws and the intolerance of the people. (The States in which slavery is abolished usually do what they can to render their territory disagreeable to the negroes as a place of residence; and as a kind of emulation exists between the different States in this respect, the unhappy blacks can only choose the least of the evils which beset them)....

The more we descend towards the South, the more difficult does it become to abolish slavery with advantage: and this arises from several physical causes which it is important to point out.

The first of these causes is the climate.... All the plants of Europe grow in the northern parts of the Union; the South has special productions of its own. It has been observed that slave-labour is a very expensive method of cultivating corn. The farmer of corn land in a country where slavery is unknown habitually retains a small number of labourers in his service, and at seed-time and harvest he hires several additional hands, who only live at his cost for a short period. But the agriculturalist in a slave State is obliged to keep a large number of slaves the whole year round, in order to sow his fields and to gather in his crops, although their services are only required for a few weeks; but slaves are unable to wait till they are hired, and to subsist by their own labour in the meantime like free laborers; in order to have their services they must be bought. Slavery, independently of its general disadvantages, is therefore still more inapplicable to countries in which corn is cultivated than to those which produce crops of a different kind. The cultivation of tobacco, of cotton, and especially of the sugar-cane, demands, on the other hand, unremitting attention: and women and children are employed in it, whose services are of but little use in the cultivation of wheat. Thus slavery is naturally more fitted to the countries from which these productions are derived....

But there is yet another motive which is more cogent than all the others: the South might, indeed, rigorously speaking, abolish slavery; but how should it rid its territory of the black population? Slaves and slavery are driven from the North by the same law, but this twofold result cannot be hoped for in the South....

In the state of Maine there is one Negro in three hundred inhabitants; in Massachusetts, one in one hundred; in New York, two in one hundred; in Pennsylvania, three in the same number; in Maryland, thirty-four; in Virginia, forty-two; and lastly, in South Carolina, fifty-five per cent. Such was the proportion of the black population to the whites in the year 1830. But this proportion is perpetually changing, as it constantly decreases in the North and augments in the South....

In the North, as I have already remarked, a twofold migration ensues upon the abolition of slavery, or even precedes that event when circumstances have rendered it probable: the slaves quit the country to be transported southwards; and the whites of the Northern states, as well as the emigrants from Europe, hasten to fill up their places. But these two causes cannot operate in the same manner in the Southern states. On the one hand, the mass of slaves is too great for any expectation of their ever being removed from the country to be entertained; and on the other hand, the Europeans and Anglo-Americans of the North are afraid to come to inhabit a country in which labour has not been reinstated in its rightful honours. Besides, they very justly look upon the States in which the proportion of the negroes equals or exceeds that of the whites, as exposed to very great dangers; and they refrain from turning their activity in that direction.

Thus the inhabitants of the South would not be able, like their Northern countrymen, to initiate the slaves gradually into a state of freedom by abolishing slavery; they have no means of perceptibly diminishing the black population, and they would remain unsupported to repress its excesses. So that in the course of a few years a great people of free negroes would exist in the heart of a white nation of equal size....

As soon as it is admitted that the whites and the emancipated blacks are placed upon the same territory in the situation of two alien communities, it will readily be understood that there are but two alternatives for the future; the negroes and the whites must either wholly part or wholly mingle. I have already expressed the conviction that I entertain as to the latter event. (This opinion is sanctioned by authorities infinitely weightier than anything that I can say; thus, for instance, it is stated in the *Memoirs of Jefferson* – as collected by M. Conseil – " Nothing is more clearly written in the book of destiny than the emancipation of the blacks; and it is equally certain that the two races will never live in a state of equal freedom under the same government, so insurmountable are the barriers which nature, habit, and opinions have established between them.")

I do not imagine that the white and black races will ever live in any country upon an equal footing. But I believe the difficulty to be still greater in the United States than elsewhere. An isolated individual may surmount the prejudices of religion, of his country, or of his race, and if this individual is a king he may effect surprising changes in society; but a whole people can not rise, as it were, above itself. A despot who should subject the Americans and their former slaves to the same yoke might perhaps succeed in commingling their races; but as long as the American democracy remains at the head of affairs, no one will undertake so difficult a task....

Thomas R. Dew, from his *Review of the Debates in the Virginia Legislature of 1831 and 1832*: (7)

The history of the world has too conclusively shown, that two races, differing in manners, customs, language, and civilization, can never harmonize upon a footing of equality. One must rule the other, or exterminating wars must be waged.... In the very few cases where the work of desolation ceased, and a commingling of races ensued, it has been found that the civilized man has sunk down to the level of barbarism, and there has ended the mighty work of civilization....

Alexis de Tocqueville, from *Democracy in America*: (8)

Such is the view that the Americans of the South take of the question, and they act consistently with it. As they are determined not to mingle with the Negroes, they refuse to emancipate them.

Not that the inhabitants of the South regard slavery as necessary to the wealth of the planter, for on this point many of them agree with their Northern countrymen in freely admitting that slavery is prejudicial to their interest; but they are convinced that, however prejudicial it may be, they hold their lives upon no other tenure....

Whatever may be the efforts of the Americans of the South to maintain slavery, they will not always succeed. Slavery, which is now confined to a single tract of the civilized earth, which is attacked by Christianity as unjust, and by political economy as prejudicial; and which is now contrasted with democratic liberties and the information of our age, can not survive. By the choice of the master, or by the will of the slave, it will cease; and in either case great calamities may be expected to ensue. If liberty be refused to the negroes of the South, they will in the end seize it for themselves by force; if it be given, they will abuse it ere long....

Thomas Jefferson to John Holmes, April 22, 1820: (9)

I can say, with conscious truth, that there is not a man on earth who would sacrifice more than I would to relieve us from this heavy reproach, in any *practicable* way. The cession of that kind of property, for so it is misnamed, is a bagatelle which would not cost me a second thought, if, in that way, a general emancipation and *expatriation* could be effected; and gradually, and with due sacrifices, I think it might be. But as it is, we have the wolf by the ears, and we can neither hold him, nor safely let him go. Justice is in one scale, and self-preservation in the other....

BOOK I – CHAPTER FIVE

The Yeast of the Pharisees

Mrs. Roger A. Pryor, wife of a Virginia congress-man, from her *Reminiscences of Peace and War*: (1)

When the famous Thirty-sixth Congress met for its long session, December 5, 1859, the whole country was in ferment over the execution of John Brown. "An indiscreet move in any direction," wrote ex-President Tyler from his plantation, "may produce results deeply to be deplored. I fear the debates in Congress, and above all the Speaker's election. If excitement prevails in Congress, it will add fuel to the flame which already burns so terrifically." He, and all patriots, might well have been afraid of increased excitement. It was evident from the first hour that the atmosphere was heavily charged. The House resolved itself into a great debating society, in which the only questions were: "Is slavery right or wrong? Shall it, or shall it not, be allowed in the territories?" The foray of the zealot and fanatic aggravated the fury of the combatants.

The member from Mississippi – L. Q. C. Lamar (afterwards Supreme Court Justice of the United States) – threw an early fire-brand by announcing on the floor of the House, "The Republicans are not guiltless of the blood of John Brown, his co-conspirators, and the innocent victims of his ruthless vengeance." Lawrence Keitt of South Carolina declared: "The South asks nothing but its rights. I would have no more, but as God as my judge, I would shatter this republic from turret to foundation-stone before I would take a tittle less." Thaddeus Stevens of Pennsylvania re-torted: "I do not blame gentlemen of the South for using this threat of rending God's creation from foundation to turret. They have tried it fifty times, and fifty times they have found weak and recreant tremblers in the North who have been affected by it, and who have acted from those intimidations." Such were a few, by comparison with those that rapidly followed, of the wild utterances of the hour. This occurred on the second day of the session. The House was in an uproar! Members from their seats crowded down into the aisles, and the clerk was powerless to preserve order. "A few more such scenes," said one, "and we shall hear the crack of the revolver and see the gleam of brandished blade."

In this spirit Congress proceeded to ballot for its Speaker, and balloted for two months (until February 1), before Mr. Sherman was abandoned (having withdrawn his name) and a compromise effected by the election of Mr. Pennington, who represented neither extreme of party.

During these two months everything was said that could be said to fan the flame. Hot disputes were accentuated by bitter personal remarks. One day a pistol accidentally fell from the pocket of a member from New York, and, thinking it had been drawn with the intention of using it, some of the members were wild with passion, crying excitedly for the sergeant-at-arms, and turning the House into a pandemonium. John Sherman, who had been the unlucky bone of contention, made this remarkable statement: "When I came here I did not believe that the slavery question would come up; and but for the unfortunate affair of Brown at Harper's Ferry I do not believe that there would have been any feeling on the subject. Northern men came here with kindly feelings, no man approving the foray of John Brown, and every man willing to say so, every man willing to admit it as an act of lawless violence."

Four years before this stormy election, Banks had been chosen Speaker after a contest longer by a few days than this. Then, as now, slavery was the point at issue; but "good humor and courtesy had marked the previous contest where now were acrimony and defiance.... Then, threats of disunion were received with laughter; now they were too manifestly sincere to be treated lightly." In four years the breach between North and South, once only a rift in the rock, had become a yawning chasm. What might it not become in four years more?

Not foreseeing the rapid change of public sentiment, the Democrats had, four years before, selected Charleston for the meeting of the convention to name their candidate for the presidency. Accordingly, on April 23, the party was convened in the "hotbed of disunion."

The Northern Democrats had heard much of the splendor and elegance in which Charlestonians lived, and of the Arabian hospitality of the South, which could ignore all animosities over the bread and salt. But Charleston turned a cold shoulder to its guests from the North. All hearts, however, and all homes were opened to the Southerners. They dined with the aristocrats, drove with richly dressed ladies in gay equipages, and were entertained generally with lavish hospitality. All this tended to widen the breach between the sections.

When the delegates left their fair entertainers for the sessions of the convention, the ladies repaired to old St. Michael's Episcopal Church, where prayers, specially ordered for the success and prosperity of the South, were daily offered. "At the same time fervent abolition preachers at the North were praying for a disruption of the Charleston convention."

Judge Douglas had written a platform that was not acceptable to the South. After its adoption seven delegates from the Southern states declared their purpose of secession. The convention, seeing that it was impossible to reach any result, adjourned May 3, to meet at Baltimore the 18th of June. The seceders resolved to meet at Richmond the second Monday of May. This initial movement awakened the alarm of at least one devoted son of the South.... In conversation with his friend Johnston, shortly after the adjournment of the Convention, [Alexander] Stephens said, "Men will be cutting one another's throats in a little while. In less than twelve months we shall be in a war, and that the bloodiest in history. Men seem to be utterly blinded to the future"....

Senator William H. Seward, of New York, leader of the newly formed Republican Party, from his speech at Rochester, New York, October 25, 1858: (2)

Our country is a theater, which exhibits, in full operation, two radically different political systems; the one resting on the basis of servile or slave labor, the other on the basis of voluntary labor of freemen.... The two systems are at once perceived to be incongruous. But they are more than incongruous - they are incompatible. They never have permanently existed together in one country, and they never can. It would be easy to demonstrate this impossibility, from the irreconcilable contrast between their great principles and characteristics. But the experience of mankind has conclusively established it....

Hitherto the two systems have existed in different states, but side by side within the American Union. This has happened because the Union is a confederation of states. But in another aspect the United States constitute only one nation. Increase of population, which is filling the states out to their very borders, together with a new and extended net-work of railroads and other avenues, and an internal commerce which daily becomes more intimate, is rapidly bringing the states into a higher and more perfect social unity or consolidation. Thus, these antagonistic systems are continually coming into closer contact, and collision results.

Shall I tell you what this collision means? They who think that it is accidental, unnecessary, the work of interested or fanatical agitators, and therefore ephemeral, mistake the case altogether. It is an irrepressible conflict between opposing and enduring forces....

Thomas Prentice Kettell, a leading economist of the time, from his book, *Southern Wealth and Northern Profits*: (3)

From the moment of the formation of the Federal Union there commenced a struggle for political power which has not ceased to be directed against the Slave States. The instrument of union, while it provided for the extinction of the slave-trade, which then formed so large a portion of Northern traffic, contained also a provision for black representation in the Southern States, stipulating that that representation should not be changed until 1808, and thereafter only by a vote of three-fourths of all the States. That provision has been the groundwork of that constant Northern aggression upon Southern interests which has so successfully gained on the federal power until now it imagines the desired three-fourths is within its reach, when the South, with its interests, will be at the feet of the abolitionists....

The gradual abolition of slavery in the old Northern States, and the rapidity with which Eastern capital, following migration, has settled the Western States, has given a large preponderance to the free interest in the national councils. Of the 26 senators that sat in the first Congress, all represented a slave interest, more or less: with the States and territories now knocking for admission, there are 72 senators, of whom 32 only represent the slave interest. That interest, from being "a unit" in the Senate, has sunk to a minority of four, and yet the majority do not cease to complain of Southern "aggression." With this rapid decline in the Southern vote in the great "conservative body" of the Senate, the representation in the lower house has fallen to one-third. How long will it be before the desired three-fourths vote, for which a large party pant, will have been obtained, and, when obtained, what will have become of those Southern rights which are even now denied by party leaders to be any rights at all?

In the last 30 years 11 Free States have been prepared for the Union; a similar progress in the next 30 years and the South will have fallen into that constitutional minority which may deprive it of all reserved rights. This circle is closing rapidly in upon it, amid a continually rising cry of abolition, pointed by bloody inroads of armed men. This is called Southern "aggression"....

The question of slavery in Territories settles itself according to the adaptation of soil to slave-labor. This is not a matter of sentiment or surmise, it is simply a matter of experience and history. The whole of the Northern Free States were once "the homes of slavery." They all possessed that "property", and they all gradually abandoned it as of no practical value. This process is now going on in the Northern Slave States....

Nine States holding slaves in 1709 abolished the institution within 30 years of that date. The reason for doing so was not philanthropic nor yet political, but simply a matter of dollars and cents. Slave-labor in that region was not worth having. This economical principle it is which governs slavery in the Territories.

Slavery will not go on to any of the present unappropriated Territory of the nation, for the reason that it would not be profitable to go there. If it should do so it would be certain to lose. Because the future States would abolish the institution on account of its inutility; and would, like Ohio, Illinois, Indiana, and Minnesota, forbid blacks from coming in at all, either bond or free.

These are fixed and well-known principles; and when a party of political hucksters profess only "one policy", that of keeping slavery out by virtue of their acts, they profess only a bald sham, which is an insult to the intelligence of the people whose votes they seek. As well might a party of political traders point to the influx and efflux of the tide, and pretend that their efforts alone prevent the farm-lands of the Atlantic from being drowned at each recurring flood. Barefaced as would be such an assumption, it is not more baseless than the pretence that Kansas was "saved to freedom" by Brown and Beecher. There is no man of intelligence who does not know that if Kansas had been made a Slave State, and any number of slaves had been carried into it, that a very short time only would elapse before those slaves would have been emancipated by State laws, and consequently "freedom" would have gained instead of losing.

If, then, we are to believe the assertion of the Black Republican leader, the "one policy" only "of which he knows" is a gross deception. It has no practical force or meaning beyond its use as a means of irritating the popular mind, in order to turn votes to the party on the strength of that exasperation; yet he denominates this sham "the great national issue between free labor and capital labor for the territories" that parties are "conducting to its proper solution."

Notwithstanding these disclaimers of the leader in the part of "moderator," seeking to retain those partisans who see more danger than profit in the gratuitous agitation of this deceptive issue, the active partisans are earnest in their deifications of John Brown, and virulent in their hatred of the South.

Mr. Seward himself seems to have been as unfortunate in his partnership with John Brown as he was with the Auburn rumseller during the Temperance campaign in New York. In the latter case he put $2000 capital into partnership to sell "paints, oils," &c, but his zealous, money-making "young partner" construed the "&c" into champagne and "fine old brandies." Mr. Seward, in his public apology, elicited by public surprise, stated that he had been overreached by his partner in drawing the papers, and could not now help himself. History does not record whether he pocketed the profits on the champagne and brandies, but the chances are that he did. The North Carolina teacher, and shrewd New York lawyer and apostle of temperance, was turned into a rumseller by the will of a journeyman painter.

In the Free-soil business he was not more fortunate. He went into business with John Brown, to deal in freedom, &c, in Kansas. John Brown, however, having got possession of his stock in trade, construed the "&c" into invading Virginia, to rob and slaughter the whites, and stampede the negroes. Mr. Seward is again in a dilemma with his "young partner". John Brown's strong doctrine is as objectionable as the Auburn partner's strong drink, and he is compelled to repudiate John Brown to satisfy the temperate people, although the partnership continues by contract, and the profits will accrue in due time....

John S. Wise, from *The End of an Era*: (4)

The Northern elections in the month succeeding John Brown's raid showed gains to the Republicans in the North. Lincoln spoke in February, 1860, at Cooper Institute, New York. His comments on Brown were looked for with anxiety. He said John Brown's effort was "peculiar;" and while he characterized it as absurd, he had no word of censure. Seward spoke soon afterwards in the Senate. He was a man of more refinement than Lincoln. He represented a constituency more highly civilized, and one in which a greater regard for law existed than in the West. He dared to say that Brown "attempted to subvert slavery in Virginia by conspiracy, ambush, invasion, and force," and to add that "this attempt to execute an unlawful purpose in Virginia by invasion, involving servile war, was an act of sedition and treason, and criminal in just the extent that it affected the public peace and was destructive of human happiness and life."

Seward's detestation of slavery was more widely known than Lincoln's. Up to that time, he had no formidable competitor for the Republican nomination for the presidency. It is not improbable that, in the then excited state of Northern feeling, the two candid admissions above quoted cost him the nomination for the presidency.

While these scenes were being enacted, a great change of feeling took place in Virginia towards the people of the North and towards the Union itself. Virginians began to look upon the people of the North as hating them, and willing to see them assassinated at midnight by their own slaves, led by Northern emissaries; as flinging aside all pretense or regard for laws protecting the slaveowner; as demanding of them the immediate freeing of their slaves; or that they prepare against further attacks like Brown's, backed by the moral and pecuniary support of the North.

During the year 1860, the Virginians began to organize and arm themselves against such emergencies. They knew that, while James Buchanan was President, the power of the federal administration could be relied upon to suppress such violence; but they also knew that his term of office was nearly at an end, and they had little hope of such protection if the federal administration fell into the hands of the Republicans....

Item from the Richmond *Dispatch*, November 9, 1860: (5)

THE PRESIDENTIAL ELECTION

It is at least a matter of congratulation that this painful and lamentable Presidential canvass just concluded has come to an end. When we looked to the North we found a party organized upon a sentiment of hostility to the social system of the South, and sustaining a nominee for the first office in the Union upon the one idea of uncompromising war upon Southern rights....

When we turned to the South we beheld a scene of discord without precedent in its history. The several parties arrayed there against one another were bitter in their denunciations of each other, and active in the raising and pressing of issues that were untimely and injurious in their effects.... Nothing could be more grateful to the common enemy, whose drilled cohorts were steadily marching to victory. The arch-fiend of the infernal regions could not gloat with more pleasurable emotions over a feud in Paradise, than did the partisans of Lincoln over the idle internal war among Southern politicians and their passionate followers....

The election of Abraham Lincoln has indeed put this

country in peril. With him comes that calamity which [President George] Washington dreaded as a wedge that would assuredly split the Union in twain, viz: a sectional party in one division of the Union founded on issues hostile to the people of the other, seizing the reins of government and dictating rulers to the nation. He saw in this an outrage, an alienation of the affection and sympathies of the States, which, sooner or later, would dissolve the Union. He was right. It can only be a question of time. Two people who are thus led to hate one another, and struggle against each other, cannot long continue to live together under the same Government.

[Ex-President Millard] Fillmore, who has filled the seat first occupied by Washington, pronounced the triumph of the sectional party at the North a sufficient cause for the secession of the Southern States from the Union....

BOOK I - CHAPTER SIX

The Irrepressible Conflict

Item from the Richmond *Whig*, March 6, 1861: (1)

COERCIVE POLICY OF THE INAUGURAL

We desire to repeat what we said on yesterday, that the coercive policy, foreshadowed in President Lincoln's Inaugural towards the seceding States, will meet with the stern and unyielding resistance of a united South. The declaration contained in that document to the effect that the Federal Government intends "to hold, occupy and possess the property and places belonging to the Government, and to collect the duties and imposts" necessarily involves war, and *war*, as remarked by Mr. Dorman in his speech in [the Virginia] Convention only yesterday, involves a total and permanent disruption of the Union.

It is too late now to discuss the rightfulness or the wrongfulness of the abstract doctrine of secession. Six or seven States have already proclaimed themselves independent of the Union, and have organized a Provisional Government, and are now in the act of discharging all the functions of a separate nationality. It is the part of wise and practical men, and it is especially the duty of the Federal Administration at Washington, to look *facts* in the face – to meet and accept the facts as they find them, and dispose of them with a view to the interests of peace and harmony. Let Lincoln carry out the policy indicated in his Inaugural, and civil war will be inaugurated forthwith throughout the length and breadth of the land.

The Gulf States, in our judgment, have acted rashly, and improperly; but considering them erring sisters, entitled to our sympathies and our aid in an emergency, Virginia can never consent, and will never consent for the Federal Government to employ coercive measures towards them. And the stupendous folly of such a policy is perfectly apparent. – For, as we have said, it would lead to certain and inevitable war, and to the complete and eternal destruction of the Union....

Let President Lincoln reconsider his determination, and let him address himself to a peaceful solution of our national difficulties, and the Union may yet be restored in all its pristine dimensions, strength and glory....

"Too late, too late! ....
For now the heathen of the Northern Sea,
Lured by the crimes and frailties of the court,
Begin to slay the folk and spoil the land."
　　　　　　　- Tennyson, Idylls of the King (2)

Item from the Richmond *Dispatch*, April 13, 1861:
(3)

THE WAR BEGINS

It will be seen that, under the military compulsion of the immense fleet and army which the Black Republican President has sent to subjugate Charleston, the Carolina forces have been forced, in self-defence, to attempt the reduction of that fort [Fort Sumter] which so long has menaced their homes and firesides, and which Lincoln had formally notified them he was about to supply with provisions, - "peaceably if he can, *forcibly if he must,*" – a notification which, backed up by an immense naval and military force, was of course a declaration of war.

The war thus inaugurated by the Executive representative of the irrepressible conflict, South Carolina and the Confederate States have sought, by every honorable means, to avoid. As long as Major Anderson [commander at Fort Sumter] remained in Fort Moultrie, in accordance with the understanding between the Carolina and Federal authorities that the military status of the harbor was not to be changed, not a Carolina hand was laid upon a single fort in the harbor. Fort Sumter was well known to be the key of the whole position, yet, though the Carolinians might easily have seized, at any time, this undefended stronghold, they stood rigidly by their pledge, until availing himself of the darkness of night, and in utter disregard of the compact between the two Governments, Major Anderson seized, occupied and possessed Fort Sumter, spiking the guns and burning the gun-carriages of Fort Moultrie, an act of war, recognized as such by all military authorities as well as by common sense, and the first act of war in that irrepressible conflict which Abraham Lincoln has now fully inaugurated.

It was only when this first act of hostilities had been perpetrated that the volunteers of Charleston took possession of Fort Moultrie and commenced the erection of defensive fortifications in the harbor. But, even then, instead of resorting to an immediate bombardment of the fort, as they would have been justified in doing, and which Maj. Anderson did not then possess the means of returning with effect, they sent Commissioners to Washington earnestly soliciting the Federal Government to restore peacefully the former state of things and place Maj. Anderson once more in Fort Moultrie. We all know how utterly fruitless was this respectful and fraternal invocation. Instead of the "bread" of peace which they asked, the Government gave them a "stone," in the *Star of the West*, crowded with armed men and death-dealing instruments of war.

Not satisfied with these efforts for a pacific solution of the difficulty, the Confederate States also sent Commissioners to Washington, while for more than a month have been endeavoring to persuade the Administration peacefully to abandon Fort Sumter. These appeals the Administration have artfully pretended to heed, and a month ago caused it to be given out that Fort Sumter was to be abandoned; whereas, it now appears that all the time they were energetically preparing men and munitions of war for its reinforcement. In the meantime, the people of Charleston have been actually supplying Major Anderson and his officers with provisions, exhibiting a spirit of forbearance and generosity unprecedented in the annals of war.

In the midst of the negotiations a fleet, larger than England keeps up in the [English] Channel, an army of three thousand soldiers, with an immense amount of munitions of war, has been suddenly sent by the Government to attack Morris Island and force provisions, and probably men, into Fort Sumter. Simultaneously with this most menacing movement, the Southern Commissioners have been cavalierly dismissed from Washington, and a formal notification sent by Lincoln to Gov. Pickens that he was about to provision Fort Sumter, peaceably, if he could; forcibly, if he must....

Edward A. Pollard, from his *Southern History of the War*: (4)

For weeks the Cabinet of Mr. Lincoln had been taxed to devise some artifice for the relief of Fort Sumter, short of open military reinforcements (decided to be impracticable), and which would have the effect of inaugurating the war by a safe indirection and under a plausible and convenient pretence. The device was at length hit upon. It was accomplished by the most flagrant perfidy. Mr. Seward had already given assurances to the Southern commissioners, through the intermediation of Judge Campbell [of Virginia], that the Federal troops would be removed from Fort Sumter....

Some time elapsed, and there was reason to distrust the promise. Colonel Lamon, an agent of the Washington government, was sent to Charleston, and was reported to be authorized to make arrangements with Governor Pickens, of South Carolina, for the withdrawal of the Federal troops from Fort Sumter. He returned without any accomplishment of his reported mission. Another confidential agent of Mr. Lincoln, a Mr. Fox, was permitted to visit Fort Sumter, and was discovered to have acted the part of a spy in carrying concealed dispatches to Major Anderson, and collecting information with reference to a plan for the forcible reinforcement of the fort. On the 7th of April, Judge Campbell, uneasy as to the good faith of Mr. Seward's promise of the evacuation of Sumter, addressed him another note on the subject. To this the emphatic and laconic reply was: "*Faith as to Sumter fully kept – wait and see.*" Six days thereafter a hostile fleet was menacing Charleston, the Lincoln government threw down the gauntlet of war, and the battle of Sumter was fought....

The advantages of delay which the Lincoln government had obtained by the pretence of the evacuation of Sumter, and the adroitness of Mr. Seward with the commissioners, had been profitably employed by it in naval and other preparations for its meditated blow on the Southern coasts....

No sooner was the hostile fleet of the Federal government safely on its way to the Southern coasts, than the perfidy of Abraham Lincoln and his advisers was openly and shamelessly consummated. The mask was dropped. The Southern commissioners who had been so long cozened, were distinctly rebuffed; and simultaneously with the appearance of the Federal fleet in the offing of the Charleston harbor, an official message, on the 8th day of April, was conveyed to Governor Pickens, of South Carolina, by Lieutenant Talbot, an authorized agent of the Lincoln government, announcing the determination of that government to send provisions to Fort Sumter, "peaceably if they can, forcibly if they must."

The message was telegraphed by General Beauregard to Montgomery, and the instructions of his government asked. He was answered by a telegram from Mr. Walker, the Secretary of War, instructing him to demand the evacuation of the fort, and, if that was refused, to proceed to reduce it. The demand was made; it was refused. Major Anderson replied that he regretted that his sense of honor and of his obligations to his government prevented his compliance with the demand. Nothing was left but to accept the distinct challenge of the Lincoln government to arms....

The fact was that the President had long ago calculated the result, and the effect on the country, of the hostile movements which he had directed against the sovereignty of South Carolina. He had procured the battle of Sumter; he had no desire or hope to retain the fort: the circumstances of the battle and the non-participation of his fleet in it were sufficient evidences, to every honest and reflecting mind, that it was not a contest for victory, and that "the sending provisions to a starving garrison" was an ingenious artifice to commence the war that the Federal Govern-ment had fully resolved upon....

Abraham Lincoln to G. V. Fox, Commander of the Fort Sumter expedition: (5)

"Washington, D. C., May 1, 1861
"Capt. G. V. Fox.

"*My Dear Sir*: I sincerely regret that the failure of the late attempt to provision Fort Sumter should be the source of any an-noyance to you.... You and I both anticipated that the cause of the country would be advanced by making the attempt to provision Fort Sumter, even if it should fail; and it is no small consolation now to feel that our anticipation is justified by the result.

"Very truly, your friend,

"A. Lincoln"

Edward A. Pollard, from his *Southern History of the War*: (6)

On the 14th day of April, Mr. Lincoln published his proclamation of war. He acted to the last in a sinister spirit. He had just assured the commissioners from Virginia, who had been deputed to ascertain the purposes of his government, that he would modify his inaugural only so far as to "perhaps cause the United States mails to be withdrawn" from the seceded States. The following proclamation was the "modification" of the inaugural:

> "Whereas the laws of the United States have been for some time past, and now are, opposed, and the execution thereof obstructed in the States of South Carolina, Georgia, Alabama, Florida, Mississippi, Louisiana, and Texas, by combinations too powerful to be suppressed by the ordinary course of judicial proceeding, or by the powers vested in the Marshals by law- "Now, therefore, I, Abraham Lincoln, President of the United States, in virtue of the power in me vested by the Constitution and the laws, have thought fit to call forth, and hereby do call forth the militia of the several States of the Union, to the aggregate number of seventy-five thousand, in order to suppress said combinations, and to cause the laws to be duly executed. The details for this object will be immediately communicated to the State authorities through the War Department…."

The trick of the government, to which we have referred, in its procurement of the battle of Sumter, is too dishonest and shallow to account for the immense reaction of sentiment in the North that ensued. That reaction is certainly to be attributed to causes more intelligent and permanent than the weak fallacy that the Lincoln government was not responsible for the hostilities in Charleston harbor, and that the South itself had dragged the government and people of Abraham Lincoln unwillingly into the inauguration of war. The problem of this reaction may be more justly solved. In fact, it involved no new fact or principle. The Northern people, including all parties, secretly appreciated the value of the Union to themselves; they knew that they would be ruined by a permanent secession of the Southern States....

Thomas Prentiss Kettell, from *Southern Wealth and Northern Profits*: (7)

The New England States, from the first, were mostly engaged in navigation and manufactures. It was there that capital first accumulated from application to those employments. Agriculture spread in two directions, vis., across the mountains to the west, and southwest from the south Atlantic States. These two agricultural branches divided naturally into free and slave labor, and both sections held the same position to New England as all the colonies had before held to the mother country.

The manufacturing and navigating States, as a matter of course, accumulated the wealth which the other sections produced, each in proportion to its productions ... and with every increase in numbers, and every extension of national territory, the New England States have had only a larger market for their wares, while the foreign competing supply has been restricted by high duties on imports....

If we were to penetrate beyond a rupture, and imagine a peaceable separation, by which the North and South should be sundered without hostilities, we might contemplate the condition and prospects of each. From what has been ... revealed to us from the returns of the census, it is quite apparent that the North, as distinguished from the South and West, would be alone permanently injured. Its fortune depends upon manufacturing and shipping; but, as has been seen, it neither raises its own food nor its own raw material, nor does it furnish freights for its own shipping. The South, on the other hand, raises a surplus of food, and supplies the world with raw materials. Lumber, hides, cotton, wool, indigo – all that the manufacturer requires – is within its own circle.

The requisite capital to put them in action is rapidly accumulating, and in the long run it would lose – after recovering from first disasters – nothing by separation. The North, on the other hand, will have food and raw materials to buy in order to employ its labor; but who will then buy its goods? It cannot supply England; she makes the same things cheaper. The West will soon be able to supply itself. The South, while having the world as an eager customer for its raw produce, will not want Northern goods....

When that moment arrives, Massachusetts, which now occupies the proudest rank in the Union, will fall back upon her own resources, and still claim to be an agricultural state, since her summer crop is granite and her winter crop is ice....

Item from the New Orleans *Daily Crescent*, January 21, 1861: (8)

THE DIFFERENCE

There is this difference between the Northern and Southern States, which illustrates the exact nature of the quarrel between the two sections: That, while the Southern States, in the Union, would have interposed no objection to the secession of any Northern State, the Northern States, on the other hand, are thrown into a perfect paroxysm of rage at the mere whisper of an intention to secede, on the part of any State of the South.

Thus, if, at any time within the last ten years, Massachusetts had threatened to leave the Union, the idea, so far from being unpalatable to the South, would have been hailed with the liveliest demonstrations of joy and satisfaction. The South would have bid her go and go quickly, and have esteemed it a happy riddance....

But, why is there such objection made to the withdrawal of the South? We are told by Abolition orators and organs that the

South is a poor, miserable region – that most of the wealth, the enterprise, and the intelligence of the nation is in the North – that the Southern people, as was said by Sumner in the Senate, are identified with, and apologists for, an institution essentially "barbaric" – that our section is unable to support a mail system, and that we are pensioners, to that extent, of the Federal government – that we are, in short, a semi-civilized, God-forsaken people, a long ways behind the "great North" in the arts, in refinement, in education, in enterprise, and in everything else that constitutes what they call "civilization." One would suppose they would be eager to be relieved of association with a people of whom they have so poor an opinion. So far the contrary, however, they are, as we have before said, mortally offended at the bare idea of our dissolving with them our political connection.

There must be a reason for this, as there is for everything else, and the reason is plain enough. All that they say about the South is false, and, what is more, they know it to be false. They know that the South is the main prop and support of the Federal system. They know that it is Southern productions that constitute the surplus wealth of the nation, and enables us to import so largely from foreign countries. They know that it is their import trade that draws from the people's pockets sixty or seventy millions of dollars per annum, in the shape of duties, to be expended mainly in the North, and in the protection and encouragement of Northern interests. They know that it is the export of Southern productions, and the corresponding import of foreign goods, that gives profitable employment to their shipping. They know that the bulk of the duties is paid by the Southern people, though first collected at the North, and that, by the iniquitous operation of the Federal Government, these duties are mainly expended among the Northern people. They know that they can plunder and pillage the South, as long as they are in the same Union with us, by other means, such as fishing bounties, navigation laws, robberies of the public lands, and every other possible mode of injustice and peculation.....

And, above and beyond all this, is the Puritanic love of mean tyranny and cold-blooded, inexorable oppression, which the Union enables them to cherish and reduce to practice – coupled with the Pharisaical boast of "holier than thou," which they are constantly uttering as a reproach to the South – both of which feelings are innate in the descendants of the Pilgrims, and have become a part of their nature, which they could not get rid of if they wished.

These are the reasons why these people do not wish the South to secede from the Union. They are enraged at the prospect of being despoiled of the rich feast upon which they have so long fed and fattened, and which they were just getting ready to enjoy with still greater *gout* and gusto. They are mad as hornets because the prize slips them just as they are ready to grasp it.....

Alexis de Tocqueville, from *Democracy in America*: (9)

If the Union were to undertake to enforce by arms the allegiance of the confederate States by military means, it would be in a position very analogous to that of England at the time of the War of Independence.

However strong a government may be, it can not easily escape from the consequences of a principle which it has once admitted as the foundation of its constitution. The Union was formed by the voluntary agreement of the States; and, in uniting together, they have not forfeited their nationality, nor have they been reduced to the condition of one and the same people. If one of the States chose to withdraw its name from the contract, it would be difficult to disprove its right of doing so; and the Federal Government would have no means of maintaining its claims directly, either by force or by right.

In order to enable the Federal Government easily to conquer the resistance which may be offered to it by any of its subjects, it would be necessary that one or more of them should be specially interested in the existence of the Union, as has frequently been the case in the history of confederations.

If it be supposed that among the states that are united in the Federal tie there are some which exclusively enjoy the principal advantages of union, or whose prosperity depends on the duration of that union, it is unquestionable that they will always be ready to support the central Government in enforcing the obedience of the others. But the Government would then be exerting a force not derived from itself, but from a principle contrary to its nature....

Great things may then be done in the name of the Federal Government, but in reality that Government will have ceased to exist....

Item in the Richmond *Whig*, April 10, 1861: (10)

A GOVERNMENT OF FORCE

Let us consider for a moment the results of a consolidated Government, resting on force, as proposed by the dominant party at the North.

In a country so extensive as this, with interests so various, separate and distinct, if not antagonistic, only one of two sorts of Government is possible – either a loose league of confederated sovereigns, held together by affection and interest, or a consolidated despotism, upheld by the sword and cemented by fear. Our ancestors attempted to establish the first, and inaugurated the old Articles of Confederation, which bore us triumphantly through the Revolution. But for the pecuniary embarrassments resulting from the war, and the necessity for raising money by a system of uniform and indirect taxation, that Confederation would have continued to the present day to bless the land with content, peace and plenty. To meet the pecuniary difficulties of the times, without departing materially from the spirit of the original league, the present Federal Agent was established.

During the seventy years of its existence, while it adhered to the principles of its foundation and respected the conflicting interests and reserved rights of the various States, its career was prosperous and it performed its mission. But now that it has been seized upon by a sectional party, it is claimed that its powers are omnipotent, its will absolute, and it must and will maintain its supremacy, in spite of States and people, at the point of the sword.... It is organizing fleets and armies to wage war upon the authors of its being – the sovereign States and the people of the Confederacy.... Surely Mr. Lincoln is entering upon a fearful career in inaugurating a war, which, he says, his oath compels him to begin, and which the same oath will forever restrain him from terminating.

The people of Virginia, speaking through their Convention, have with almost unanimity protested against the Federal Government, which is in part their Government, inaugurating any such disastrous and bloody drama.... They have borne much for the preservation of an Union of equal and sovereign States – and, perhaps, they may be willing to bear more, while hope remains; but when the General government shall make war upon a sovereign member of the Confederacy, and convert a Government of consent into one of force, they will imitate the example of Henry and Washington, and re-assert that sovereignty which those illustrious men established for them....

Governor John Letcher's letter of reply to Lincoln's call for Virginia troops: (11)

Executive Department
Richmond, Va. April 16th, 1861

Hon. Simon Cameron, Secretary of War.

Sir: I received your telegram of the 15th, the genuineness of which I doubted. Since that time I have received your communication, mailed the same day, in which I am requested to detach from the militia of the State of Virginia "the quota designated in a table," which you append, "to serve as infantry or riflemen for the period of three months, unless sooner discharged."

In reply to this communication, I have only to say, that the militia of Virginia will not be furnished to the powers at Washington, for any such use or purpose as they have in view. Your object is to subjugate the Southern States, and a requisition made upon me for such an object – an object, in my judgment, not within the purview of the Constitution, or the act of 1795 – will not be complied with. You have chosen to inaugurate civil war, and having done so, we will meet it, in a spirit as determined as the Administration has exhibited towards the South.

Respectfully
John Letcher

From the *Declaration of Independence*, July 4, 1776: (12)

Governments long established should not be changed for light and transient causes.... But when a long train of abuses and usurpations, pursuing invariably the same Object evinces a design to reduce them under absolute Despotism, it is their right, it is their duty, to throw off such Government, and to provide new Guards for their future security....

Virginia's *Ordinance of Secession*, adopted in Convention, April 17, 1861: (13)

An ORDINANCE to repeal the ratification of the Constitution of the United States of America, by the State of Virginia, and to resume all the rights and powers granted under said Constitution.

The people of Virginia, in their ratification of the Constitution of the United States of America, adopted by them in convention on the twenty-fifth day of June in the year of our Lord one thousand seven hundred and eighty-eight, having declared that the powers granted under the said Constitution were derived from the people of the United States, and might be resumed whensoever the same should be perverted to their injury and oppression; and the Federal government having perverted said powers, not only to the injury of the people of Virginia, but to the oppression of the Southern slave-holding states:

Now, therefore, we, the people of Virginia do declare and ordain, that the ordinance adopted by the people of this state in convention on the twenty-fifth day of June in the year of our Lord one thousand seven hundred and eighty-eight, whereby the Constitution of the United States of America was ratified, and all acts of the General Assembly of this state ratifying or adopting amendments to said Constitution, are hereby repealed and abrogated; that the union between the State of Virginia and the other states under the Constitution aforesaid is hereby dissolved and that the State of Virginia is in the full possession and exercise of all the rights of sovereignty which belong and appertain to a free and independent state....

BOOK II

SUMMER (1862)

Waken, lords and ladies gay,
On the mountain dawns the day;
All the jolly chase is here
With hawk and horse and hunting-spear;
Hounds are in their couples yelling,
Hawks are whistling, horns are knelling,
Merrily merrily mingle they,
'Waken, lords and ladies gay'....
   - Sir Walter Scott, "Hunting Song" (1)

RIGHT *Lt. Gen. Thomas J. "Stonewall" Jackson* – Courtesy of Library of Congress

Summer Thunder

Lt. Gen. Jubal A. Early, from his "Lee Memorial Address" at Washington and Lee University, January 19, 1872: (1)

The commencement of hostilities in Charleston harbor, the proclamation of Lincoln, calling for troops to make an unconstitutional war on the seceded states, and the consequent secession of Virginia, found General [Robert E.] Lee a colonel in the United States Army, with a character and reputation which would have insured him the highest military honors within the gift of the United States government. In fact, it has been said that the command of the army intended for the invasion of the South was tendered him. However, rejecting all overtures made to him, as soon as he learned the action of his native state, in a dignified manner, and without parade or show, he tendered his resignation, with the determination to share the fate of his state, his friends, and kindred.

The then governor at once, with the unanimous consent of the Convention of Virginia, tendered him the command of all the forces of the state. This he accepted, and promptly repaired to Richmond, to enter upon the discharge of his duties....

Lt. Col. Walter H. Taylor, an officer on Gen. Robert E. Lee's staff, from *Four Years with General Lee*: (2)

Under the direction of General Lee ... the Virginia volunteers were in a wonderfully short time organized, armed, equipped, and sent to the front: so that when the Confederate authorities assumed control of affairs after the State had formally joined the Confederacy, Governor Letcher was enabled to turn over to them the "Army of Virginia," volunteers and provisional, thoroughly organized and ready for work, and around which, as a nucleus, was collected what afterward became the historic "Army of Northern Virginia."

The capital of the Confederacy was removed from Montgomery to Richmond, and the various departments of the Government immediately transferred to the latter city; the War Department carried on the process of organization and preparation; the functions of General Lee as general-in-chief of the Army of Virginia terminated, and he was created one of the five generals provided for by a law of Congress, in the Army of the Confederate States. Brigadier General G. T. Beauregard and General J. E. Johnston, already in the field, were assigned to the command of the troops in Virginia – the former having the "Army of the Potomac" (Confederate States Army) and the latter the forces then collected in the lower Valley of Virginia; these two armies were subsequently united and won the first battle of Manassas....

Mrs. Roger A. Pryor, from *Reminiscences of Peace and War*: (3)

The month of July, 1861, found me with my little boys at "The Oaks" – the residence of Dr. Izard Bacon Rice, in Charlotte County, seventy miles from Richmond, and miles away from the nearest railroad depot. There I might have enjoyed a peaceful summer with my kind host – a fine type of a Christian gentleman, sometime an Old-Line Whig and fierce Union man, now an ardent advocate of state's rights, and a stanch supporter of the new Confederacy. I might – as I had often done before – have revelled in the fine trees; the broad acres of tobacco in their summer prime, when the noble plant was proudly flinging out its banners before its fall; the old garden with its box-edged crescents, stars, and circles, - I might have dreamed away the summer in perfect contentment but for General Beauregard. Distant as was his army, a message from his guns reached my summer retreat more than a hundred miles away.

Dr. Rice lived in a large, old-fashioned house, on a plantation of two thousand acres or more. An oak grove, alive with chattering squirrels which had been held sacred for two generations, surrounded the house. The squirrels held conventions in the trees, and doubtless expressed their opinions of the family below, whom they had good reason to consider inferior beings, inasmuch as they were slow-motioned, heavy creatures, utterly destitute of grace and agility, and with small appreciation of hickory-nuts.

The Doctor cultivated tobacco, and when I arrived the fields stretched as far as the eye could reach, now a vast level sea of green, now covering the low, gently rounded, undulating hills as they sloped down to the Staunton River. There was never a season when these fields were not alive with laborers of every age; for the regal plant so beloved of men – and ranking with opium and hemp as a solace for the ills of mankind – has enemies from the hour it peeps from the nursery of the hot bed. It can never be forgotten a moment. Children can hunt the fly which seeks to line the leaf with eggs, or destroy the unhatched eggs, or aid the great army which must turn out in haste when the ravenous worm is born. The earth must be turned frequently at the roots, the flower buds pinched off, the shoots or "suckers" removed. The Doctor's tobacco field was an enlivening spectacle, and very picturesque did the ebony faces of the little workers look, among the broad leaves. No lady's garden was kept so clean, so free from sticks, errant bits of paper, or debris of any kind.

I do not claim that Dr. Rice (my uncle) was a typical planter – as far as the government of his slaves was concerned. He had inherited liberal ideas with these inherited slaves. His grandfather, David Rice, had written the first published protest in this country against slavery as "inconsistent with religion and policy." His father had ruled a plantation where severe punishment was unknown, where the cheerful slaves rarely needed it. The old gentleman was considered eccentric – and eccentric it surely was for a master to punish a fault by commanding the culprit to stand in his presence while he recited a long passage from Homer or Virgil! The punishment was effective. For fear of it, the fault was rarely repeated.

It was my uncle's custom to assemble every slave on his plantation on Sunday morning, and to speak a few words to each one, commending the women if their families appeared in clean, well-kept garments, rewarding with a pair of shoes the urchins reported by "Uncle Moses" as having been orderly and useful, exchanging a pleasant jest here and there.

He presented a tight, comfortable house to every newly married pair, with timber for the bridegroom to add to it, or to enclose the piece of land for a garden or a poultry yard which went with it. Every mother at the birth of a child was presented with a pig. The plantation, which was large and fruitful, and from which nothing but tobacco and wheat was ever sold, yielded vegetables, poultry, mutton, beef, bacon in lavish abundance, while the orchards and vines were equally productive.

Some hundreds of the negroes of the neighborhood were members of the Presbyterian church of the whites. In the old church books may be seen to-day records of their marriages and funerals, and how (for example) "Lovelace Brown was brought before the session for hog-stealing and suspended for one month." But there were better records than this. These Presbyterian negroes were at one time led by an eminent patriarch, Uncle Abel, who deserves more than a passing notice. He had been taught to read and had been well drilled in the Shorter Catechism. But his marriage ceremonies were always read from the Episcopal Prayer-book, every word of which he held sacred, not to be changed or omitted to suit any modern heresy. "I M, take thee N," was the formula for Jack or Peter, Dilsey or Dicey – and "with this ring I thee wed" must be pronounced with solemnity, ring or no ring, the latter being not at all essential.

My uncle's old family coach, punctual to the minute, swept around the circle on the lawn every Sunday morning, with Uncle Peter proudly guiding the horses from his high perch. And high-swung was the coach, to be ascended (as we ascended our four poster beds) by three carpeted steps, - in the case of the carriage, folding steps, which were tucked inside after we had disposed of ourselves, with our ample hoops. There was plenty of room inside. Pockets lined the doors, and these were filled by my aunt with beaten biscuit and sugarcakes "for the little darkies on the road."

Arriving at the church, the gentlemen from the adjacent plantations, who had been settling the affairs of the nation under the trees, came forward to hand us from our carriage, after the manner of old-time cavaliers and sedan-chairs; and my aunt and I would be very gracious, devoutly hoping in our hearts that my uncle and his sons would not forget a reciprocal courtesy when Mrs. Winston Henry, Mrs. Paul Carrington, and Mrs. Sarah Car-rington should arrive.

The women all seated themselves on the right side of the church, while the men, during the singing of a preliminary hymn, came in like a processional and took the left as their portion, - all of which (except the advertisements on the church doors) was conducted precisely according to the customs of Revolutionary times, when Patrick Henry and John Randolph, now sleeping a few miles away, were themselves (we trust) churchgoers.

Church dinners at home were simple, but abundant, - so that if three or four carriages should arrive from distant planta-tions in the neighborhood, there could be welcome refreshment for all, but on the great days when my uncle and aunt received the neighborhood, when the Carringtons and Patrick Henry's sons, John and Winston, came with their families to spend the day, the dinner was something to be remembered. Perhaps a description verbatim from an old family servant will be better than anything I can furnish from memory.

"Yes, sir! We had fine dinners in them days. The butter

was moulded like a temple with pillars, and a rose stuck in the top. There was a wreath of roses roun' all the dessert dishes. Viney biled the ham in cider. We had roas' pig, biled turkey, chickens fried an' briled, spring lam', ducks an' green goslin'. An' every cut-glass dish in the house was full of preserves, an' the great bowl full of ice-cream, an' floatin' island, an' tipsy-cake, an' cheese-cakes, an' green sweetmeats, an' citron. John was bothered where to set all the dishes."

Our guests would remain late, that they might have the cool evening hours for their long drives. Mr. John Henry, with his family of gifted sons and beautiful daughters, lived at Red Hill, the home of his father, the great orator and patriot, under the trees his father had planted and near the grave where he sleeps. Mr. Winston Henry had also an interesting family, and lived in an old colonial house not far away, surrounded by grounds filled in summer with pomegranates and gardenias, and with lemon and orange trees in tubs, also great *trees* of heliotrope, and vines of jessamine – a paradise of beauty and sweetness. Rosalie Henry would bring her guitar to my uncle's and sing for us by the hour. She was so loved, so cherished by her parents, that they gave her a bedroom over their own, to which she ascended by a stairway from their own apartment – all that they might be near her. But one morning early, pretty Rosalie changed gowns with her maid, put a pail on her head, and slipped past her trusting, adoring parents to join her lover in the jessamine bower, and in a bridal robe of linsey-woolsey was married at the next town! Then it was that my good uncle had his opportunity. The sublime teaching of forgiveness was respected from his kindly lips.

In the early summer of '61 Virginia planters were not all *d'accord* on political questions; and like Agag, it behooved us to "walk delicately" in conversation. One thing they would not endure. Politics were to be kept out of the pulpit. Never had the pastor such attentive congregations; they were watching him, keenly alive to the remotest hint or allusion to the war. His business was with the spiritual kingdom of God. He must not interfere with

Caesar's. He found it expedient to omit for the present the warlike aspirations of David, in which he beseeches the Lord's attention to his enemies, and, among other things calculated to comfort and soothe his pious feelings, prays that they may be as "stubble before the wind," as "wood before fire," and be "rooted forever out of the land of the living."

"Enemies" were not to be alluded to in the pulpit. Nor, indeed, not yet in private! It was proper and in good taste to speak of them as "Federals"; but at no very distant day these same polite gentlemen called them "enemies" with a will; when scornfully disposed, they were "Yankees," and when they wished to be positively insulting, "Yanks."

Across the river from the Oaks was "Mildendo," the home of the Carrington family. From this home went every man capable of bearing arms – Fontaine, the fine young surgeon so well placed in the United States Navy, and his brother, the grave head of the house upon whom everybody depended; and one, a cousin, leaving his bride at the altar. Patrick Henry's grandsons all enlisted. Mr. Charles Bruce left his baronial castle on Staunton Hill near the Oaks, equipped the "Staunton Hill Artillery Company" at his own expense, placed himself at its head and shared all its hardships. His brother, Mr. James Bruce, cut up his rich carpets and curtains for the soldier's blankets. These were but a few of the gallant neighbors of my uncle, who exchanged homes of luxury for the hardships of war – all of whom probably shared General Lee's keen sorrow at the necessity forced upon Virginia to withdraw her allegiance from the Union.

My uncle had a son already in the cavalry service – and another, Henry, a fine young fellow of sixteen, was at Hampden-Sidney College, Virginia. Presently a letter from the latter filled the family at the Oaks with – yes, anxiety – but at the same time a proud sense of how old Revolutionary "blood will tell." Henry was on the march! At the first tocsin of war the students of Hampden-Sidney had rushed to arms – most of them under age; and when their president, the venerated Rev. John Atkinson, found they would go, he placed himself at their head as their captain. Military tactics had not been included in his theological training. So promptly had he responded to the call of his country he had no opportunity to drill his young soldiers according to the rules of Hardee and Jomini; but he did more for them than this. His fatherly care and his example of courage, fortitude, and faith in the cause inspired them to bear hardships which were severe almost beyond their powers of endurance.

Notwithstanding the inexperience of their captain, these boys, fresh from their college halls, were often publicly complimented as they headed the column in the long marches over the mountains of Virginia.

When they were called to Richmond their patriotic ardor received a shock. Governor Letcher seriously took under consideration the propriety of sending them back to school on account of their youth. A committee from the company waited upon him, and he was finally prevailed upon to allow them to go to the front.

They soon learned what war was – these beardless college boys – and bore themselves gallantly in several engagements. But their military career was brief. McClellan flanked their position at Rich Mountain, July 12, 1861, and cut off every avenue of retreat. The whole command, after a sharp engagement, were made prisoners of war. For the time being the boys felt their military career to have been an inglorious failure.

While they were thus disappointed and depressed, a Federal officer, presumably a lieutenant, visited them in the prison camp. He said he had heard so much of the boy soldiers led by their college president that he wished to make their acquaintance.

The boys were not by way of being over anxious to receive visits from their victors. The officer asked, "Why in the world are you here?"

"We are here to *fight!*" said they. "What do you suppose we came for?"

"Well, boys," said the officer, pleasantly, "make yourselves easy. I'll send you home to your mothers in a few days."

The officer was General McClellan!

The company was paroled, but was not exchanged for a year. This prolonged parole, they always thought, was due to General McClellan's influence in order to give them a whole year at college.

They all returned to the army after their exchange, but never as the "Hampden-Sidney Boys." They never forgot the little interview with the General. He won all their hearts.

Our own Hampden-Sidney boy, Henry Rice, soon afterward wrote from a hospital in Richmond that he was ill with fever. My uncle ordered him home, and I took the great family coach and Uncle Peter and went to the depot, fourteen miles away, to fetch him. He looked so long, that I doubted whether I could bestow him in the carriage; and as he was too good a soldier for me to suggest that he be "doubled up," I entered the carriage first, had his head and shoulders placed in my lap, then closed the door and swung his long legs out of the window!

My uncle was a fine specimen of a Christian gentleman – always courteous, always serene. I delighted in following him around the plantation on horseback. When he winnowed his wheat, Uncle Moses, standing like an emperor amid the sheaves, filled the hearts of my little boys with ecstasy by allowing them to ride the horses that turned the great wheel. Finally the wheat was packed in bags, and we stood on the bank of the river to see it piled into flat-bottomed boats on the way to market.

The next morning Moses appeared at the dining room door while we were at breakfast.

"Good morning, Moses," said my uncle. "I thought you were going with the wheat."

"Dar ain't no wheat," said the old man. "Hit's all at de bottom of the river."

"How did that happen?"

"We jest natchelly run agin a snag; when de boat turn over, hit pulled all de others down. "Cose you know, Marster, dey was tied together, an' boat ain' got no eyes to see snags."

"Well – get out your chains and grappling hooks, Moses, and save all you can. It will do to feed the chickens."

"Why, Uncle!" I exclaimed, "how calmly you take it."

"Certainly," said he; "because I've lost my crop is that any reason I should lose my temper? Here, Pizarro, have our horses saddled. We'll go down to the river and encourage Moses to resurrect his wheat." (Pizarro was John's son. John had studied with the boys of the family, and knew some history and Latin. One of the women bore the classic name of "Lethe"; others were "Chloe" and "Daphne"; another name, frequently repeated, was "Dicey" – a survival, according to Mr. Andrew Lang, of the myth of Orpheus and Eurydice, which was found among the Indians and the Virginia negroes of colonial times. Orpheus seems to have perished from their traditions, but Dicey is still a favorite name. The descendants of Lethe and Pizarro still live at the Oaks. A late achievement shows their progress under new conditions, the baptismal records having been enriched with "Hazel-Kirke-Florida-Bell-Armazinda-Hodge," more imposing if less suggestive than the "Homicide" and "Neuralgia" of a neighboring county.)

This precise type of a Virginia plantation will never appear again, I imagine. I wish I could describe a plantation wedding as I saw it that summer. But a funeral of one of the old servants was peculiarly interesting to me. "Aunt Matilda" had been much loved, and when she found herself dying, she had requested that the mistress and little children should attend her funeral. "I ain' been much to church," she urged, "I couldn't leave my babies. I ain' had dat shoutin' an' hollerin' religion, but I gwine to heaven jes' de same" – a fact of which nobody who knew Aunt Matilda could have the smallest doubt.

We had a long, warm walk behind hundreds of negroes, following the rude coffin in slow procession through the woods, singing antiphonally as they went one of those strange, weird hymns not to be caught by any Anglo-Saxon voice.

It was a beautiful and touching scene, and at the grave I longed for an artist (we had no kodaks then) to perpetuate the picture. The level rays of the sun were filtered through the green leaves of the forest, and fell gently on the dusky, pathetic faces, and on the simple coffin surrounded by orphan children and relatives, very dignified and quiet in their grief.

The spiritual patriarch of the plantation presided. Old Uncle Abel said: -

"I ain' gwine keep you all long. 'Tain' no use. We can't do nothin' for Sis' Tildy. All is done for her, an' she done preach her own fune'al sermon. Her name was on dis church book here, but dat warn' nothin', 'doubt 'twas on de Lamb book too!

"Now whiles dey fillin' up her grave I'd like you all to sing a hymn Sis' Tildy uster love, but you all know I bline in one eye, an' de sweat done got in de other; so's I can't see to line it out, an' I dunno as any o' you all ken do it" – and the first thing I knew, the old man had passed his well-worn book to me, and there I stood, at the foot of the grave, "lining out": -

"Asleep in Jesus, blessed sleep

From which none ever wakes to weep," –

Words of immortal comfort to the great throng of negro mourners who caught it up, line after line, on an air of their own, full of tears and tenderness, - a strange, weird tune no white person's voice could ever follow.

Among such scenes I passed the month of June and the early part of July, and then General Beauregard reminded us that we were at war, and had no right to make ourselves comfortable.

Dr. Rice, on the afternoon of the 21st, had betaken himself to his accustomed place under the trees, to escape the flies, - the pest of Southern households in summer, - and had lain down on the grass for his afternoon nap. He suddenly called out excitedly:

"There's a battle going on – a fierce battle – I can hear the can-nonading distinctly. Here – lie down – you can here it!" "Oh, no, no, I can't" I gasped. "It may be at Norfolk."

Like Jessie, who had heard the pibroch at the siege of Lucknow, he had heard, with his ear to the ground, the firing at Manassas. The battle of Bull Run was at its height … one hundred and fifty miles away.…

John S. Wise, from *The End of an Era*: (4)

Around the telegraph offices in Norfolk, great throngs of citizens and soldiers stood, roused to the highest pitch of excite-ment, as bulletin after bulletin was read aloud announcing a great Confederate triumph.

Men whose names had never been heard before leaped at one bound into the front rank of the world's heroes, in the minds of that delirious audience. Beauregard, Joe Johnston, Stonewall Jackson, Bee, and Bartow were the names on every tongue. The magnitude of the engagement was represented as equal to the greatest of ancient or modern battles. The throngs gloated in the stories of unprecedented carnage. One telegram announced a field so covered with the dead bodies of gayly dressed Union Zouaves that it resembled a French poppy farm. The conduct of the Southern troops was represented as surpassingly brave and chivalric, while that of "the Yankees" was referred to as corre-spondingly base and cowardly. The boast that one Southerner could whip ten Yankees seemed fully verified. The prediction fol-lowed that within a month the Southern army would be encamped about New York, and that it would dictate terms of peace within sixty days.…

As the summer advanced, no other startling battles oc-curred.… Altogether, a decided reaction had taken place since the wonderful battle of Manassas. It had not been followed up by the extermination of "the Yankees," as I expected it would be.

Although but two hundred and sixty-nine Confederate soldiers had been killed at Manassas, many of them were our friends. But the deaths in battle were as nothing compared with other deaths. We were beginning to dread measles and mumps and typhoid fever and dysentery in the camps. We were learning the ghastly truth that, for every man who dies in actual battle, a dozen pass away ingloriously by disease.

The skeleton had not yet clutched any of our family; but, my! how many of our friends were already in mourning! And the war seemed no nearer to its end than when it began....

BOOK II - CHAPTER TWO

"Heavily the Low Sky Raining/ Over Towered Camelot...."

John M. Daniel, editorial from the Richmond *Examiner*, January 16, 1862: (1)

For a period uncertain in duration, whether of days, weeks, or months, the season commands a truce. This is the true winter. The first campaign is ended, and a time has come when it is no longer unsafe to review results and to consider with candor the situation of our affairs.

The campaign has been strictly defensive. We have gained nothing, for we have attempted no gain. That we have lost comparatively little of actual territory during the latter six months, is due only to the difficulties of invasion in a country like this, the necessity for time to prepare half a million of soldiers, the courage of the Southern volunteers, and the individual cowardice of the Northern mercenaries. It is, however, undeniable that the defensive policy, besides the moral strain on our army that awaits repeated and endless attack, and the exhaustion of a country which is the scene of war, has given the enemy an uninterrupted opportunity to prepare a gigantic host, and to arrange it at leisure for the full trial of relative strength, when the seasons permit the resumption of hostilities.

While the political leaders of the South have been reposing in dreams of approaching peace, and while our accomplished captains of engineers have been expending their remarkable scientific ingenuity in the erection of works as wonderful, and almost as extensive, and quite as valuable, as the Chinese Wall to resist invading forces from a given direction, the enemy have gradually and at leisure gathered up their immense resources and concentrated their tremendous energies to envelop the Confederacy with their armies and fleets, and to penetrate the interior from some one of many alternative points. Although they can now do nothing, they have their general programme in perfect order for execution when the weather changes in the ordinary course of the earth round the sun; and at this moment we find ourselves in the face of superior forces where-ever we look, whether to the north, the east, or the west, or the south itself.

General Sidney Johnston has to strain every nerve to prevent the military as well as geographical heart of the country from slipping out of his grasp. Generals Joseph Johnston and Beauregard are held by McClellan on the Potomac as in a vise. A gigantic armament is ready to attempt the descent of the Mississippi, and their fleets on the Atlantic coast and the Gulf are too freshly before the public attention to require remembrance. Such are the fruits of a policy purely defensive. Without even the hesitancy which would come of a possible interruption, the enemy have thus surrounded the Southern Confederacy.

Maj. Jed Hotchkiss, from *Confederate Military History*: (2)

The advance of McClellan's army, moved from Washington by transport, reached Fort Monroe the latter part of March, and on the 2^d of April, McClellan in person ordered an advance up the peninsula.... General Magruder, of the Confederate army ... opposed his progress nearly at its beginning....

On the 6th and 7th, after a personal reconnaissance, the Federal commander prepared for a regular siege of the Confederate works; distributing his near 100,000 men along their front, with his numerous batteries in favorable positions. Magruder, with his little army of 11,000, bravely maintained his ground for ten days, keeping back his engineering antagonist and vigilantly watching his regular approaches. By maintaining this bold front he gave Johnston time to bring his forces from the Rappahannock and concentrate them on the Peninsula, and thus effectively bar the way of McClellan's host to Richmond....

Huger evacuated Norfolk May 9th, after destroying the navy yard, and fell back toward Petersburg. The now famous ram *Virginia* was blown up by her gallant crew on the 11th and her men hurried to Drewry's Bluff on the James, to take charge of the guns at the fortifications which General Lee, in the meantime, had prudently constructed at that point. The *Virginia* out of the way, the Federal gunboats ascended the James and attacked Drewry's Bluff, eight miles below Richmond, on the 15th. The channel of the James had been filled with sunken ships and other obstructions, and the gunboats met with a most spirited resistance from the guns in the works on the bluff, which repulsed their attack and compelled them to fall back down the river.

This naval attack in his rear induced Johnston to retreat across the Chickahominy on the 15th, and place his army in front of the defensive works, three miles to the east of Richmond, which had been thrown up in 1861 for the defense of that city.... McClellan reached the Chicahominy on the 19th, and on the 20th moved two corps, about two-fifths of his army, across the swamp-bordered river at Bottom's Bridge, the crossing of the Williamsburg and Richmond turnpike, which he followed to Seven Pines, within eight miles of Richmond.... A general deployment followed, with his left resting on White Oak Swamp and his right on the Chicka-hominy....

Constance Cary Harrison, from "Richmond Scenes in '62": (3)

And now we come to the 31st of May, 1862, when the eyes of the whole continent turned to Richmond. On that day Johnston assaulted the Federals, who had been advanced to Seven Pines. In face of recent reverses, we in Richmond had begun to feel like the prisoner of the Inquisition in Poe's story, cast into a dungeon of slowly contracting walls. With the sound of guns, therefore, in the direction of Seven Pines, every heart leaped as if deliverance were at hand. And yet there was no joy in the wild pulsation, since those to whom we looked for succor were our own flesh and blood, barring the way to a foe of superior numbers, abundantly provided, as we were not, with all the equipments of modern warfare, and backed by a mighty nation as determined as ourselves to win. Hardly a family in the town whose father, son, or brother was not part and parcel of the defending army.

When on the afternoon of the 31st it became known that the engagement had begun, the women of Richmond were still going about their daily vocations quietly, giving no sign of the inward anguish of apprehension. There was enough to do now in preparation for the wounded; yet, as events proved, all that was done was not enough by half. Night brought a lull in the cannonading. People lay down dressed upon beds, but not to sleep, while the weary soldiers slept upon their arms. Early next morning the whole town was on the street. Ambulances, litters, carts, every vehicle that the city could produce, went and came with a ghastly burden; those who could walk limped painfully home, in some cases so black with gunpowder they passed unrecognized. Women with pallid faces flitted bareheaded through the streets searching for their dead and wounded. The churches were thrown open, many people visiting them for a sad communion-service or brief time of prayer; the lecture-rooms of various places of worship were crowded with ladies volunteering to sew, as fast as fingers could fly, the rough beds called for by the surgeons. Men too old

or infirm to fight went on horseback or afoot to meet the returning ambulances, and in some cases served as escort to their own
dying sons.

By afternoon of the day following the battle, the streets
were one vast hospital. To find shelter for the sufferers a number
of unused buildings were thrown open. I remember, especially,
the St. Charles Hotel, a gloomy place, where two young girls went
to look for a member of their family, reported wounded. We had
tramped in vain over pavements burning with the intensity of the
sun, from one scene of horror to another, until our feet and brains
alike seemed about to serve us no further. The cool of those vast
dreary rooms of the St. Charles was refreshing; but such a spectacle! Men in every stage of mutilation lying on the bare boards,
with perhaps a haversack or an army blanket beneath their heads,
- some dying, all suffering keenly, while waiting their turn to be
attended to. To be there empty-handed and impotent nearly broke
our hearts. We passed from one to the other, making such slight
additions to their comfort as were possible, while looking in every
upturned face in dread to find the object of our search. This sorrow, I may add, was spared, the youth arriving at home later with
a slight flesh wound.

The condition of things at this and other improvised hospitals was improved next day by the offerings from many churches
of pew-cushions, which, sewn together, served as comfortable
beds; and for the remainder of the war their owners thanked God
upon bare benches for every "misery missed" that was "mercy
gained." To supply food for the hospitals the contents of larders
all over town were emptied into baskets; while cellars long sealed
and cobwebbed, belonging to the old Virginia gentry who knew
good Port and Madeira, were opened by the Ithuriel's spear of
universal sympathy. There was not much going to bed that night,
either; and I remember spending the greater part of it leaning
from my window to seek the cool night air, while wondering as to
the fate of those near to me. There was a summons to my mother
about midnight. Two soldiers came to tell her of the wounding of

one close of kin; but she was already on duty elsewhere, tireless and watchful as ever.

Up to that time the younger girls had been regarded as superfluities in hospital service; but on Monday two of us found a couple of rooms where fifteen wounded men lay upon pallets around the floor, and, on offering our services to the surgeons in charge, were proud to have them accepted and to be installed as responsible nurses, under direction of an older and more experienced woman. The constant activity our work entailed was a relief from the strained excitement of life after the battle of Seven Pines.

When the first flurry of distress was over, the residents of those pretty houses standing back in gardens full of roses set their cooks to work, or, better still, went themselves into the kitchen, to compound delicious messes for the wounded, after the appetizing old Virginia recipes. Flitting about the streets in the direction of the hospitals were smiling, white-jacketed negroes, carrying silver trays with dishes of fine porcelain under napkins of thick white damask, containing soups, creams, jellies, thin biscuit, eggs *a la crème*, boiled chicken, etc., surmounted by clusters of freshly gathered flowers. A year later we had cause to pine after these culinary glories when it came to measuring out, with sinking hearts, the meager portions of milk and food we could afford to give our charges.

As an instance, however, that quality in food was not always appreciated by the patients, my mother urged upon one of her sufferers (a gaunt and soft-voiced Carolinian from the "piney woods district") a delicately served trifle from some neighboring kitchen.

"Jes ez you say, old miss," was the weary answer; "I ain't a-contradictin' you. It mout be good for me, but my stomick's kinder sot agin it. There ain't but one thing I'm sorter yarnin' arter, an' that's a dish o' greens en bacon fat, with a few molarses poured onto it."

From our patients, when they could syllable the tale, we had accounts of the fury of the fight, which were made none the less horrible by such assistance as imagination could give to the facts. I remember they told us of shot thrown from the enemy's batteries, that plowed their way through lines of flesh and blood before exploding in showers of musket-balls to do still further havoc. Before these awful missiles, it was said, our men had fallen in swaths, the living closing over them to press forward in the charge.

It was at the end of one of these narrations that a piping voice came from a pallet in the corner: "They fit right smart, them Yanks did, I tell *you*!" and not to laugh was as much of an effort as it had just been not to cry….

Day by day we were called to our windows by the wailing dirge of a military band preceding a soldier's funeral. One could not number those sad pageants; the coffin crowned with cap and sword and gloves, the riderless horse following with empty boots fixed in the stirrups of an army saddle; such soldiers as could be spared from the front marching after with arms reversed and crape-enfolded banners; the passers-by standing with bare, bent heads. Funerals less honored outwardly were continually occurring. Then and thereafter the green hillsides of lovely Hollywood were frequently upturned to find resting-places for the heroic dead….

Spite of its melancholy uses, there was no more favorite walk in Richmond than Hollywood, a picturesquely beautiful spot, where high hills sink into velvet undulations, profusely shaded with holly, pine, and cedar, as well as by trees of deciduous foliage. In spring the banks of the stream that runs through the valley were enameled with wild flowers, and the thickets were full of May-blossom and dogwood. Mounting to the summit of the bluff, one may sit under the shade of some ample oak, to view the spires and roofs of the town, with the white colonnade of the distant Capitol. Richmond, thus seen beneath her verdant foliage "upon hills, girdled by hills," confirms what an old writer felt called to exclaim about it, "Verily, this city hath a pleasant seat." On the right, below this point, flows the rushing yellow river, making ceaseless turmoil around islets of rock whose rifts are full of birch and willow, or leaping impetuously over the bowlders of granite that strew its bed. Old-time Richmond folk used to say that the sound of their favorite James (or, to be exact, "Jeems") went with them into foreign countries, during no matter how many years of absence, haunting them like a strain of sweetest music; nor would they permit a suggestion of superiority in the flavor of any other fluid to that of a draught of its amber waters.

So blent with my own memories of war is the voice of that tireless river, that I seem to hear it yet, over the tramp of rusty battalions, the short imperious stroke of the alarm-bell, the clash of passing bands, the gallop of eager horsemen, the roar of battle, the moan of hospitals, the stifled note of sorrow! ....

BOOK II – CHAPTER THREE

The Coming of Arthur

Lt. Col. Walter Taylor, from *Four Years with General Lee*: (1)

On the last day of May the battle of Seven Pines, or Fair Oaks, was delivered, and General Johnston was wounded. On that afternoon the President and General Lee had gone out on the lines, and were present and under a severe fire as the troops of General Whiting went into action. Maj. Gen. G. W. Smith was next in rank to General Johnston, and assumed command of the army after the wounding of the latter. The next day, by order of the President, General Lee took personal command of the Army of Northern Virginia. He proceeded at once to make its position secure against attack, and to enhance its efficiency and strength, by every means in his power, so as to justify aggressive movements....

Maj. Jed Hotchkiss, from *Confederate Military History*: (2)

Undaunted courage, coupled with rare caution, characterized the new Confederate general commanding. Desiring to be fully informed in reference to the rear as well as the front of the great host beleaguering Richmond, Lee took his bold and ever-alert cavalry leader, J. E. B. Stuart, into his councils, and dispatched him on the 12th with 1,200 veteran cavalry to reconnoiter McClellan's rear....

Maj. Heros Von Borcke, a Prussian volunteer on the staff of Gen. J. E. B. Stuart, from his *Memoirs of the Confederate War for Independence*: (3)

June 12, 1862. – It was two o'clock in the morning, and we were all fast asleep, when General Stuart's clear voice awoke us with the words, "Gentlemen, in ten minutes every man must be in his saddle!"

In half the time all the members of the staff were dressed, and the horses had been fed; and the ten minutes were scarcely up when we galloped off to overtake the main body, which we reached by about five o'clock. Our command was composed of parts of the different regiments of the brigade, and consisted of about 2500 cavalry, with two pieces of horse-artillery. None of us knew where we were going; General Stuart only communicated the object of the expedition to the colonels commanding; nevertheless every one followed our honoured leader with perfect confidence. We marched the whole day long without halting, and towards evening bivouacked near the little town of Taylorsville in Hanover County, where we were already within the enemy's lines. At daybreak we again mounted our horses, and our vanguard was soon reported to have met with a party of the enemy's dragoons, who on their approach had hurried off in hasty flight. Without waiting to pursue them, we continued our march, greeted everywhere with enthusiasm by the inhabitants, especially by the ladies, who for a long time had seen none other than Federal troops.

I was in company with Stuart the whole time, constantly near the vanguard, and could note that every operation was initiated and superintended by the General himself. A few miles from Hanover Court-house we surprised a picket of the enemy's cavalry, every man of which fell into our hands from the suddenness of our attack. Whilst we were occupied with sending the prisoners to the rear, our advance-guard came back at a run, hotly pursued by a large body of the enemy's dragoons. Our leading squadron spurred immediately forward to meet the attack, and, having obtained General Stuart's permission, I joined them as with loud war-cries they hurled themselves against the blue masses of the enemy. The Yankees were not able to withstand the impetuous onset of the Virginia horsemen, and, after a *melee* of a very few minutes, there commenced a most exciting chase, which was continued for nearly three miles. Friend and foe were soon enveloped in blinding clouds of dust, through which pistol and carbine shots were seen darting to and fro like flashes of lightning. The larger number of the enemy escaped, thanks to their fresher animals, but we took many of them prisoners, and their dead and wounded men and horses encumbered the road as we pushed along.

Half an hour later our advance-guard again came in collision with the enemy, who had rallied, and, with strong reinforcements, were awaiting us. Two squadrons of the 9th Virginia Cavalry were immediately sent forward to the attack, and I received orders from General Stuart to hasten with our main column to the scene of action. I rode at once to bring on the main column; but though I used the utmost speed to get back in time to take part in the charge, when I arrived at the scene of the sharp conflict the work had already been done. The enemy's lines were broken and in full flight, leaving many of their dead and wounded, and a large number of prisoners, among whom were several officers, in our hands. We had to lament the loss of the gallant Captain Latane, who, while boldly leading his men, fell pierced by five bullets. In a few seconds the 1st Virginia Cavalry had arrived, and we instantly dashed forward in pursuit.

The enemy made one more attempt to rally, but their lines were broken by our furious attack; they fled in confusion, and we chased them in wild pursuit across an open field, through their camp, and far into the woods. When we had returned to their camp the work of destruction began. Every one tried to rescue for himself as much as possible of the articles of luxury with which the Yankees had overloaded themselves, but few succeeded in the end; for, in accordance with the well-laid plan of our leader, flames flashed up, now in one place, now in another, and in a few minutes the whole camp was enveloped in one blaze, hundreds of tents burning together presenting a wonderfully beautiful spectacle. Many horses and mules, and two captured standards, were all that we carried off with us. After half an hour's halt our destroying cavalry again set forth; our track of blood and fire pointing out to the enemy the path which we had taken.

We now found ourselves in the heart of the enemy's position, and their encampments lay around us on all sides. At one point of our journey, the house occupied by the Federal Commander-in-Chief, General McClellan, as his headquarters, surrounded by the white tents of a very large camp, was plainly visible at the distance of about two and a half miles. Our situation would have been one of extraordinary peril, had not the boldness and rapidity of our movements disabled and paralysed our adversaries.

On either side of the road we constantly seized upon unsuspecting Federal soldiers, who had no idea of the close proximity of the dreaded Stuart until collared by his horsemen. A considerable number of wagons laden with provisions and goods fell into our hands, among them one containing the personal stores of General McClellan, with his cigars, wines, and other dainties. But we could not be burdened with booty, so the entire train was committed to the flames, the champagne popped bootlessly, and the cabanas wasted their fragrance on the air. Three transport-ships which lay in the river Pamunkey near at hand, laden with wheat, corn, and provisions from all quarters, were seized by us, together with the guard and the agents stationed there, and ere long the flames mounting towards heaven proclaimed how complete was our work of destruction. A brigade of the enemy's cavalry here sought to intercept our way and to detain us till the troops, which were marching upon us from all sides, could arrive; but it was broken by our first attack, and crossed our path no more.

Thus towards evening we reached the railroad which was so useful to the enemy in giving them communication with the north; and just as the demolition of the road-bed was about to begin, the train was seen coming up. Without delay General Stuart posted a portion of his men on either side of the embankment, with orders to fire if the train refused to stop at the station. The train moved slowly nearer and nearer, puffing off the steam, and we could soon perceive that it was laden with soldiers, most of them being in open carriages. As the command to stop was disregarded, but on the contrary the movement of the train was accelerated, firing began along our whole line. The engine-driver was shot down by Captain Farley, to whom I had lent my blunderbuss; but before the deadly bullet reached him he had put the train in somewhat quicker motion, so that we could not make ourselves masters of it.

A battle of the strangest description now arose. Some of the soldiers in the train returned our fire, others sprang out to save themselves by flight, or lay down flat at the bottom of the carriages. The train, though its motion had been quickened, was not going at so rapid a pace that we could not keep up with it by galloping hard. Meantime, having had my hat almost knocked off my head by one of the enemy's bullets, I became so wildly excited that, without heeding our own fire, I spurred my horse over the embankment, and very soon had discharged all the five charges of my revolver at the foe. We heard later that few of the occupants of the train had escaped unhurt; the greater part were either killed or severely wounded. I reproached myself afterwards with having so given the reins to my passion; but after all I only acted in obedience to orders and the requirements of war. After having done as much injury as we could to the railroad, we proceeded on our march, whilst the last beams of the sun lighted up the scene of destruction.

It had been a hard ride and a hard day's work, and my parched tongue was cleaving to the roof of my mouth, when one of our men galloped up to me, and held out a bottle of champagne, saying, "Captain, you did pretty hot work to-day. I got this bottle of champagne for you out of McClellan's wagon. It will do you good." Never in my life have I enjoyed a bottle of wine so much....

Maj. Jed Hotchkiss, from *Confederate Military History*: (4)

Starting from Richmond, [Stuart] followed the Brook turnpike northward to Ashland, then turned eastward by way of Hanover Court House, and followed the main road down the south side of the Pamunkey, a few miles in the rear of McClellan's far-stretching army, crossing the York River Railroad at Tunstall's, making captures, destroying stores, and breaking the enemy's line of communication as he went; then, turning southward, he crossed the swollen Chickahominy, near Providence Forge, and continued to the banks of the James at Charles City, whence he returned by the river road to Richmond, having in forty-eight hours, with the loss of but a single man, the brave Latane, whom he left in the hands of noble Virginia women for burial, ridden entirely around the Federal army and gathered information of incalculable value to Lee in maturing his plans....

Lt. Col. Walter Taylor, from *Four Years with General Lee*: (5)

The brilliant achievements of the army under General ["Stonewall"] Jackson, in the Shenandoah Valley, had so startled and paralyzed the Federal authorities, and had excited such fears for the safety of Washington, as to remove all apprehension of any immediate trouble from the enemy heretofore operating in the

Valley, and to render improbable the junction of the army under McDowell with that of McClellan.

General Lee, quick to observe and profit by the advantage to be derived from this propitious state of affairs, conceived the plan of drawing Jackson's command to his aid, swiftly and secretly, in order that he might, when thus reinforced, fall with all his strength upon the enemy's right flank, and compel him to a general engagement.

The necessary orders were given. General Jackson moved with all possible celerity, and when he had reached Ashland, General Lee, having left Generals Magruder, Holmes, and Huger, with about twenty-eight thousand men, in the defenses of Richmond, on the 26th of June moved to the north side of the Chickahominy River with the remainder of his army, and took the initiative in the engagements embraced in the seven days' battles, from which resulted the complete discomfiture of the army under General McClellan, and its retreat to the protection of the fleet operating in James River....

Major Robert Stiles, from *Four Years Under Marse Robert*: (6)

Our battery was among the 28,000 men left on the Richmond side of the Chickahominy to defend the capital, to occupy the attention of McClellan's troops on this side, and to prevent their recrossing to the aid of their hard-pressed comrades on the other; but the real defenders of the city were the men who stormed the bloody heights at Gaines' Mill and the positions at Mechanicsville and Cold Harbor. We were in General Magruder's command and were kept most of the time hitched up and ready to move at a moment's warning. We were subjected now and then to fire from Federal batteries, suffered some loss of horses and equipment, and several of our men were wounded, but there were no serious casualties.

On the 29th of June – Sunday, I think it was – General Magruder advanced his troops along the Nine-Mile road to feel the enemy, when the main thing that struck us was the immense quantity of abandoned stores and equipment, indicating how abundant had been the supply of the Federal forces and how great the demoralization of their retreat. Near Savage Station there must have been acres covered by stacks of burning boxes of bacon, crackers, and desiccated vegetables – "desecrated veg-etables," our boys called them. To us poorly-equipped and half-starved rebels it was a revelation....

On Sunday evening, not far from Savage Station, I had been struck directly over the heart by a spent ball, which glanced from a buckle, but blackened my breast and nauseated me some-what. Next morning, still feeling badly and the battery remaining stationary for a time, I had retired a little from the line and was half reclining at the foot of a huge pine that stood on the edge of the Williamsburg road. Hearing the jingle of cavalry accoutre-ments toward the Chickahominy, I looked up and saw a half-dozen mounted men, and riding considerably in advance a solitary horseman, whom I instantly recognized as the great wizard of the marvelous Valley Campaign which had so thrilled the army and the country.

Jackson and the little sorrel stopped in the middle of the road, probably not fifty feet off, while his staff halted perhaps a hundred and fifty yards in his rear. He sat stark and stiff in the saddle. Horse and rider appeared worn down to the lowest point of flesh consistent with effective service. His hair, skin, eyes, and clothes were all one neutral dust tint, and his badges of rank so dulled and tarnished as to be scarcely perceptible. The "mangy little cadet cap" was pulled so low in front that the visor cut the glint of his eyeballs.... Not a muscle quivered as he resumed his steady gaze down the road toward Richmond. He was the ideal of concentration, - imperturbable, resistless. I remember feeling that if he were not a very good man he would be a very bad one. By a ludicrous turn of the association of ideas, the old darkey minister's illustration of faith flashed through my brain: "Bredren, ef de Lord tell me to jump through a stone wall, I's gwine to jump at it; jumpin' at it 'longs to me, goin' through it 'longs to God." The man before me would have jumped at anything the Lord told him to jump through.

A moment later and his gaze was rewarded. A magnificent staff approached from the direction of Richmond, and riding at its head, superbly mounted, a born king among men. At that time General Lee was one of the handsomest of men, especially on horseback, and that morning every detail of the dress and equipment of himself and horse was absolute perfection. When he recognized Jackson he rode forward with a courier, his staff halting. As he gracefully dismounted, handing his bridle rein to his attendant, and advanced, drawing the gauntlet from his right hand, Jackson flung himself off his horse and advanced to meet Lee, Little Sorrel trotting back to the staff, where a courier secured him.

The two generals greeted each other warmly, but wasted no time upon the greeting. They stood facing each other, some thirty feet from where I lay, Lee's left side and back toward me, Jackson's right and front. Jackson began talking in a jerky, impetuous way, meanwhile drawing a diagram on the ground with the toe of his right boot. He traced two sides of a triangle with promptness and decision; then starting at the end of the second line, began to draw a third projected toward the first. This third line he traced slowly and with hesitation, alternately looking up at Lee's face and down at his diagram, meanwhile talking earnestly; and when at last the third line crossed the first and the triangle was complete, he raised his foot and stamped it down with emphasis, saying, "We've got him!" then signaled for his horse, and when he came, vaulted awkwardly into the saddle and was off. Lee watched him a moment, the courier brought his horse, he mounted, and he and his staff rode away.

The third line was never drawn – so we never "got" Mc-Clellan…. The understanding in the army at the time was that

Huger and Holmes were to have drawn it, but their commands lost their way in the almost trackless forest.... As before stated, General Lee left but twenty-eight thousand men on the Richmond side of the Chickahominy when he crossed to the other side to attack McClellan, and of course looked to these fresh troops, when his victorious but decimated and worn-out soldiers had driven the enemy into their arms, to fall upon the Federal general and gather the fruits of victory. But here are more than one-third of these fresh troops, and the very ones Lee had arranged should cut off the retreat of his gallant foe, that never got into action at all, and McClellan was permitted to reach and occupy the strong position which saved his army and cost the lives of thousands of ours. And even this was not all. Magruder, a most vigorous officer, to whose command we were attached, lost his way and thus delayed the attack and gave McClellan further time for his dispositions. And when at last we did attack, it was in a disconnected and desultory fashion....

According to his own report of June 20, 1862, McClellan had three hundred and forty pieces of field artillery. I see no reason for doubting that a very large proportion of these were massed upon Malvern Hill. Nothing human can long withstand the fire of such a mass of artillery concentrated, as the Federal guns at Malvern Hill were, upon very short attacking lines of infantry. Colonel Taylor says divisions were marched forward at different times, each attacking independently and each in turn repulsed. I think it was even worse than this, and that in some cases single brigades advanced to the attack and were almost literally swept backward by what seemed to be the fire of a continuous line of battle of artillery.

The effect of these repeated bloody repulses can hardly be conceived. One fearful feature was the sudden and awful revulsion of feeling among our soldiers, inspired by six days of constant victory and relentless pursuit of a retreating foe. The demoralization was great and the evidences of it palpable everywhere. The roads and forests were full of stragglers; commands were inextricably confused, some, for the time, having actually disappeared. Those who retained sufficient self-respect and sense of responsibility to think of the future were filled with the deepest apprehension. I know that this was the state of mind of some of our strongest and best officers; in fact, I do not know of any general officer in the army, save one, who did not entertain the gloomiest forebodings, and I recall hearing at the time, or rather a day or so afterwards, substantially the same story of that one which ... was related by Dr. Hunter McGuire, Jackson's medical director...:

"At Malvern Hill, when a portion of our army was beaten and to some extent demoralized, Hill and Ewell and Early came to tell [Jackson] that they could make no resistance if McClellan attacked them in the morning. It was difficult to wake General Jackson, as he was exhausted and very sound asleep. I tried it myself, and after many efforts, partly succeeded. When he was made to understand what was wanted he said: 'McClellan and his army will be gone by daylight,' and went to sleep again. The generals thought him mad, but the prediction was true"....

The story illustrates two of the greatest and most distinguishing traits and powers of Jackson as a general: he did not know what demoralization meant, and he never failed to know just what his adversary thought and felt and proposed to do. In the present instance, not only did all that Jackson said and implied turn out to be true, that McClellan was thinking only of escape, and never dreamed of viewing the battle of Malvern Hill in any other aspect, but in an incredibly short time our army had recovered its tone and had come to take the same view of the matter.

Indeed, as I believe, nothing but another untoward accident prevented McClellan surrendering his entire army to Lee, notwithstanding his successful defense at Malvern Hill.... Stuart, Lee's chief of cavalry, following up McClellan's movements after Malvern Hill, from the heights above Westover, overlooked the entire Federal army huddled together in the river bottoms of and adjacent to Westover plantation, apparently in a state of utter disorganization and unpreparedness, and he could not resist the temptation of dropping a few shells among them, which produced a perfect stampede among the troops and wagons, but at the same time had the effect of calling the attention of the Federal commanders to the fact that the position of their army was utterly untenable without command of the heights from which these shells had been fired, and they immediately sent a heavy force to take possession of them. Stuart at once informed General Lee and received word that Jackson and Longstreet were *en route* to support him; but again the guides proved incompetent, and Longstreet was led six or seven miles out of the way, and Stuart, after resisting as long as he could, was compelled to yield possession of the heights, which were promptly occupied and fortified by an adequate Federal force....

"Stuart, glorious Stuart," as Colonel Taylor justly calls him, while his boyish indiscretion in firing into the huddled masses of the enemy from Evelington Heights, before informing General Lee of the situation, was apparently the cause of the loss of another great opportunity – yet it should not be forgotten, in this connection, that the great plan of the Seven Days battles owed its inspiration, or at least its completion and perfection, to the information derived from Stuart's marvelous ride around McClellan's entire army just in advance of Lee's attack, more than to any other source outside the imperial intellect of the Commander-in-Chief himself. Stuart was a splendidly endowed cavalry leader, his only fault being a tendency to indulge too far his fondness for achievements that savored of the startling, the marvelous, and the romantic.

One more general reflection: Whatever effect the Seven Days' battles may have had upon other reputations, Federal or Confederate – and there were upon our side generals whose names stood high upon the roster of our main army when these operations began, but never again appeared upon it after they closed – yet there is one name and fame which these seven days gave to history and to glory, as to which the entire world stands agreed, and all the after chances and changes of the war but expanded the world's verdict. When we contemplate Lee's great plan and the qualities of leadership which these operations revealed in him, we know not which most to admire – the brilliance, the comprehensiveness, or the almost reckless audacity of the scheme and of the man. It is a singular fact, and one which seems to demand explanation, that the prominent impression which Lee invariably seems to make is that of roundness, balance, perfection; and yet unquestionably his leading characteristic as a general is aggressive audacity. Take for example his leaving but 28,000 of 80,000 men between McClellan and Richmond, and with the other 52,000 crossing a generally impassable stream and attacking McClellan's 105,000 in entrenched positions. Mayhap old Jubal Early, who knew Lee and knew war as well as any other man on either side, has the right of it and suggests the true explanation when he says, speaking of this very operation: "Timid minds might regard this as rashness, but it was the very perfection of a profound and daring strategy."

And when we attempt to measure the effect of these Seven Days' battles – when we note that within less than one month from the day he took command of an army with which he had no previous personal connection, Lee had completely secured its confidence and correctly estimated its capabilities, had conceived and perfected his great plan and every detail essential to its successful execution, had begun to put it into operation and actually delivered his first great blow; when we note further that within a week after that blow was struck Richmond was entirely relieved and within a few weeks more Washington was in serious peril, and the United States Government had called for three hundred thousand more men; when, we say, all this is considered, we may well ask when did the weight of one great Captain's sword, only this and nothing more, cause the scales of war to dip with such a determined, downward sag? ….

The Brand Excalibur

Lt. Col. Walter Taylor, from *Four Years with General Lee*: (1)

Although defeated, the army under General McClellan was still a formidable force, and was being constantly strengthened. Its proximity to the Confederate capital, and its unassailable position, the facility with which it could be transferred across James River for operations on the south side, the capacity of the North indefinitely to recruit its ranks, and of the Government to repair and increase its equipment, rendered the situation one of profound solicitude, and presented to the Confederate commander the alternative of remaining a passive observer of his adversary's movements, or of devising a campaign which would compel the withdrawal of the hostile army from its position of constant menace.

With a just conception of the inordinate fear which possessed the mind of the Federal civil authorities for the safety of their capital, he concluded that seriously to threaten that city, either by strategic maneuvers or by a decisive blow struck at the army in its front, would be the surest way of effecting the removal of McClellan's army from its position on James River.

With this view he sent General Jackson in advance with his two divisions, followed by that of A. P. Hill, to engage General Pope, who commanded the Federal army in Northern Virginia, intending, as soon as his anticipations of the effect of this move were realized, to follow promptly with the bulk of his army.

In vindication of his sagacity, information was soon received of the transfer of troops from McClellan's army on James River to Washington.

Leaving two divisions of infantry and a brigade of cavalry at Richmond, he now moved with the rest of the army to join General Jackson, who had already presented a rebel front to the astonished gaze of Major-General John Pope, unaccustomed to such a sight, and had commenced at Cedar Run, on the 9th of August, that series of brilliant maneuvers and engagements which so dazed the Federal commander, and so startled and alarmed the authorities at Washington....

Maj. Jed Hotchkiss, from *Confederate Military History*: (2)

The battle of Cedar Run, as General Lee says in his report, "effectually checked the progress of the enemy for the time," but the pressure from Washington was so great that Pope had to respond with an advance.... Lee, in expectation of this, had, on the 13th of August, ordered Longstreet, with his division and two brigades under Hood, to move to Gordonsville, and R. H. Anderson to follow him, anticipating by a day McClellan's movement from Harrison's Landing toward Fort Monroe. At the same time Stuart was ordered to move the main body of his cavalry toward Orange Court House, covering the right of Longstreet's movement and placing his cavalry upon the right of Lee's army when concentrated in Orange.... Lee, in person, followed and joined his army in Orange near the middle of August, and on the 19th gave orders for an advance, having determined to strike Pope and defeat him before the great force under McClellan could join him....

The morning of the 21st found Lee's 50,000 veterans on the south bank of the Rappahannock.... Pope's 55,000 men held the commanding ground on the north bank.... Lee's military genius, and his conferences with Jackson, convinced him that the proper movement was one that should turn Pope's right and place the Confederates in his rear, cutting him off from the old time highway that led through the Piedmont country, by Warrenton, toward Washington. Moreover, "the strength of the hills" lay in that direction; for within sight, looking to the northward and westward, were the outlying ridges of the coast range, the Rappahannock and Bull Run mountains, behind which concealed movements could be made in the desired direction.

The first step in this strategic movement was to get the mobile left wing of his army, under the energetic and always-ready Jackson, behind these covering low mountain ranges ... without the knowledge of Pope. To accomplish this, Lee adopted a series of novel advances. While Jackson and Stuart were engaging the attention of Pope along the Rappahannock, north of the railroad, he moved Longstreet from his right, by concealed roads, and placed him in Jackson's rear, leaving the latter free to fall back after dark, giving place to Longstreet, and march to a position farther up the river, but still holding on to Longstreet's left. This first exchange of positions was made during the night of the 21st, or rather the early morning of the 22nd, and that day, preceded by cavalry, Jackson reached the neighborhood of Warrenton Springs.... On this same 22nd, Lee initiated one of the boldest of his deceiving strategic movements. During the forenoon he dispatched Stuart, with the main body of his cavalry, by concealed roads behind his army, to Waterloo Bridge, four miles above Warrenton Springs, held by Jackson, and where the graded highway from Warrenton to Little Washington crosses the Rappahannock. There Stuart, with 1,500 men and two guns, crossed the river and began a rapid march for Pope's rear, to break the railway leading to Washington and gather information, just as he had recently done in his grand ride around McClellan at Richmond.

With a good road to march on, he reached Warrenton unopposed, in the afternoon. After halting there for a short rest, he continued eastward, by Auburn Mills, to Catlett's station, on the

Orange and Alexandria railroad, intending to destroy the bridge over Cedar creek near that place. The downpour that had swelled the Rappahannock, caught Stuart on the march, and he reached his objective in the midst of rain and darkness; but an intercepted and captured negro led him to a camp where were the headquarters wagons of General Pope. These Stuart quickly captured with one of the Federal commander's staff and his personal baggage and official papers.

His efforts to destroy the wagon trains and the railroad bridge were but partially successful, in consequence of the rain and darkness. He began his return march before daylight of the 23d, bringing off 300 prisoners, and recrossed the Rappahannock in the evening of the same day, without molestation, after having taught Pope a second lesson on the subject of rear guards, and infused an element of fear into the Federal army as to the safety of his lines of retreat; also bringing off the captured correspondence between Pope and Halleck, which informed Lee fully concerning the strength and the plans of his antagonist....

The heavy rain of the night of the 22nd interrupted Jackson's movement.... During the night of the 24th, Longstreet's batteries took the place of Jackson opposite Warrenton Springs, as did also his troops, leaving Jackson free to begin his movement on the morning of the 25th, which he did, at an early hour, leaving his baggage train behind and taking with him only ambulances and ordnance wagons. His troops carried in their haversacks scant rations for three days, Jackson confident of being able to abundantly supply them from the enemy's stores.

Starting from the vicinity of Jeffersonton, to which he fell back in giving place to Longstreet, Jackson marched for some distance to the northwestward, along the great highway leading to the Valley, by way of Chester Gap, and his bronzed veterans were elated with the conviction that they were again bound for the scene of their victories of the preceding spring; but, when a short distance beyond Amissville, their course was turned from the northwest to the northeast, they looked questioningly one to the other, as to whither they were going, led by Lieutenant Boswell and portions of the noted Black Horse cavalry through their Fauquier home-land. Jackson pressed steadily forward, through the long August day, without a halt, until he had covered 25 miles and reached the vicinity of Salem, on the Manassas Gap Railroad, just as the sun sank behind the Blue Ridge to his left.

At dawn of the 26th, Jackson's men were again puzzled on finding themselves marching to the southeast, following the line of the Manassas Gap Railroad, through Thoroughfare Gap, to Gainesville, where Stuart joined them with his cavalry and led the way from that hamlet directly to Bristoe Station, on the Orange & Alexandria Railroad, which they reached about dark, after a march of 24 miles, without having met opposition on the way.

Jackson and his 22,000 enthusiastic men, and Stuart with wide-awake and jolly cavalry, were now in Pope's rear and on his line of communication, which they proceeded to destroy, capturing trains moving toward Washington and breaking up detached Federal encampments along the railway. Not satisfied with this, and desiring not only to reap the spoils stored at Manassas but to guard against movements from Washington, Jackson sent Trimble's brigade of infantry and Stuart with a portion of his cavalry, through the darkness, four miles further to Manassas Junction, which they reached and captured after a brief resistance....

Maj. Heros von Borcke, from *Memoirs of the Confederate War for Independence*: (3)

The plateau of Manassas presents an area of about three miles square, over which the Yankees had built an irregular town of storehouses, barracks, huts, and tents, which was fortified on all sides by continuous redoubts. Here were collected stores and provisions, ammunition and equipments for an army of 100,000 men (besides an enormous quantity of luxuries unknown to warfare), the capture of which was a most important success to our arms.

The sight that was presented to me at the moment of my arrival was truly a magnificent one. In front, rapidly advancing, were the long lines of our cavalry, their pennons fluttering gaily in the morning air, and moving in company with them might be seen the horse-artillery, from whose pieces, as well as from the guns we had captured in the redoubts and were now serving with admirable effect, dense clouds of white smoke were spread over the plain; on the left Jackson's veteran columns were pushing forward at a double quick, while in the distant view the blue masses of the enemy were in rapid flight towards the glimmering woods.

I found General Stuart exceedingly delighted with his success. He had taken the troops guarding the place completely by surprise, capturing the greater part of them and twelve pieces of artillery in the redoubts without much fighting, and had just routed three brigades of infantry that had been sent from Alexandria as reinforcements. The enemy in their flight had left behind their dead and wounded and more than 1500 runaway negroes – men, women, and children. The quantity of booty was very great, and the amount of luxuries absolutely incredible….

We were occupied throughout the day in collecting as much of the booty as we could carry off with us, and preparing the rest for destruction. During the afternoon we received reports that the Federal army was moving rapidly upon us from various points, and very soon Ewell's division, which formed Jackson's rear, was hotly engaged with their advance-guard. The main body of our infantry commenced now to march off quietly in the direction of Centreville, turning afterwards towards the Stone Bridge and Sudley's Mill, while the cavalry remained on the plains to apply the torch to the captured property….

Just as the sun was disappearing behind the range of distant hills that formed the western horizon, the flames were rising from a hundred different points of the plain, bringing out vividly each one of a legion of dark figures which were moving about, in the midst of the conflagration, to assist in spreading the fire, and fanning it into fury wherever it languished. The glow reflected from all these burning buildings, tents, and railway cars, with the red glare from the mouths of the cannon, and the sparkling of the bursting shells as seen against the darkening forest, made up a spectacle of strange mysterious splendour....

Lt. Gen. Jubal A. Early, from his "Lee Memorial Address," January 19, 1872: (4)

Pope now found it necessary to look out for his supplies and his line of retreat, and then ensued that series of engagements called "the second battle of Manassas." Pope had already been joined by two corps of McClellan's army, Porter's and Heintzelman's, the one by the way of Fredericksburg, and the other over the railroad; and Jackson's three divisions, numbering less than twenty thousand men, after cutting the railroad, and destroying several trains of cars and immense stores at Manassas, which could not be removed for want of transportation, withstood for two days, beginning on the 28th of August, Pope's entire army, reinforced by Reno's eight thousand men, and McClellan's two corps, while General Lee was moving up with Longstreet's and Anderson's commands.

Never did General Jackson display his leading characteristics more conspicuously than on this occasion, and he fully justified the confidence of the commanding general, in intrusting him with the execution of one of the most brilliant and daring strategic movements on record....

Maj. Robert Stiles, from *Four Years Under Marse Robert*: (5)

While I have … no personal reminiscence to relate … of the Manassas … campaign of '62, yet an account was given me of the very crisis and climax…. One of the most promising of the younger officers of the Army of Northern Virginia … Col. Edward Willis, of the Twelfth Georgia Regiment [once a Captain on Jackson's staff] … began to talk of the campaign against Pope, which he regarded as Jackson's masterpiece, and as he had been closely with Jackson through it all, I considered what he said of value, as it certainly was of surpassing interest.

He first expatiated at some length upon the masterly – I had almost said dastardly – way in which Jackson managed to find out all Pope's plans and purposes, and yet to elude and delude and deceive and defraud him in the most heartless and malignant fashion as to his own movements and designs. Part of the time, while waiting for Lee and Longstreet, Jackson was in extreme peril, dodging between and against the huge Federal Army corps, rushing blindly like avalanches to crush him. On one or two occasions, I think Willis said, he even went so far as to sacrifice his skirmish line, that is, arrange to have them captured by Pope's troops in a particular position, from which even the skirmishers themselves, as well as their captors, would naturally infer that "Old Jack" was marching in a certain direction and about a certain time would be about a certain place, when quite the reverse was the actual truth. In short, it must be admitted that all of Jackson's dealings with Pope, about this time, were disingenuous in the extreme. Someone, not Willis, has said substantially that they embodied a continuous, tortuous, twisted, aggravated, protracted *lie* – over fifty miles long.

But at last, as Willis said, all these tactics of deception were exhausted! Jackson was straight in front, in the famous position in the railroad cut, and Pope's whole army moved upon him. They advanced in imposing array, with several lines of battle – bands playing, flags flying, and their artillery, following the second line, slowly firing as they approached. Just as his dispositions – the best he could make for resisting such an onslaught – were complete, Jackson heard from Longstreet, who promised him aid in two hours. The shock could be delayed, however, only a few moments, and Jackson, feeling the imminence of the crisis, started down his lines to communicate to his troops, worn with fatigue and suspense, his own heaven-born faith and fire and Longstreet's assurance of help. I understood from Willis that he rode along the line with him, and that all he said was:

"Two hours, men, only two hours; in two hours you will have help. You must stand it for two hours."

It was the crisis of the campaign, and both sides fully appreciated it. The enemy came right on until within two hundred yards, and then broke into the rush of the charge.... A hundred yards nearer and the full fire from Jackson's line burst upon them ... the advancing lines halted and wavered throughout their length – a moment more and the whole magnificent array had melted into a mass of fugitives.

Again Jackson rode down his lines: "Half an hour men, only half an hour; can you stand it half an hour?"

And now, as Willis said, it seemed as if some of his men exhaled their very souls to him in shouts, while others, too much exhausted to cheer, took off their hats and gazed at him in adoration as he passed. The enemy, reformed, began again to advance, and Jackson quickened his horse's gait. "They are coming once more, men; you must stand it once more; you must stand it half an hour."

Could they have stood it? We shall never know – for before the mighty wave broke again into the crest and foam of the actual charge, the Texas brigade was in on Jackson's right and Old Pete and Old Jack together swept them in the counter-charge like chaff before the whirlwind....

Lt. Col. Walter Taylor, from *Four Years with General Lee*: (6)

Vanquished at Manassas, General Pope next essayed to make a stand in the fortified lines about Centreville; but another *detour* by General Jackson, under General Lee's orders, caused a further retreat in the direction of Washington, and in the early days of September the Federal army – now embracing the combined forces of McClellan and Pope – was retired within the line of fortifications constructed on the Virginia side of the river, for the protection of the Federal capital....

The Knights of the Round Table

Maj. Heros von Borcke, from his *Memoirs of the Confederate War for Independence*: (1)

General Lee had now decided not to attack the enemy in their strong fortifications around Alexandria, but boldly to carry the war into the enemy's territory, or at least into the fertile plains of Maryland. Many advantages, it was hoped, might be secured by this policy. For a considerable period he would be able there to subsist his army, relieved from the necessity of protecting his lines of communication for supplies. The confident belief was also entertained that our army would be increased by 20,000 to 25,000 recruits, who were supposed to be only awaiting the opportunity of taking up arms against the Federal Government. Being so rein-forced, our commander-in-chief doubted not that he might easily strike a blow against Baltimore, or even Washington, or transfer the theatre of military operations across the border into the rich agricultural region of Pennsylvania.

On the morning of the 5th September there was again presented throughout the Confederate camps a scene of bustling activity. Every regiment was preparing for the march, officers were riding to and fro, and the long artillery-trains were moving off along the turnpike, their rumbling noise combining with the rattle of the drums and the roll of the bugles to wake the echoes for miles around. Our destination was *northward*, and as we rode onward towards the little town of Leesburg, inspirited by this fact, our horses exhibiting new life from yesterday's repose, many a youthful hero looked forward to his triumphant entry into the Federal capital, or to a joyous reception at the hands of the fair women of Baltimore, whose irrepressible sympathies had been always with the South.

After a march of several hours the column reached Leesburg, and the streets of the village were at once so compactly filled with troops, artillery, and waggon-trains, that General Stuart determined to make a detour with his cavalry, which had been halted about a mile distant, in preference to proceeding through the place. It was necessary, however, for the General to repair for final instructions to the headquarters of General Lee in the town, and in this ride he was accompanied by his Staff....

About two o'clock in the afternoon we received orders to move on, and after a dusty and very much impeded march of two hours, winding through infantry columns, and compelled frequently to halt, we reached the Potomac at White's Ford, where the cavalry were to cross. The banks of this noble river, which is of great width at this point, rise to the height of about sixty feet above the bed of the stream, and are overshadowed by gigantic trees of primeval growth, the trunks and branches of which are enwrapped with luxuriant vines, that, after reaching the very top, fall in graceful streamers and festoons to the ground, thus presenting tangles of tender verdure rarely seen in the forests of Europe. At White's Ford the Potomac is divided into two streams by a sandy strip of island in the middle. This island is half a mile in length, and offered us a momentary resting-place half-way in our passage of the river. It was, indeed, a magnificent sight as the long column of many thousand horsemen stretched across this beautiful Potomac. The evening sun slanted upon its clear placid waters, and burnished them with gold, while the arms of the soldiers glittered and blazed in its radiance. There were few moments, perhaps, from the beginning to the close of the war, of excitement more intense, of exhilaration more delightful, than when we ascended the opposite bank to the familiar but now strangely thrilling music of "Maryland, my Maryland"....

Maj. Jed Hotchkiss, from *Confederate Military History*: (2)

By the 7th of the month, Lee had concentrated the most of his army in the vicinity of Frederick City, in a land teeming with abundance. He had issued the most stringent orders, forbidding depredations on private property and requiring his quartermasters to purchase and pay for supplies for the army.

On the 8th he issued a stirring proclamation, calling upon the men of Maryland to join the men of his command, gathered within their borders from their sister Southern States; appealing to their manhood to avail themselves of this opportunity to reassert their sovereign rights and join in securing the independence of the South, assuring them that his army had only come to aid them in throwing off a foreign yoke and to enable them "again to enjoy the inalienable rights of freemen and restore independence and sovereignty to their State." In closing he said:

"This, citizens of Maryland, is our mission, so far as you are concerned. No constraint upon your free will is intended; no intimidation will be allowed within the limits of this army at least. Marylanders shall once more enjoy their ancient freedom of thought and speech. We know no enemies among you, and will protect all, of every opinion. It is for you to decide your destiny freely and without constraint. This army will respect your choice, whatever it may be; and while the Southern people will rejoice to welcome you to your natural position among them, they will only welcome you when you come of your own free will."

This magnanimous declaration fell upon cold ears, for the Piedmont region, in which Frederick is situated, contained few sympathizers with the Confederate cause. The majority of its people were contented and well-to-do owners of small farms, most of them of German descent, whose affiliations were more with Pennsylvania to the north than with Virginia to the south of them. It would have been quite different had Lee arrived among the men of Midland or Tidewater Maryland....

Lt. Col. Walter H. Taylor, from *Four Years with General Lee*: (3)

At Frederick City ... General Lee conceived his plan of operations, embracing the capture of Harper's Ferry, and a subsequent concentration of the army to join issue in a grand battle with General McClellan, who had again vaulted into the headquarters-saddle of the Federal army, vacated by General Pope.

An order of battle was issued, stating in detail the position and duty assigned to each command of the army. General Jackson was to undertake the reduction and capture of Harper's Ferry, and had assigned to him for this purpose his own two divisions, and those of A. P. Hill, Anderson, and McLaws. Longstreet's two divisions, under Jones and Hood, and D. H. Hill's division, remained to hold in check the army under McClellan pending Jackson's operations....

After the evacuation of Frederick City by our forces, a copy of General Lee's order was found in a deserted camp by a soldier, and was soon in the hands of General McClellan.... The God of battles alone knows what would have occurred but for the singular accident mentioned; it is useless to speculate on this point, but certainly the loss of this battle order constitutes one of the pivots on which turned the event of the war.

Notwithstanding this unfortunate circumstance, the stubborn and heroic defense of the South Mountain Pass by Longstreet and D. H. Hill, and Jackson's complete success at Harper's Ferry, including the gallant resistance made at Crampton's Gap by portions of McLaws's and Anderson's commands against the assaults of Franklin's corps, enabled General Lee to unite his forces at Sharpsburg in time to give battle, on the 17th of September, to his old adversary; but under altogether different circumstances from such as were anticipated.

Longstreet and D. H. Hill in resisting the assaults of the bulk of McClellan's army had suffered very heavily. Jackson had been compelled, after considerable fighting, to hasten from Harper's Ferry (which place was surrendered to him on the 15th), by forced marches of extraordinary character, to join Lee, who had remained with Longstreet. The route from Harper's Ferry was strewed with foot-sore and weary men, too feeble to keep up with the stronger and more active; and, instead of going into battle with full ranks, the brigades were but as regiments, and in some cases no stronger than a full company....

Mary Bedinger Mitchell, from "A Woman's Recollections of Antietam": (4)

September, 1862, was in the skies of the almanac, but August still reigned in ours; it was hot and dusty. The railroads in the Shenandoah Valley had been torn up, the bridges had been destroyed, communication had been made difficult, and Shepherdstown, cornered by the bend of the Potomac, lay as if forgotten in the bottom of somebody's pocket. We were without news or knowledge, except when some chance traveler would repeat the last wild and uncertain rumor that he had heard. We had passed an exciting summer. Winchester had changed hands more than once; we had been "in the Confederacy" and out of it again, and were now waiting, in an exasperating state of ignorance and suspense, for the next move in the great game.

It was a saying with us that Shepherdstown was just nine miles from everywhere. It was, in fact, about that distance from Martinsburg and Harper's Ferry – oft-mentioned names – and from Williamsport, where the armies so often crossed, both to and from Maryland. It was off the direct road between those places and lay, as I said, at the foot of a great sweep in the river, and five miles from the nearest station on the Baltimore and Ohio railroad. As no trains were running now, this was of little consequence; what was more important was that a turnpike road – unusually fine for that region of stiff, red clay – led in almost a straight line for thirty miles to Winchester on the south, and stretched northward, beyond the Potomac, twenty miles to Hagerstown. Two years later it was the scene of "Sheridan's ride." Before the days of steam this had been part of the old posting-road between the Valley towns and Pennsylvania, and we had boasted a very substantial bridge. This had been burned early in the war, and only the massive stone piers remained; but a mile and a half down the Potomac was the ford, and the road that led to it lay partly above and partly along the face of rocky and precipitous cliffs. It was narrow and stony, and especially in one place, around the foot of "Mount Misery," was very steep and difficult for vehicles. It was, moreover, entirely commanded by the hills on the Maryland side, but it was the ford over which some part of the Confederate army passed every year, and in 1863 was used by the main body of infantry on the way to Gettysburg. Beyond the river were the Cumberland Canal and its willow-fringed tow-path, from which rose the soft and rounded outlines of the hills that from their farther slopes looked down upon the battle-field of Antietam. On clear days we could see the fort at Harper's Ferry without a glass, and the flag flying over it, a mere speck against the sky, and we could hear the gun that was fired every evening at sunset.

Shepherdstown's only access to the river was through a narrow gorge, the bed of a small tributary of the Potomac, that was made to do much duty as it slipped cheerily over its rocks and furnished power for several mills and factories, most of them at the time silent. Here were also three or four stone warehouses, huge empty structures, testifying mutely that the town had once had a business. The road to the bridge led through this cleft, down an indescribably steep street skirting the stream's ravine to whose sides the mills and factories clung in most extraordinary fashion; but it was always a marvel how anything heavier than a wheelbarrow could be pulled up its tedious length, or how any vehicle could be driven down without plunging into the water at the bottom.

In this odd little borough, then, we were waiting "developments," hearing first that "our men" were coming, and then that they were not coming, when suddenly, on Saturday, the 13th of September, early in the morning, we found ourselves surrounded by a hungry horde of lean and dusty tatterdemalions, who seemed to rise from the ground at our feet. I did not know where they came from, or to whose command they belonged; I have since been informed that General Jackson recrossed into Virginia at Williamsport, and hastened to Harper's Ferry by the shortest roads. These would take him some four miles south of us, and our haggard apparitions were perhaps a part of his force. They were stragglers, at all events, - professional, some of them, but some worn out by the incessant strain of that summer. When I say that they were hungry, I convey no impression of the gaunt starvation that looked from their cavernous eyes. All day they crowded to the doors of our houses, with always the same drawling complaint: "I've been a-marchin' an' a-fightin' for six weeks stiddy, and I ain't had n-a-r-thin' to eat 'cept green apples an' green cawn, an' I wish you'd please to gimme a bite to eat."

Their looks bore out their statements, and when they told us they had "clean gin out," we believed them, and went to get what we had. They could be seen afterward asleep in every fence corner, and under every tree, but after a night's rest they "pulled themselves together" somehow and disappeared as suddenly as they had come. Possibly they went back to their commands, possibly they only moved on to repeat the same tale elsewhere. I know nothing of numbers, nor what force was or was not engaged in any battle, but I saw the troops march past us every summer for four years, and I know something of the appearance of a marching army, both Union and Southern. There are always stragglers, of course, but never before or after did I see anything comparable to the demoralized state of the Confederates at this time. Never were want and exhaustion more visibly put before my eyes, and that they could march or fight at all seemed incredible.

As I remember, the next morning – it was Sunday, September 14th – we were awakened by heavy firing at two points on the mountains. We were expecting the bombardment of Harper's Ferry, and we knew that Jackson was before it. Many of our friends were with him, and our interest there was so intense that we sat watching the bellowing and smoking heights, for a long time, before we became aware that the same phenomena were to be noticed in the north. From our windows both points could be observed, and we could not tell which to watch more keenly. We knew almost nothing except that there was fighting, that it must be very heavy, and that our friends were surely in it somewhere, but whether at South Mountain or Harper's Ferry we had no means of discovering. I remember how the day wore on, how we staid at the windows until we could not endure the suspense; how we walked about and came back to them; and how finally, when night fell, it seemed cruel and preposterous to go to bed still ignorant of the result.

Monday afternoon, about 2 or 3 o'clock, when we were sitting about in disconsolate fashion, distracted by the contradictory rumors, our negro cook rushed into the room with eyes shining and face working with excitement. She had been down in "de ten-acre lot to pick a few years ob cawn," and she had seen a long train of wagons coming up from the ford, and "dey is full ob wounded men, and de blood runnin outen dem dat deep," measuring on her outstretched arm to the shoulder. This horrible picture sent us flying to town, where we found the streets already crowded, the people all astir, and the foremost wagons, of what seemed an endless line, discharging their piteous burdens. The scene speedily became ghastly, but fortunately we could not stay to look at it. There were no preparations, no accommodations – the men could not be left in the street – what was to be done?

A Federal soldier once said to me, "I was always sorry for your wounded; they never seemed to get any care." The remark was extreme, but there was much justice in it. There was little mitigation of hardship to our unfortunate armies. We were fond of calling them Spartans, and they were but too truly called upon to endure a Spartan system of neglect and privation. They were generally ill-fed and ill-cared for. It would have been possible at this time, one would think, to send a courier back to inform the town and bespeak what comforts it could provide for the approaching wounded; but here they were, unannounced, on the brick pavements, and the first thing was to find roofs to cover them. Men ran for keys and opened the shops, long empty, and the unused rooms; other people got brooms and stirred up the dust of ages; then swarms of children began to appear with bundles of hay and straw, taken from anybody's stable. These were hastily disposed in heaps, and covered with blankets – the soldier's own, or blankets begged or borrowed. On these improvised beds the sufferers were placed, and the next question was how properly to dress their wounds. No surgeons were to be seen. A few men, detailed as nurses, had come, but they were incompetent, of course. Our women set bravely to work and washed away the blood or stanched it as well as they could, where the jolting of the long rough ride had disarranged the hasty binding done upon the battle-field. But what did they know of wounds beyond a cut finger, or a boil? Yet they bandaged and bathed, with a devotion that went far to make up for their inexperience. Then there was the hunt for bandages. Every housekeeper ransacked her stores and brought forth things new and old. I saw one girl, in despair for a strip of cloth, look about helplessly, and then rip off the hem of her white petticoat. The doctors came up, by and by, or I suppose they did, for some amputating was done – rough surgery, you may be sure. The women helped, holding the instruments and the basins, and trying to soothe or strengthen. They stood to their work nobly; the emergency brought out all their strength to meet it.

One girl who had been working very hard helping the men on the sidewalks, and dressing wounds afterwards in a close, hot room, told me that at one time the sights and smells (these last were fearful) so overcame her that she could only stagger to the staircase, where she hung, half conscious, over the banisters, saying to herself, "Oh, I hope if I faint some one will kick me into a corner and let me lie there!" She did not faint, but went back to her work in a few moments, and through the whole of what followed was one of the most indefatigable and useful. She was one of many; even children did their part.

It became a grave question how to feed so many unexpected guests. The news spread rapidly, and the people from the country neighborhoods came pouring in to help, expecting to stay with friends who had already given up every spare bed and every inch of room where beds could be put up. Virginia houses are very elastic, but ours were strained to their utmost. Fortunately some of the farmers' wives had been thoughtful enough to bring supplies of linen, and some bread and fruit, and when our wants became better known other contributions flowed in; but when all was done it was not enough.

We worked far into the night that Monday, went to bed late, and rose early next morning. Tuesday brought fresh wagonloads of wounded, and would have brought despair, except that they were accompanied by an apology for a commissariat. Soon more reliable sources of supply were organized among our country friends. Some doctors also arrived, who – with a few honorable exceptions – might as well have staid away. The remembrance of that worthless body of officials stirs me to wrath. Two or three worked conscientiously and hard, and they did all the medical work, except what was done by our own town physicians. In strong contrast was the conduct of the common man detailed as nurses. They were as gentle as they knew how to be, and very obliging and untiring. Of course they were uncouth and often rough, but with the wounded and dying about us every day, and with the necessity that we were under for the first few days, of removing those who died at once that others not yet quite dead might take their places, there was no time to be fastidious; it required all our efforts to be simply decent, and we sometimes failed in that.

We fed our men as well as we could from every available source, and often had some difficulty in feeding ourselves. The townspeople were very hospitable, and we were invited here and there, but could not always go, or hesitated, knowing every house was full. I remember once, that having breakfasted upon a single roll and having worked hard among sickening details, about 4 o'clock I turned wolfishly ravenous and ran to a friend's house down the street. When I got there I was almost too faint to speak, but my friend looked at me and disappeared in silence, coming back in a moment with a plate of hot soup. What luxury! I sat down then and there on the front doorstep and devoured the soup as if I had been without food for a week.

It was known on Tuesday that Harper's Ferry had been taken, but it was growing evident that South Mountain had not been a victory. We had heard from some of our friends, but not from all, and what we did hear was often most unsatisfactory and tantalizing. For instance, we would be told that some one whom we loved had been seen standing with his battery, had left his gun an instant to shake hands and send a message, and had then stepped back to position, while our civilian informant had come away for safety, and the smoke of conflict had hidden battery and all from view. As night drew nearer, whispers of a great battle to be fought the next day grew louder, and we shuddered at the prospect, for battles had come to mean to us, as they never had before, blood, wounds, and death.

On the 17th of September cloudy skies looked down upon the two armies facing each other on the fields of Maryland. It seems to me now that the roar of that day began with the light, and all through its long and dragging hours its thunder formed a background to our pain and terror. If we had been in doubt as to our friends' whereabouts on Sunday, there was no room for doubt now....

George M. Neese, from *Three Years in the Confederate Horse Artillery*: (5)

September 17 - Early this morning the cannon commenced booming on the fields around Sharpsburg in Washington County, Maryland. Sharpsburg is about three miles from Shepardstown, and from our camp we plainly heard the opening guns of the great battle that raged fearfully all day between General Lee's forces and General McClellan's whole army. At times the artillery fire was so fierce and heavy that it sounded like one continual roar of thunder rumbling and rolling across the sky. The Musketry fire was equally severe and raged furiously, almost incessantly all day, and its hideous deathly crash vied with the deafening roar of the thundering artillery. It is utterly incomprehensible and perfectly inconceivable how mortal men can stand and live under such an infantry fire as I heard to-day. Judging from the way the musketry roared the whole surrounding air between the lines must have been thick with flying lead. This morning my gun was still in Martinsburg undergoing repairs, which circumstance alone kept us from the battle-field to-day, for twice during the day an urgent despatch came for us to hasten to the front and help to play in the bloody act that was in full glow and raging over the fields around Sharpsburg.

About three o'clock this afternoon my gun arrived from Martinsburg ready for fight, and we started immediately for the fiery vortex of battle that was still raging with unabated fury. Our progress was necessarily slow, and the ford in the Potomac is rough and narrow and the river was full of wagons going and coming. The road all the way between the river and the battle-field was crowded with ordnance wagons and ambulances. Shepherdstown seemed to be full of our wounded when we passed through.....

Maj. Heros von Borcke, from his *Memoirs of the Confederate War for Independence*: (6)

Jackson commanded our left wing. General Lee himself had taken charge of the centre, and Longstreet commanded the right. Of our cavalry, Robertson's brigade, under Colonel Munford, was detached to the extreme right, Fitz Lee's and Hampton's were held in reserve on the extreme left, which, as before stated, rested on the Potomac. The fighting commenced soon after daybreak, and was raging in full fury on the left with Jackson's corps at seven o'clock in the morning.... The enemy concentrated the whole weight of his attack upon Jackson's centre, which for a time gave way, and was driven back through a large patch of forest that had been gallantly defended. But the grim Stonewall soon rallied his men, and, having been reinforced, drove back the Yankees in his turn for several miles with great slaughter.

About midday ... the fighting in Jackson's front had ceased a little ... but on our right, where, up to this moment, all had been comparatively quiet, the firing grew louder and more continuous. Longstreet, hard pressed by superior numbers of the enemy, had been giving way slowly, but defending the ground like a wounded lion, foot by foot, until, receiving reinforcements at the outskirts of Sharpsburg, he recovered his lost ground after a severe and sanguinary combat....

Lt. Col. Walter Taylor, from *Four Years with General Lee*: (7)

The fighting was heaviest and most continuous on the Confederate left. It is established upon indisputable Federal evidence that the three corps of Hooker, Mansfield, and Sumner, were completely shattered in the repeated but fruitless efforts to turn this flank, and two of these corps were rendered useless for further aggressive movements. The aggregate strength of the attacking columns at this point reached forty thousand men, not counting the two divisions of Franklin's corps, sent at a late hour in the day to rescue the Federal right from the impending danger of being itself destroyed; while the Confederates, from first to last, had less than fourteen thousand men on this flank, consisting of Jackson's two divisions, McLaw's division, and the two small divisions, of two brigades each, under Hood and Walker, with which to resist their fierce and oft-repeated assaults.

As a wall of adamant the fourteen thousand received the shock of the forty thousand; and the latter, staggered by the blow, reeled and recoiled in great disorder.

The disproportion in the centre and on our right was as great as, or even more decided than, on our left....

From such informal reports as were received at the time, and from my own observation and knowledge, I estimated the effective strength of the Confederate army at Sharpsburg at thirty-seven thousand men – twenty-nine thousand infantry and eight thousand cavalry and artillery. But I am now satisfied, after reference to the official reports of the Maryland campaign ... that my estimate was excessive....

General McClellan, in his official report, states that he had in action, in the same engagement, eighty-seven thousand one hundred and sixty-four of all arms.

Those thirty-five thousand Confederates were the very flower of the Army of Northern Virginia, who, with indomitable courage and inflexible tenacity, wrestled for the mastery, in the ratio of one to three of their adversaries; and with consummate skill were they maneuvered and shifted from point to point, as different parts of the line of battle were in turn assailed with greatest impetuosity. The right was called upon to go to the rescue of the left; the centre was reduced to a mere shell in responding to the demands for assistance from the right and left; and A. P. Hill's command, the last to arrive from Harper's Ferry, reached the field just in time to restore the wavering right. At times it appeared as if disaster was inevitable, but succor never failed, and night found Lee's lines unbroken and his army still defiant....

Lt. Gen. John B. Gordon – at that time a Colonel commanding an Alabama regiment at the center of the Confederate line – from his *Reminiscences of the Civil War*: (8)

I was not at the front when, near nightfall, the awful carnage ceased; but one of my officers long afterward assured me that he could have walked on the dead bodies of my men from one end of the line to the other ....

Before I was wholly disabled and carried to the rear, I walked along my line and found an old man and his son lying side by side. The son was dead, the father mortally wounded. The gray-haired hero called to me and said: "Here we are. My boy is dead, and I shall go soon; but it is all right." Of such were the early volunteers....

Lt. Col. Walter Taylor, from *Four Years with General Lee*: (9)

The army of General McClellan had been too severely handled and was too badly broken to justify a renewal of the attack.... The 18th of September, the day after the battle, passed therefore without any serious engagement. General Lee's army, as may be inferred, was in no condition to take the offensive – and on the night of that day it recrossed the Potomac River into Virginia....

BOOK III

AUTUMN (1863)

Waken, lords and ladies gay,
The mist has left the mountain gray,
Springlets in the dawn are steaming,
Diamonds on the brake are gleaming;
And foresters have busy been
To track the buck in thicket green;
Now we come to chant our lay
'Waken, lords and ladies gay"….
　　　　　　　- Sir Walter Scott, "Hunting Song" (1)

RIGHT *Maj. Gen. James Ewell Brown "Jeb" Stuart* – Courtesy of Library of Congress

The Bonny Light Horseman

Maj. Heros von Borcke, from his *Memoirs of the Confederate War for Independence*: (1)

The cavalry had to cover the line along the Potomac from Williamsport to Harper's Ferry, Hampton's brigade being stationed near Hainsville, Fitz Lee's near Shepherdstown, and Robertson's under Colonel Munford, near Charlestown, opposite Harper's Ferry; which latter stronghold, after everything valuable had been removed from it, had been given up to the enemy....

Our headquarters [at the Dandridge plantation] were situated on a hill beneath a grove of lofty umbrageous oaks of primitive growth, which extended, on the right, towards the large mansion-house, the thick brick walls of which, in the blush of the early sunlight, were just visible in little patches of red through the rich verdure of the embosoming garden. At the foot of this hill, skirting a main road to which the slope was smooth and gradual, ran the bright little river Opequan, its limpid waters breaking through and tumbling over cliffs and rocks, thus forming a cascade of considerable height, with rainbows in its spray as the sun changed every falling drop into a ruby or a diamond. This lovely *entourage* was now enlivened and diversified by the white tents of our encampment, the General's, with its fluttering battle-flag, in the centre, by the smoke of the camp-fires where the negroes were busily engaged in cooking breakfasts, by the picturesque groups of officers and men who were strolling about or cleaning their arms, and by the untethered horses and mules which were quietly grazing all over the ground.

One may be pardoned some extravagance of language in attempting to describe a scene which brought a feeling of thankful happiness to the soldier, weary of the excitement, the toil, the hardships, and the anguish of war. We had now plenty of food for our exhausted animals, which had undergone so much fatigue and privation, and our own commissariat was far more abundant than it had been for many weeks. The long mess-table, at which we dined together in the open air, was loaded with substantials that seemed dainties and luxuries to us, who often for days together had gone without food, and at best could secure only a meagre repast.

The plantation of "The Bower" had been long in the possession of the family of Dandridge, one member of which, more than a century ago, was the pretty widow Martha Custis, *nee* Dandridge, afterwards the wife of George Washington, whose beauty and amiability have been preserved in history and fiction, who was delineated by the pencil of Stuart in one generation, and the pen of Thackery in another. Nowhere, perhaps, in the wide limits of the State, could one have formed a better idea of the refined manners and profuse hospitable life of dear old Virginia, and before the breaking-out of the war "The Bower" had rarely been without its guests.

The proprietor at the time I knew the place was a kind-hearted intelligent gentleman of fifty or thereabouts, whose charming wife retained, in a remarkable degree for America, the personal attractiveness of her youthful bloom. The rest of the numerous family consisted of grown and growing sons and daughters and nieces. Of the boys, three were in the army fighting bravely for cause and country. The girls, some of whom were exceedingly handsome, and all of whom were pleasing and accomplished, remained beneath the rooftree of the old homestead. With these amiable people I soon contracted a very intimate friendship, which time nor distance can ever weaken.

Frequently, when the mocha, of which we had captured a large supply from the enemy, was smoking invitingly on our breakfast-table, we had the pleasure of greeting the proprietor as a welcome guest at our morning meal at headquarters; later in the day a lady's skirt might even be seen in the streets of our en-campment; but regularly every night we proceeded with our band to the house, where dancing was kept up till a late hour. The mu-sical director of our band was a private of one of the regiments, whom Stuart had detached to his military family for his musical talent alone, Bob Sweeney, a brother of the celebrated banjo-play-er, Joe Sweeney, forerunner of all the Christy's; - Bob Sweeney, who also played this favorite instrument of the family with amaz-ing cleverness; who knew sentimental, bibulous, martial, nautical, comic songs out of number; who was carried about with him by the General everywhere; who will have a conspicuous place in some of our later adventures; and who, after having safely passed through many accidents of war, died at last of small-pox, regretted by everybody, but most of all by "Jeb" Stuart.

Bob was assisted by two of our couriers who played the violin, musicians of inferior merit; but his chief reliance was in Mu-latto Bob, Stuart's servant, who worked the bones with the most surprising and extraordinary agility, and became so excited that both head and feet were in constant employment, and his body twisted about so rapidly and curiously that one could not help fearing that he would dislocate his limbs and fly to pieces in the midst of the breakdown.

General Stuart was himself always the gayest and noisi-est of the party, starting usually at the close of the festivity the famous song –

> "If you want to have a good time,
> Join in the cavalry,
> Join in the cavalry," &c. –

The whole of the excited company, young and old, uniting in the chorus, the last notes of which sounded far through the still air of the night as we walked back to our tents. General Stuart did not like it at all if any one of his Staff officers withdrew himself from these innocent merry-makings, after the fatigues of the day, to seek an early rest, and would always rouse him from his slumbers to take part in the revelry....

I had now taken up my quarters in the same tent with my comrade, Captain Blackford, who had a wonderful talent for making himself comfortable; and in a short time we had so improved our *habitat* that it was quite a model establishment. My former tent (one of the so-called dog-tents), which was very narrow and contracted, insomuch that when I lay in it at full length either my head or my feet must be exposed to the night air and the dews, I turned over to our two negroes William and Gilbert, who enlarged it greatly, and it now stood immediately in the rear of our own....

For days afterwards there was perfect quiet at our headquarters. No cannonade shook the air, and the lazy, listless life we led was in harmony with the serenity of the season, which charmed us with the repose and loveliness of the American *Fall*. The wooded hills and rich fields around "The Bower" abounded in game – partridges, pheasants, wild turkeys, hares, and grey squirrels – so that I could indulge to the fullest extent my passion for sport....

At headquarters we had some very agreeable guests, among whom were Colonel Bradley T. Johnston, and an intimate friend of General Stuart and myself, Colonel Brien, who had formerly commanded the 1st Virginia Cavalry, and had resigned his commission in consequence of his failing health. Every evening before starting for the mansion-house we all assembled – guests, officers, couriers, and negroes – around a roaring wood-fire in the center of our encampment, where Sweeney, with his banjo, gave us selections from his *repertoire*, which were followed by a fine quartette by some of our soldiers, who had excellent voices, the *al fresco* concert always concluding with the famous chorus of "Join in the cavalry" already mentioned, which was much more noisy than melodious. But every evening the negroes would ask for the lively measures of a jig or a breakdown – a request invariably granted; and then these darkies danced within the circle of spectators like dervishes or lunatics – the spectators themselves applauding to the echo.

On the 7th a grand ball was to take place at "The Bower," to which Mr. D. had invited families from Martinsburg, Shepherd-stown, and Charlestown, and in the success of which we all felt a great interest. As an exceptional bit of fun, Colonel Brien and I had secretly prepared a little Pantomime, "The Pennsylvania Farmer and his Wife," in which the Colonel was to personate the farmer and I the spouse. Accordingly, when the guests had all assembled and the ball was quite *en train*, the immense couple entered the brilliantly lighted apartment – Brien enveloped in an ample greatcoat, which had been stuffed with pillows until the form of the wearer had assumed the most enormous proportions; I dressed in an old white ball-dress of Mrs. D.'s that had been enlarged in every direction, and sweetly ornamented with half-a-bushel of artificial flowers in my hair.

Our success greatly outran our expectations. Stuart, ex-ploding with laughter, scrutinized me closely on all sides, scarcely crediting the fact that within that tall bundle of feminine habili-ments dwelt the soul of his Chief of Staff. Again and again we were made to repeat our little play in dumb show, until, getting tired of it and wishing to put a stop to it, I gracefully fainted away and was carried from the room by Brien and three or four assis-tants, amid the wild applause of the company, who insisted on a repetition of the fainting scene. When, in a few moments, I made my appearance in uniform, the laughter and applause recom-menced, and Stuart, throwing his arms around my neck in a bur-lesque of pathos, said, "My dear old Von, if I could ever forget you as I know you on the field of battle, your appearance as a woman would never fade from my memory." So the joyous night went on with dancing and merriment, until the sun stole in at the windows, and the reveille sounding from camp reminded us that the hour of separation had arrived....

Maj. Jed Hotchkiss, from *Confederate Military History*: (2)

To engage McClellan's attention and gather a supply of fresh horses from the farmers of Pennsylvania, Lee, on the 10th of October, dispatched the raid-loving Stuart, with 1,800 horsemen, across the Potomac at Williamsport, and thence along the western side of Cumberland Valley, to Chambersburg, where he halted on the morning of the 11th. Thence sweeping to the eastward, across the South Mountain, he returned through the Piedmont region, and by noon of the 12th again crossed the Potomac into Virginia, after a rapid and extensive ride, not only with a fresh supply of much-needed horses, but with full information as to what was going on in and around McClellan's army, of which he had made a complete circuit.

This bold and memorable ride so irritated the Federal government that it peremptorily ordered McClellan to choose a line of attack and move against Lee in Virginia....

McClellan determined to draw Lee from the Valley, by crossing to the east of the Blue Ridge and then following along its eastern foot, and see what military results could be secured in the Piedmont region, which had hitherto only been tried at Cedar Run. Crossing the Potomac October 23rd, he successively occupied, with detachments, the gaps of the Blue Ridge, making demonstrations across the same toward the Shenandoah, thus guarding his flanks as his army marched southward.

Lee was not slow to comprehend the plans of his opponent, which involved a new "on to Richmond." He immediately sent Longstreet to place his newly-constituted First Corps athwart the front of McClellan's advance. Crossing the Blue Ridge at Chester Gap, he placed his command in the vicinity of Culpeper Court House, where he arrived November 6th, the very day that McClellan's advance arrived at Warrenton....

Jackson, with the Second Corps of the Army of Northern Virginia (also recently organized....), was left in the Shenandoah

Valley, to remain, as long as he could prudently do so, as a protection to that great Confederate granary, and as a menace to McClellan's right, as he would hesitate to push far into Virginia so long as that ever-ready fighter and unconquerable leader remained in the lower valley....

With his usual boldness, Lee did not hesitate to post the two wings of his army 60 miles apart, as the crow flies, well satisfied that with Longstreet's ability as a stubborn fighter when once in position, he could resist a front attack from McClellan and trust to Jackson to descend the mountains in ample time to fall on the enemy's flank and join in the fray, knowing also that the Federal authorities would hesitate to push forward the Army of the Potomac and leave Jackson so near the gateway to the Federal capitol....

McClellan now occupied Pope's former position, behind the Rappahannock, with fully 125,000 men; 80,000 held the defense of Washington, and 22,000 watched the portals of the Shenandoah Valley in the vicinity of Harper's Ferry. Lee had less than 72,000 in the two corps of the Army of Northern Virginia and in his cavalry corps, under Stuart, to again meet this great Army of the Potomac.

Not satisfied with the tardy movements of McClellan, Lincoln supplanted him in command, at Warrenton, with Burnside, who at once hastened to execute an "on to Richmond," by way of Fredericksburg, thinking that by taking advantage of a shorter line of movement he could reach his objective without being intercepted by Lee; but when, on the 15th, he pressed his advance toward Fredericksburg, the alert Stuart promptly reported his movement to Lee, and the latter, with equal promptness, foresaw his plans of campaign and hurried Longstreet forward from Culpeper and placed him at Fredericksburg, across Burnside's track, in a strong position on the south bank of the Rappahannock, before Burnside's pontoons arrived on the Stafford Heights, on the northern bank of that river, thus frustrating the Federal plan of campaign.

Jackson, who had been busy in the Valley breaking up the line of the Baltimore & Ohio Railroad and keeping the Federal authorities uneasy as to his whereabouts, promptly obeyed Lee's order to follow after Longstreet, but by ways farther to the westward. By making demonstrations at Chester and Thornton Gaps, of the Blue Ridge, he mystified those watching his movements by marching up the Valley to New Market, thence taking the great highway leading across the Massanutton, the south fork of the Shenandoah, the Blue Ridge at Fisher's Gap and by Madison Court house, to the vicinity of Orange Court House, and thence by the road to Fredericksburg.... He arrived in the vicinity of Fredericksburg near the end of November, having successfully concealed his march, and went into camp between Fredericksburg and Guiney's Station....

Thousands of Lee's army were barefooted and destitute of clothing suitable for the rigors of the early winter, and many were even without muskets; and yet, Lee said, in a letter of that time, of his army of 72,000 veterans, that it was "never in better health or in better condition for battle than now."

Interrupted in carrying out his intentions, Burnside took ample time to muster his 116,000 men and 350 pieces of artillery, many of them guns of long range, upon the commanding plateau north of the Rappahannock, known as Stafford Heights, from which he looked down upon the heroic town of Fredericksburg – trembling in expectancy of destruction between the two great contending armies on either side of it....

A Dismal Concert of Doom

Maj. Heros von Borcke, from his *Memoirs of the Confederate War for Independence*: (1)

Fredericksburg, one of the oldest places in Virginia, was before the war a pretty town of about 5000 inhabitants, which enjoyed a considerable local trade, and was distinguished for the hospitality and refinement that belonged to its society. It was now comparatively deserted. The larger part of its citizens had been driven off by the continued threats of bombardment which had hung like a Damocles's sword above their heads for several weeks, and the few who had been compelled to remain behind plainly exhibited in their features that the apprehension of doom was pressing like an iron weight upon their hearts. The knowledge on their part that more than a hundred hostile cannon, planted on the dominating "Shepherd's Heights" of Stafford, over the river, bore directly on their unfortunate town, might well have given disquietude to this community of non-combatants.

A lively contrast was presented, however, in the demeanour of Barksdale's Mississippi Brigade, stationed at Fredericksburg, the men of which were wandering carelessly about, talking and laughing, as if there were no Yankees within the radius of a thousand miles from them, or making themselves at home in several of the largest houses which had been quite converted into barracks.

As the river was not more than 200 yards wide, we could distinctly see each one of the numerous Yankee sentinels who were pacing to and fro in their light-blue overcoats on the opposite bank, and who frequently engaged in amicable conversation with their adversaries across the stream, as it had been agreed that the firing by pickets at each other should be stopped for the time as a useless waste of ammunition. The Federals and Confederates were still nearer together at the site of the railway bridge which had been burnt at an earlier period of the war, leaving on either side the dismantled abutments and the timbers, extending to one or two piers, which were occupied by pickets.... The different brigades of our cavalry were now separated, guarding the numerous fords of the Rappahannock, which rendered necessary a picket-line of more than fifty miles in length....

11ᵗʰ December. - I had enjoyed but a few minutes of repose, enveloped in my warm blankets, when I was waked from sleep by a dull heavy noise, which, in the earliest moments of consciousness, I believed to have been produced by the thawing and sliding down of the snow that had accumulated on the top of my tent. I was quickly undeceived, however, by my negro servant Henry, who, appearing at my tent door, informed me in a single abrupt sentence of the true condition of affairs. "Major," said Henry, "de Yankees is shelling Fredericksburg. I done saddled your horse, and de General is ready for to start." This intelligence brought me in an instant to my feet. Inserting my legs into my huge cavalry-boots, I soon emerged from the tent, and in a few minutes I galloped off with the General and the other members of the Staff in full haste for the front....

Reaching our lines, we found General Lee on an eminence which, rising considerably above the other heights, a few hundred yards to the right of the Telegraph Road, afforded a view over nearly the whole plain before, and gave our great commander the opportunity of watching closely the operations of the enemy, and controlling the movement of his own army in accordance therewith.... Longstreet and several other generals were also assembled here, looking anxiously towards Fredericksburg, as yet concealed from their sight by a dense fog which hung heavily over the little valley.

Information had been received here that under cover of the fog the enemy had endeavoured to lay his pontoon bridges across the river, but that, by the accurate and effective fire of Barksdale's Mississippi brigade, the Federal engineers and working parties had been driven off with heavy loss, and all their efforts had been so far unsuccessful. The cannonade which had so rudely roused us from our slumbers had been nothing more than an artillery duel between some of the Federal batteries and a like number of our own, and had now ceased altogether; and the quiet of the morning was disturbed only by the repeated cracks of Barksdale's rifles sounding over from the river, from which we knew that the enemy's bridge-building was still resisted with spirit. The frequent reports which reached us from that quarter were as favourable as could be desired – "All right! the enemy have been driven back, with severe loss, from their pontoons."

So several hours passed wearily away, oppressing every one of us with an anticipation of the sad spectacle we should soon be compelled to witness in the bombardment of the town.

Already the Telegraph Road leading up to the heights from Fredericksburg was thronged with a confused mass of fugitives, men, women, and children, who had not been willing or able to leave their homesteads before, bearing with them such of their effects as they could bring away, and as they most wished to save, many of which, having been dropped in the haste and terror of their exodus, marked the line of their flight as far as the eye could reach.

Ten o'clock came, and the hammers of the church-clocks were just sounding the last peaceful stroke of the hour when suddenly, at the signal of a single cannon-shot, more than 150 pieces of artillery, including some of the enemy's most ponderous guns, opened their iron mouths with a terrific roar, and hurled a tempest of destruction upon the devoted town. The air shook, and the very earth beneath our feet trembled at this deafening cannonade, the heaviest that had ever yet assailed my ears. The thick fog still prevented us from obtaining a satisfactory view of the bombardment; but the howling of the solid shot, the bursting of the shells, the crashing of the missiles through the thick walls, and the dull sound of falling houses, united in a dismal concert of doom....

Maj. Robert Stiles, from *Four Years Under Marse Robert*: (2)

Tennyson is in error when he says, in "Locksley Hall," that "Woman is the lesser man." She is the greater man. A good woman is better than a good man, and a bad woman is worse; a brave woman is braver than any man ever was. During the bombardment I was sent into Fredericksburg with a message for General Barksdale. As I was riding down the street that led to his headquarters it appeared to be so fearfully swept by artillery fire that I started to ride across it, with a view of finding some safer way of getting to my destination, when, happening to glance beyond that point, I saw walking quietly and unconcernedly along the same street I was on, and approaching General Barksdale's headquarters from the opposite direction, a lone woman. She apparently found the projectiles which were screaming and exploding in the air, and striking and crashing through the houses, and tearing up the streets, very interesting – stepping a little aside to inspect a great, gaping hole one had just gouged out in the sidewalk, then turning her head to note a fearful explosion in the air. I felt as if it really would not do to avoid a fire which was merely interesting, and not at all appalling, to a woman; so I stiffened my spinal column as well as I could and rode straight down the street toward headquarters and the self-possessed lady; and having reached the house I rode around back of it to put my horse where he would at least be safer than in front.

As I returned on foot to the front the lady had gone up on the porch and was knocking at the door. One of the staff came to hearken, and on seeing a lady, held up his hands, exclaiming in amazement: "What on earth, madam, are you doing here? Do go to some safe place if you can find one." She smiled and said, with some little tartness: "Young gentleman, you seem to be a little excited. Won't you please say to General Barksdale that a lady at the door wishes to see him." The young man assured her General Barksdale could not possibly see her just now; but she persisted. "General Barksdale is a Southern gentleman, sir, and will not refuse to see a lady who has called upon him."

Seeing that he could not otherwise get rid of her, the General did come to the door, but actually wringing his hands in excitement and annoyance. "For God's sake, madam, go and seek some place of safety. I'll send a member of my staff to help you find one." She again smiled gently, - while old Barksdale fumed and almost swore, - and then she said quietly: "General Barksdale, my cow has just been killed in my stable by a shell. She is very fat and I don't want the Yankees to get her. If you will send someone down to butcher her, you are welcome to the meat"....

Maj. Heros von Borcke, from his *Memoirs of the Confederate War for Independence*: (3)

Very soon the exact site of the unhappy town was indicated, even through the fog, by a rising column of smoke and dust, and the flames of burning buildings broke out of the dark overhanging canopy with reddening glare, while the bursting bombs flashed athwart the gloom like the arrowy lightening in a thundercloud. Our batteries did not respond to the guns of the enemy with a single shot. It was evident enough that nothing could be done to save the place from the desolation to which it had been fore-doomed by the wanton barbarity of the Federal commander. The horrible din lasted for two hours, and was succeeded by perfect silence – the silence of a solitude. About noon, a gentle breeze, springing up just as the roar of the latest guns died away, lifted the veil which had mysteriously shrouded the valley, and the sun, breaking through the clouds, seemed to mock with its garish splendour the smoking ruins it revealed. Sad indeed was the scene that presented itself to our gaze, and to the eyes, filled with tears, of the mournful fugitives whose once happy homes lay before them, shattered or smouldering; and every heart of the thousands of brave Confederate soldiers who witnessed it burned for revenge.....

Maj. Robert Stiles, from *Four Years Under Marse Robert*: (4)

Really I saw then and see now no justification for it. True the town was occupied by armed men, - Barksdale and his men, our old brigade, - but then the fire did not drive them out; in the nature of things, and especially of the Mississippi brigade, of course it would not, and it did drive out the women and children, many of them. I never saw a more pitiful procession than they made trudging through the deep snow, after the warning was given and as the hour drew near. I saw little children tugging along with their doll babies, - some bigger than they were, - but holding their feet up carefully above the snow, and women so old and feeble that they could carry nothing and could barely hobble themselves. There were women carrying a baby in one arm and its bottle, its clothes, and its covering in the other. Some had a Bible and a tooth brush in one hand, a picked chicken and a bag of flour in the other. Most of them had to cross a creek swollen with winter rains, and deadly cold with winter ice and snow. We took the battery horses down and ferried them over, taking one child in front and two behind and sometimes a woman or a girl on either side with her feet in the stirrups, holding on by our shoulders. Where they were going we could not tell, and I doubt if they could....

Maj. Heros von Borcke, from his *Memoirs of the Confederate War for Independence*: (5)

It may be supposed that we thought with great anxiety of our Mississippi brigade, which had all the time been exposed to this *feu d'enfer*; but the sharp crack of their rifles soon gave us the gratifying assurance that these gallant fellows, unmindful of the death and anguish which shot and shell had been spreading amid their ranks, had firmly maintained their ground, and were ready to meet the enemy's attack; and a little later we received the satisfactory report that a renewed attempt of the Federals to force the building of their bridges had been defeated. But General Lee knew very well that he would not be able to prevent the passage of the river by the Federal army; and having entertained from the beginning no idea of seriously contesting this, he now gave orders for Barksdale's brigade to withdraw gradually from the town, and to keep up only a feigned resistance. Accordingly, about 2 P. M., Fredericksburg was altogether abandoned by our men, after a sanguinary fight had been maintained for a considerable time in the streets.

During the rest of the afternoon and evening, the pontoon bridges having been completed, the dense masses of the Federal army commenced to move over to our side of the river....

Maj. Robert Stiles, from *Four Years Under Marse Robert*: (6)

The Twenty-first Mississippi was the last regiment to leave the city. The last detachment was under the command of Lane Brandon, already mentioned as my *quandam* classmate at Yale, and son of old Colonel Brandon, of the Twenty-first, who behaved so heroically at Malvern Hill. In skirmishing with the head of the Federal column – led, I think, by the Twentieth Massachusetts –

Brandon captured a few prisoners and learned that the advance company was commanded by Abbott, who had been his chum at Harvard Law School when the war began.

He lost his head completely. He refused to retire before Abbott. He fought him fiercely and was actually driving him back. In this he was violating orders and breaking our plan of battle. He was put under arrest and his subaltern brought the command out of town.

Buck Denman ... a Mississippi bear hunter and a superb specimen of manhood, was color sergeant of the Twenty-first and a member of Brandon's company. He was tall and straight, broad-shouldered and deep-chested, had an eye like an eagle and a voice like a bull of Bashan, and was full of pluck and power as a panther. He was rough as a bear in manner, but withal a noble, tender-hearted fellow, and a splendid soldier. The enemy, finding the way now clear, were coming up the street, full company front, with flags flying and bands playing, while the great shells from the siege guns were bursting over their heads and dashing their hurtling fragments after our retreating skirmishers. Buck was behind the corner of a house taking sight for a last shot. Just as his fingers trembled on the trigger, a little three-year-old, fair-haired, baby girl toddled out of an alley, accompanied by a Newfoundland dog, and gave chase to a big shell that was rolling lazily along the pavement, she clapping her little hands and the dog snapping and barking furiously at the shell.

Buck's hand dropped from the trigger. He dashed it across his eyes to dispel the mist and make sure he hadn't passed over the river and wasn't seeing his own baby girl in a vision. No, there is the baby, amid the hell of shot and shell, and here come the enemy. A moment and he has grounded his gun, dashed out into the storm, swept his great right arm around the baby, gained cover again, and, baby clasped to his breast and musket trailed in his left hand, is trotting after the boys up to Marye's Heights.

And there behind that historic stone wall, and in the lines hard by, all those hours and days of terror was that baby kept, her fierce nurses taking turns patting her, while the storm of battle raged and shrieked....

Maj. Heros von Borcke, from his *Memoirs of the Confederate War for Independence*: (7)

All along Mayre's Heights runs a sunken road, fenced in with stone wall on either side, which in itself constituted a most formidable defensive work for our troops; a little higher up the hill there was a regular line of intrenchments, the defenders of which might fire over the heads of those below them, and the crest was occupied by the numerous pieces of the famous Washington Artillery, under their gallant commander Colonel Walton; so that the assailants were received with a triple sheet of fire, which swept them away by hundreds.

The Federals certainly behaved with the utmost gallantry. Line after line moved forward to the assault, only to recoil again and again from the murderous tempest of shot, shell, and bullets, and to strew yet more thickly with dead and wounded the crimsoned field, which was afterwards most appropriately named "the slaughter-pen." Pickett's division was but little engaged here, the wider open space of ground giving ample opportunity to our artillery to play upon the hostile columns, scattering them and throwing them into disorder even before they could form their lines of attack....

An hour of anxiety and doubt passed away, until at five o'clock we saw scattered fugitives straggling to the rear, their numbers augmenting every moment, until whole regiments, brigades, and divisions, in utter confusion and bewildered flight, covered the plain before us.... Yes; there was no doubt about it – they were running; and all the efforts of their officers, whom we could distinctly see using their sabres against their own men to check the precipitate retreat, were unavailing. All discipline was lost for the moment, and those thousands of troops whom an hour before we had seen advancing in beautiful military order, now presented the spectacle of a stampeded and demoralised mob....

Not one of our generals was aware of the magnitude of the victory we had gained, of the injury we had inflicted upon the enemy, and of the degree of demoralisation in the hostile army, everybody regarding the work as but half done, and expecting a renewal of the attack the following morning. Of our own army only one-third had been engaged, and our loss did not exceed 1800 in killed and wounded. Most of these belonged to A. P. Hill's division, and had fallen during the first attack in the morning on the spot where our lines had for some time been broken. We had to mourn the loss of two general officers, Maxey Gregg of South Carolina, and Thomas R. R. Cobb of Georgia, who fell on Mayre's Heights. At his side, General Cooke, a brother of Mrs. Stuart, was dangerously wounded in the forehead. The Federal loss was not less than 14,000 in killed and wounded (we took only 800 prisoners), and in this frightful aggregate of casualties was to be reckoned the loss of many officers of rank....

General Lee has been much criticised, and chiefly by English writers, for not having assumed the offensive in this battle; but every one who knows how exceedingly difficult it had become, already at that time, to fill the ranks of the Confederate army, and how valuable each individual life in that army must have been considered, and, on the other hand, what reckless prodigality of life characterised the Federal Government and the Federal commanders, caring little that 20,000 or 30,000 men should be killed in a campaign, when as many more Germans and Irishmen could be readily put in their places, - I say that every one who bears in mind these facts will agree with me in thinking that our commander-in-chief acted with great consideration and wisdom....

Maj. Robert Stiles, from *Four Years Under Marse Robert*: (8)

When the struggle was over and the enemy had withdrawn to his strongholds across the river, and Barksdale was ordered to reoccupy the town, the Twenty-first Mississippi, having held the post of danger in the rear, was given the place of honor in the van and led the column. There was a long halt, the brigade and regimental staff hurrying to and fro. The regimental colors could not be found.

Denman stood about the middle of the regiment, baby in arms. Suddenly he sprang to the front. Swinging her aloft above his head, her little garments fluttering like the folds of a banner, he shouted, "Forward, Twenty-first, here are your colors!" and without further order, off started the brigade toward the town, yelling as only Barksdale's men could yell. They were passing through a street fearfully shattered by the enemy's fire, and were shouting their very souls out – but let Buck himself describe the last scene in the drama:

"I was holding the baby high, Adjutant, with both arms, when above the racket I heard a woman's scream. The next thing I knew I was covered with calico and she fainted on my breast. I caught her before she fell, and laying her down gently, put her baby on her bosom. She was most the prettiest thing I ever looked at, and her eyes were shut; and – and – I hope God'll for-give me, but I kissed her just once"....

BOOK III - CHAPTER THREE

"The War You Have Demanded"

Abraham Lincoln's *Emancipation Proclamation* of September 22, 1862: (1)

BY THE PRESIDENT OF THE UNITED STATES OF AMERICA

A PROCLAMATION

I, Abraham Lincoln, President of the United States of America and Commander in Chief of the Army and Navy thereof, do hereby proclaim and declare that hereafter, as heretofore, the war will be prosecuted for the object of practically restoring the constitutional relation between the United States and each of the States and the people thereof in which States that relation is or may be suspended or disturbed.

That it is my purpose, upon the next meeting of Congress, to again recommend the adoption of a practical measure tendering pecuniary aid to the free acceptance or rejection of all slave States, so called, the people whereof may not then be in rebellion against the United States, and which States may then have voluntarily adopted, or thereafter may voluntarily adopt, immediate or gradual abolishment of slavery within their respective limits; and that the effort to colonize persons of African descent with their consent upon this continent or elsewhere, with the previously obtained consent of the governments existing there, will be continued.

That on the 1st day of January, A.D. 1863, all persons held as slaves within any State or designated part of a State the people whereof shall then be in rebellion against the United States shall be then, thenceforward, and forever free; and the executive government of the United States, including the military and naval authority thereof, will recognize and maintain the freedom of such persons and will do no act or acts to repress such persons, or any of them, in any efforts they may make for their actual freedom....

A commentary by John M. Daniel, from the Richmond *Examiner*, September 29, 1862: (2)

The Government of the United States has shot its bolt. The proclamation of Abraham Lincoln, which we publish this morning, decreeing the unconditional abolition of slavery in all the States which shall not submit to his power by the first of January next, is the fulfillment of a menace made ever since the commencement of the war. Enormous results have been, and are, calculated as its consequences. It is scarcely necessary to say to any one who knows the public mind in the South, that it will have absolutely no effect at all, either one way or other, on the conduct of the States. The only serious importance which it possesses consists in the indubitable indication that the Northern Government is resolved to pursue the affair to its extremity – intends to stop at nothing in the prosecution of this war. What we have hitherto seen is but the prelude of the war which will now begin – the war of extermination ... the call for the insurrection of four millions of slaves, and the inauguration of a reign of hell upon earth!

Lincoln's *Proclamation* suspending the writ of *habeas corpus*, appearing in the Richmond *Enquirer*, September 29, 1862: (3)

ANOTHER PROCLAMATION FROM ABRAHAM
"Proclamation

"Whereas, it has become necessary to call into service, not only volunteers, but also portions of the militia of the States by draft, in order to suppress the insurrection existing in the United States, and disloyal persons are not adequately restrained by the ordinary process of law from hindering this measure, and from giving aid and comfort in various ways to the insurrection. Now, therefore, be it ordered, that during the existing insurrection, and as a necessary measure for suppressing the same, all rebels and insurgents, their aiders and abettors within the United States, and all persons discouraging volunteer enlistments, resisting militia drafts, or guilty of any disloyal practice, affording aid and comfort to the rebels against the authority of the United States, shall be subject to martial law, and liable to trial and punishment by court martial or military commission.

"2d. That the writ of *habeas corpus* is suspended in respect to all persons arrested, or who are now, or hereafter during the rebellion shall be imprisoned in any fort, camp, arsenal, military prisons, or other place of confinement, by any military authority, or by the sentence of any court martial or military person."

A commentary appearing in the Richmond *Enquirer*, September 30, 1862: (4)

PROCLAMATION THE SECOND

Lincoln's second proclamation, also published yesterday, makes him, if submitted to, as completely the master of his people as any Czar ever was of the Russians. He orders military proceedings against any person who may be *charged* of a particular offence, and puts him in prison beyond the power of the *habeas corpus* to liberate him. That is to say every man in the North breathes free air by the grace and pleasure of Lincoln. Thus is all freedom utterly crushed out!

This Proclamation was probably intended to intimidate all opposition to the Proclamation for servile war. There are men in the North who have always declared that they would never sink so low as that, and the tidings from there is that there is great commotion in consequence of it. It is only necessary for the meanest menial of the Administration to charge a political opponent with aiding and abetting the insurrection and forthwith he is thrust in prison, to be tried at pleasure by a Court Martial! Behold "the best Government that the world ever saw!"

A despotism more debasing and crushing, it is impossible to conceive....

A commentary by John M. Daniel on the passage of the "Negro Soldiers' Bill" by the US House of Representatives, from the Richmond *Examiner*, February 9, 1863: (5)

Dispatches of Friday last announced that the "negro soldiers' bill" had passed the Yankee House of Representatives by a vote of 88 to 54. "The slaves of loyal persons," says the dispatch, "are not to be received, and no recruiting officers are to be sent into the Border States without the permission of their governors. Mr. Stevens said three hundred thousand men would leave the army in May. We could not raise fifty thousand white men. Conscription was impossible."

What a confession is here! More than twenty millions of white people, educated in common schools, accustomed from childhood to those practical exercises by which the wits are supposed to be sharpened and the body invigorated, and priding themselves upon their endowments, make war upon less than one-third of their number of semi-barbarian Southerners, slothful, ignorant, enervated, depraved; and after two years of war such as no people ever waged and none ever endured (so vast is its magnitude and so vehement and malignant its energy), the stronger power is forced by the stern necessity of constant defeat and the inherent wickedness of the cause, to appeal from its own race and section to African slaves for help. How shameful the admission of weakness – how ridiculous the appeal for aid! Three hundred thousand white men, trained in the art of modern warfare, throw down their arms in disgust in May, and their places are to be filled with negroes….

Ida M. Tarbell, from *The Life of Abraham Lincoln*: (6)

It was plain to the President that hereafter, if he was to have the men he needed, military service must be compulsory. Nothing could have been devised which would have created a louder uproar in the North than the suggestion of a draft. All through the winter of 1862-3, Congress wrangled over the bill ordering it…. The bill passed, however, and the President signed it in March, 1863.

At once there was put into operation a huge new military machine, the Bureau of the Provost-Marshal-General, which had for its business the enrollment of all the men in the United States whom the new law considered capable of bearing arms and the drafting enough of them to fill up the quota assigned to each State. This bureau was also to look after deserters….

The quotas assigned the States led to endless disputes between the governors and the War Department; the drafts caused riots; an inferior kind of soldier was obtained by draft-ing, and deserters increased…. The draft bore heavily on districts where the percentage of death among the first volunteers had been large, and often urgent pleas were made to the President to release a city or county from the quota assigned. The late Joseph Medill, the editor of the Chicago *Tribune*, once told me how he and certain leading citizens of Chicago went to Lincoln to ask that the quota of Cook County be reduced….

"I shall never forget how he suddenly lifted his head and turned on us a black and frowning face. 'Gentlemen,' he said, in a voice full of bitterness, 'after Boston, Chicago has been the chief instrument in bringing this war on the country. The Northwest has opposed the South as New England has opposed the South. It is you who are largely responsible for making blood flow as it has. You called for Emancipation, and I have given it to you. Whatever you have asked you have had. Now you come here begging to be let off from the call for men which I have made to carry out the war you have demanded. You ought to be ashamed of yourselves…. Go home, and raise your 6,000 extra men….'"

BOOK III - CHAPTER FOUR

Children of the Mist

Maj. Jed Hotchkiss, from *Confederate Military History*: (1)

[T]he Second Corps went into winter quarters, in Caroline County, in the forests just back from the front of the wooded bluffs of the Rappahannock, and Jackson established his headquarters at Moss Neck, near Fredericksburg, while Longstreet's corps occupied the left from the rear of Fredericksburg up the Rappahannock to the vicinity of Banks' Ford, above Fredericksburg.

Later in December, Stuart made a cavalry reconnaissance around Burnside's right and rear, to within a few miles of Washington and Fairfax and Occoquan. The larger portion of Longstreet's corps was sent south of the James, with its advance in the vicinity of Suffolk, to winter where subsistence was plentiful. The Federal army went into winter quarters along the line of the railway from Fredericksburg to Aquia Creek, with its base of supplies at that Potomac landing, which was easily accessible by ship and steamer. Thus these two great armies, with their camp-fires in sight of each other, disposed themselves in winter quarters in the extensive forests behind the big plantations that bordered both banks of the Rappahannock, and each addressed itself to the work of preparation for another trial of arms during the coming year; the one fairly rioting in the abundance of its supplies of men and material, of all kinds, gathered from nearly the whole world, which was at its command, while the other could only strengthen its great poverty of men and resources by husbanding the scantiest of fare and of military stores, by strengthening its patriotic courage and devotion, and by increasing its trust in Divine Providence by constant religious observances and supplications and prayers from nearly every member of its army, from its humblest private to the noble Christian soldier that led and, by example, encouraged them....

Maj. Robert Stiles, from *Four Years Under Marse Robert*: (2)

The religious interest among Barksdale's men began about the time of, or soon after, the battle of Fredericksburg, which was about the middle of December, '62, and continued with unabated fervor up to and through the battle of Chancellorsville and even to Gettysburg. In addition to the labors of the regimental chaplains, the ablest and most distinguished ministers in Virginia, of all denominations, delighted to come up and speak to the men.... And while I greatly enjoyed the many powerful sermons we heard from distinguished ministers, yet I was still more impressed by the simple song and prayer and experience meetings of the men, which were generally held for at least an hour before the regular service began....

I remember that one of these private soldiers, in illustrating and enforcing the folly of living in this world as if we were to live in it forever, asked his comrades what they would think of the good sense or even the sanity of one of their number who should to-morrow morning send to Richmond for an elegant wrapper, velvet smoking cap and slippers, and when they came, throwing away his blanket and stout shoes and clothes, should insist upon arraying himself in "these butterfly things" in the face of the fact that the next moment the long roll might turn him out into the deep snow or the guns of the enemy batter down his cantonment over his head.

Another, speaking of the trivial things to which a man gives his heart and for which he may lose his soul, speculated with the finest fancy as to what it was, and how very a trifle it may have been, that turned the heart and the gaze of Lot's wife back towards Sodom and turned her breathing body into a dead pillar of salt.

And still another – a great, broad-shouldered, double-jointed son of Anak, with a head like the Farnese Jove and a face and frame indicative of tremendous power, alike of character and of muscle – delivered himself of his "experience" in one of the most graphic and moving talks I ever listened to. He said in substance:

"Brethren, I want you to know what a merciful, forgiving being the Lord is, and to do that I've got to tell you what a meanspirited liar I am. You remember that tight place the brigade got into, down yonder at ____, and you know the life I lived up to that day. Well, as soon as ever the Minies began a-singing and the shell a-bursting around me, I up and told the Lord that I was sorry and ashamed of myself, and if He'd cover my head this time we'd settle the thing as soon as I got out. Then I got to fighting and forgot all about it, and never thought of my promise no more at all till we got into that other place, up yonder at ____; you remember it, tighter than the first one. Then, when the bullets begun a hissing like rain and the shell was fairly tearing the woods to pieces, my broken promise come back to me. Brethren, my coward heart stopped beating and I pretty nigh fainted. I tried to pray and at first I couldn't; but I just said, 'Look here, Lord, if You will look, I feel I have lied to you and that you won't believe me again, and may be you oughtn't to; but I don't want to go to hell, and I'm serious and honest this time, and if You do hear me now, we'll meet just as soon as I get out safe, and we certainly will settle things.'

"Well, brethren, He did all I asked of Him, the Lord did; and what did I do? Brethren, I'm ashamed to say it, but I lied again, and never thought one thing about it at all till one day we was shoved into the very worst place any of us ever was in. Hell gaped for me, and here come the two lies I had told and sat right down upon my heart and my tongue. Of course I couldn't pray, but at last I managed to say, 'Lord! Lord! I deserve it all if I do go there, right now, and I can't pray and I won't lie any more. You can do as you please, Lord; but if You do.... But, no, I won't lie any more, and I won't promise, for fear I should lie. It's all in your hands, Lord – hell or mercy. I've got no time to talk any more about it. I've got to go to killing Yankees. But, oh Lord! Oh Lord! – no, I daresn't, I daresn't; for I won't lie any more; I won't go down there with a fresh lie on my lips; but, oh Lord! oh Lord!'

"And so it was, brethren, all through that dreadful day; fighting, fighting, and not daring to pray.

"But, brethren, He did it, He did it; and the moment the thing was over I wouldn't give myself time to lie again, so I just took out and ran as hard as ever I could into the deep, dark woods, where God and me was alone together, and I threw my musket down on the ground and I went right down myself, too, on my knees, and cried out, 'Thank you, Lord; thank you, Lord! But I'm not going to get up off my knees until everything's settled between us;' and neither I didn't, brethren. The Lord never held it over me at all, and we settled it right there"....

Col. John S. Mosby, from "A Bit of Partisan Service": (3)

When the year 1863 arrived Fredericksburg had been fought, and the two armies, in winter quarters, were confronting each other on the Rappahannock. Both sides sought rest; the pickets on the opposite banks of the river had ceased firing and gone to swapping coffee and tobacco. The cavalry had been sent to the rear to forage. But "quiet to quick bosoms is a hell." I did not want to rust away my life in camp, so I asked Stuart to give me a detail of men to go over to Loudoun County, where I thought I could make things lively during the winter months. Always full of enterprise, Stuart readily assented, and I started off on my career as a partisan. At the time I had no idea of organizing an independent command, but expected to return to Stuart when the campaign opened in the spring. I was indifferent to rank, and would have been as contented to be a lieutenant as a colonel.

I was somewhat familiar with the country where I began operations, having picketed there the year before. The lines of the troops attached to the defenses of Washington extended from about Occoquan, on the lower Potomac, through Centreville, in Fairfax County, to the Falls of the upper Potomac, and thence as far west as Harper's Ferry. This was a long line to defend, and, before I went there, had not been closely guarded. I began on the picket-lines; my attacks were generally in the night-time, and usually the surprise compensated for the disparity in numbers. They would be repeated the next, and often during the same night at a different point, and this created a vastly exaggerated idea of my force. Some conception may be formed of the alarm it produced from a fact stated by General Hooker, that in the spring of 1863 the planks on Chain Bridge were taken up every night to keep me out of Washington. At that time I could not muster over twenty men. A small force moving with celerity and threatening many points on a line can neutralize a hundred times its own number. The line must be stronger at every point than the attacking force, else it is broken. At that time Hooker asked that the cavalry division belonging to the defenses of Washington be sent to the front to reinforce Pleasanton when he crossed the Rappahannock to engage Stuart in the great cavalry combat of June 9th. It was refused on the ground that it was necessary to keep it where it was, in order to protect the communication between the army and Washington.

A few days before that fight we struck the railroad within two miles of this cavalry camp, and captured and burned a train of supplies going up to Pleasanton. The 3,000 men who came after me could not run any faster than the twenty with me. We vanished like the children of the mist....

Lt. Col. Walter Taylor, from *Four Years with General Lee*: (4)

Active operations were resumed in the spring…. General Lee, with fifty-seven thousand troops of all arms, intrenched along the line of hills south of the Rappahannock, near Fredericksburg, was confronted by General Hooker, with the Army of the Potomac, one hundred and thirty-two thousand strong, occupying the bluffs on the opposite side of the river.

On the 29th of April the Federal commander essayed to put into execution an admirably-conceived plan of operations…. A formidable force, under Sedgwick, was thrown across the river below Fredericksburg, and made demonstrations of an intention to assail the Confederate front. Meanwhile, with great celerity and secrecy, General Hooker, with the bulk of his army, crossed at the upper fords, and, in an able manner and wonderfully short time, had concentrated four of his seven army corps, numbering fifty-six thousand men, at Chancellorsville, about ten miles west of Fredericksburg.

His purpose was now fully developed to General Lee who, instead of awaiting its further prosecution, immediately determined on the movement the least expected by his opponent. He neither proceeded to make strong his left against attack from the direction of Chancellorsville, nor did he move southward, so as to put his army between that of General Hooker and the Confederate capital; but, leaving General Early, with about nine thousand men, to take care of General Sedgwick, he moved with the remainder of his army, numbering forty-eight thousand men, toward Chancellorsville. As soon as the advance of the enemy was encountered, it was attacked with vigor, and very soon the Federal army was on the defensive in its apparently impregnable position.

It was not the part of wisdom to attempt to storm this stronghold; but Sedgwick would certainly soon be at work in the rear, and Early, with his inadequate force, could not do more than delay and harass him. It was, therefore, imperatively necessary to strike – to strike boldly, effectively, and at once. There could be no delay. Meanwhile two more army corps had joined General Hooker, who now had about Chancellorsville ninety-one thousand men – six corps, except one division ... which had been left with Sedgwick, at Fredericksburg. It was a critical position for the Confederate commander, but his confidence in his trusted lieutenant and brave men was such that he did not long hesitate. Encouraged by the counsel and confidence of General Jackson, he determined still further to divide his army; and while he, with the divisions of Anderson and McLaws, less than fourteen thousand men, should hold the enemy in his front, he would hurl Jackson upon his flank and rear, and crush and crumble him as between the upper and nether millstone....

Maj. Hunter McGuire, Jackson's Medical Director, from *The Confederate Cause and Conduct in the War Between the States*: (5)

Never can I forget the eagerness and intensity of Jackson on that march to Hooker's rear. His face was pale, his eyes were flashing. Out from his thin compressed lips came the terse command: "Press forward, press forward." In his eagerness, as he rode he leaned over on the neck of his horse as if in that way the march might be hurried. "See that the column is kept closed and that there is no straggling," he more than once ordered – and "Press on, press on" was repeated again and again. Every man in the ranks knew that we were engaged in some great flank movement, and they eagerly responded, and pressed on at a rapid gait....

The fiercest energy possessed the man, and the fire of battle fell strong upon him. When he arrived at the Plank Road he sent this, his last message, to Lee: "The enemy has made a stand at Chancellorsville. I hope as soon as practicable to attack. I trust that an ever kind Providence will bless us with success"....

Capt. James Power Smith, a member of Jackson's staff, from "Stonewall Jackson's Last Battle": (6)

Rodes' division, at the head of the column, was thrown into line of battle, with Colston's forming the second line and A. P. Hill's the third.... It must have been between 5 and 6 o'clock in the evening, Saturday, May 2d, when these dispositions were completed. Upon his stout-built, long-paced little sorrel, General Jackson sat, with visor low over his eyes and lips compressed, and with his watch in his hand. Upon his right sat General Robert E. Rodes, the very picture of a soldier, and every inch all that he appeared. Upon the right of Rodes sat Major Blackford.

"Are you ready, General Rodes?" said Jackson.

"Yes, sir!" said Rodes, impatient for the advance.

"You can go forward then," said Jackson.

A nod from Rodes was order enough for Blackford, and then suddenly the woods rang with the bugle call, and back came the responses from bugles on the right and left, and the long line of skirmishers, through the wild thicket of undergrowth, sprang eagerly to their work, followed promptly by the quick steps of the line of battle. For a moment all the troops seemed buried in the depths of the gloomy forest, and then suddenly the echoes waked and swept the country for miles, never failing until heard at the headquarters of Hooker at Chancellorsville – the wild "rebel yell" of the long Confederate lines....

Maj. Heros von Borcke, from his *Memoirs of the Confederate War for Independence*: (7)

The whole of the 11th corps had broken at the first shock of the attack; entire regiments had thrown down their arms, which were lying in regular lines on the ground, as if for inspection; suppers just prepared had been abandoned; tents, baggage, waggons, cannons, half-slaughtered oxen, covered the foreground in chaotic confusion, while in the background a host of many thousand Yankees were discerned scampering for their lives as fast as their limbs could carry them, closely followed by our men, who were taking prisoners by the hundreds, and scarcely firing a shot....

Capt. James Power Smith, from "Stonewall Jackson's Last Battle": (8)

When Jackson had reached the point where his line now crossed the turnpike, scarcely a mile west of Chancellorsville, and not a half a mile from a line of Federal troops, he had found his front line unfit for the farther and vigorous advance he desired, by reason of the irregular character of the fighting, now right, now left, and because of the dense thickets, through which it was impossible to preserve alignment. Division commanders found it more and more difficult as the twilight deepened to hold their broken brigades in hand.

Regretting the necessity of relieving the troops in front, General Jackson had ordered A. P. Hill's division, his third and reserve line, to be placed in front. While this change was being effected, impatient and anxious, the general rode forward on the turnpike, followed by two or three of his staff and a number of couriers and signal sergeants. He passed the swampy depression and began the ascent of the hill toward Chancellorsville, when he came upon a line of the Federal infantry lying on their arms.

Fired at by one or two muskets (two musket-balls from the enemy whistled over my head as I came to the front), he turned and came back toward his line, upon the side of the road to his left.

As he rode near to the Confederate troops, just placed in position and ignorant that he was in the front, the left company began firing to the front, and two of his party fell from their saddles dead – Captain Boswell, of the Engineers, and Sergeant Cunliffe, of the Signal Corps.

Spurring his horse across the road to his right, he was met by a second volley from the right company of Pender's North Carolina brigade. Under this volley, when not two rods from the troops, the general received three balls at the same instant.... As he lost his hold upon the bridle-rein, he reeled from the saddle, and was caught by the arms of Captain Wilbourn, of the Signal Corps. Laid upon the ground, there came at once to his succor General A. P. Hill and members of his staff.... Couriers were sent for Dr. Hunter McGuire, the surgeon of the corps and the general's trusted friend, and for an ambulance.

Being outside of our lines, it was urgent that he should be moved at once. With difficulty litter-bearers were brought from the line near by, and the general was placed upon the litter.... A moment after, artillery from the Federal side was opened upon us ... and the litter-bearer at my side was struck and fell, but, as the litter turned, Major Watkins Leigh, of Hill's staff, happily caught it. But the fright of the men was so great that we were obliged to lay the litter and its burden down....

Soon the firing veered to the other side of the road.... Again we resorted to the litter, and with difficulty bore it through the bush, and then under a hot fire along the road. Soon an ambulance was reached, and stopping to seek some stimulant at Chancellor's (Dowdall's Tavern), we were found by Dr. McGuire, who at once took charge of the wounded man....

Lt. Col. Walter Taylor, from *Four Years with General Lee*: (9)

The flank movement of Jackson's wing was attended with extraordinary success. On the afternoon of the 2nd of May he struck such a blow to the enemy on their extreme right as to cause dismay and demoralization to their entire army; this advantage was promptly and vigorously followed up the next day, when Generals Lee and Stuart (the latter then in command of Jackson's wing) joined elbows; and after most heroic and determined effort, their now united forces finally succeeded in storming and capturing the works of the enemy.

Meantime Sedgwick had forced Early out of the heights at Fredericksburg, and had advanced toward Chancellorsville, thus threatening the Confederate rear. General Lee having defeated the greater force, and driven it from its stronghold, now gathered up a few of the most available of his victorious brigades, and turned upon the lesser.

On the 3rd of May Sedgwick's force was encountered in the vicinity of Salem Church, and its further progress checked by General McLaws, with the five brigades detached by General Lee for this service – including Wilcox's, which had been stationed at Banks' Ford. On the next day General Anderson was sent to reinforce McLaws with three additional brigades. Meanwhile, General Early had connected with these troops, and in the afternoon, so soon as dispositions could be made for attack, Sedgwick's lines were promptly assailed and broken – the main assault being made on the enemy's left by Early's troops. The situation was now a critical one for the Federal lieutenant. Darkness came to his rescue, and on the night of the 4th he crossed to the north side of the river.

On the 5th General Lee concentrated for another assault on the new line taken up by General Hooker; but on the morning of the 6th it was ascertained that the enemy, in General Lee's language, "had sought safety beyond the Rappahannock," and the river flowed again between the hostile hosts.

Glorious as was the result of this battle to the Confederate arms, it was accompanied by a calamity in the contemplation of which the most brilliant victory of that incomparable army must ever be regarded as a supreme disaster. The star of Confederate destiny reached its zenith on the 2nd day of May, when Jackson fell wounded at the head of his victorious troops; it began to set on the 10th of May, when Jackson was no more....

Maj. Hunter Mcguire, from *The Confederate Cause and Conduct in the War Between the States*: (10)

Mrs. Jackson arrived to-day, and nursed him faithfully to the end.... The General's joy at the presence of his wife and child was very great, and for him unusually demonstrative.... About daylight, on Sunday morning, Mrs. Jackson informed him that his recovery was very doubtful, and that it was better that he should be prepared for the worst. He was silent for a moment, and then said: "It will be infinite gain to be translated to Heaven".... Colonel Pendleton came into the room about one o'clock, and he asked him, "Who is preaching at headquarters to-day?" When told that the whole army was praying for him, he replied, "Thank God – they are very kind." He said: "It is the Lord's Day; my wish is fulfilled. I have always desired to die on Sunday,"

His mind now began to fail and wander, and he frequently talked as if in command upon the field, giving orders in his old way.... A few moments before he died he cried out in his delirium, "Order A. P. Hill to prepare for action! Pass the infantry to the front rapidly! Tell Major Hawks" – then stopped, leaving the sentence unfinished. Presently, a smile of ineffable sweetness spread itself over his pale face, and he said quietly, and with an expression, as if of relief, "Let us cross over the river, and rest under the shade of the trees"....

BOOK III - CHAPTER FIVE

"Let Us Cross Over the River…."

Lt. Col. Walter Taylor, from *Four Years with General Lee*: (1)

From the very necessities of the case, the general theory upon which the war was conducted on the part of the South was one of defense. The great superiority of the North in men and material made it indispensable for the South to husband its resources as much as possible, inasmuch as the hope of ultimate success which the latter entertained, rested rather upon the dissatisfaction and pecuniary distress which a prolonged war would entail upon the former – making the people weary of the struggle – than upon any expectation of conquering a peace by actually subduing so powerful an adversary.

Nevertheless, in the judgment of General Lee, it was a part of a true defensive policy to take the aggressive when good opportunity offered; and by delivering an effective blow to the enemy, not only to inflict upon him serious loss, but at the same time to thwart his designs of invasion, derange the plan of campaign contemplated by him, and thus prolong the conflict.

The Federal army, under General Hooker, had now reoccupied the heights opposite Fredericksburg, where it could not be attacked except at a disadvantage. Instead of quietly awaiting the pleasure of the Federal commander in designing and putting into execution some new plan of campaign, General Lee determined to maneuver to draw him from his impregnable position and if possible to remove the scene of hostilities beyond the Potomac. His design was to free the State of Virginia, for a time at least, from the presence of the enemy, to transfer the theatre of war to Northern soil, and, by selecting a favorable time and place in which to receive the attack which his adversary would be compelled to make on him, to take the reasonable chances of defeating him in a pitched battle; knowing full well that to obtain such an advantage there would place him in position to attain far more decisive results than could be hoped for from a like advantage gained in Virginia.

But even if unable to attain the valuable results which might be expected to follow a decided advantage gained over the enemy in Maryland or Pennsylvania, it was thought that the movement would at least so far disturb the Federal plan for the summer campaign as to prevent its execution during the season for active operations.

In pursuance of this design, early in the month of June, General Lee moved his army northward by way of Culpeper, and thence to and down the Valley of Virginia to Winchester.

The army had now been reorganized into three army corps, designated the First, Second, and Third Corps, and commanded respectively by Lieutenant Generals Longstreet, Ewell, and A. P. Hill.

The Second Corps was in advance, and crossed the branches of the Shenandoah, near Front Royal, on the 12th of June. Brushing aside the force of the enemy under General Milroy, that occupied the lower Valley – most of which was captured and the remnant of which sought refuge in the fortifications at Harper's Ferry – General Ewell crossed the Potomac River with his three divisions in the latter part of June, and, in pursuance of the orders of General Lee, traversed Maryland and advanced into Pennsylvania.

General A. P. Hill, whose corps was the last to leave the line of the Rappahannock, followed with his three divisions in Ewell's rear. General Longstreet covered these movements with his corps; then moved by Ashby's and Snicker's Gaps into the Valley and likewise crossed the Potomac River, leaving to General Stuart the task of holding the gaps of the Blue Ridge Mountains with his corps of cavalry....

Maj. Robert Stiles, from *Four Years Under Marse Robert*: (2)

I do not remember where I overtook Ewell's corps, but think I entered Pennsylvania with them. General Lee had issued stringent orders against plundering and, certainly in the main, the men carefully observed these orders. I was constantly told by the inhabitants that they suffered less from our troops than from their own, and that if compelled to have either, they preferred having "the rebels" camped upon their lands. I saw no plundering whatever, except that once or twice I did see branches laden with fruit broken from cherry trees.

Of course, it goes without saying that the quartermasters, especially of artillery battalions, were, confessedly and of malice aforethought, horse thieves. It was, perhaps, adding insult to injury to offer to pay for the horses, as we did, in Confederate money; yet occasionally the owners took it, as "better then nothing" – how better it would be difficult to say. I felt sorry for the farmers, some of whom actually concealed their horses in their dwelling houses, or, rather, attempted to conceal them, for we became veritable sleuth-hounds in running down a horse, and were up to all the tricks and dodges devised to throw us off the track.

After all, we gained very little by our horse stealing. The impressed animals were, for the most part, great, clumsy, flabby Percherons or Conestogas, which require more than twice the feed our compact, hard-muscled little Virginia horses required, and yet could not do half the work they did, nor stand half the hardship and exposure. It was pitiable, later, to see these great brutes suffer when compelled to dash off at full gallop with a gun, after pasturing on dry broom sedge and eating a quarter of a feed of weevil-eaten corn. They seemed to pine for the slow draft and full feed of their Pennsylvania homes....

By this time the reader has doubtless learned that things were not likely to be dull when our old friend [Brigadier-General] "Extra Billy" [Smith, ex-Governor of Virginia] was about; that in fact there was apt to be "music in the air" whenever he was in charge. On the occasion below described, the old Governor seemed to be rather specially concerned about the musical part of the performance.

We were about entering the beautiful Pennsylvania town of York, General Smith's brigade in the lead. Under these conditions, feeling sure there was likely to be a breeze stirring about the head of the column, I rode forward so as to be near the General and not to miss the fun. As we approached the population seemed to be very generally in the streets, and I saw at a glance that the old Governor had blood in his eye. Turning to Fred, his aide, - who was also his son, and about the strongest marked case of second edition I ever saw, - he told him to "Go back and look up those tooting fellows," as he called the brigade band, "and tell them first to be sure their drums and horns are all right, and then to come up here to the front and march into town tooting 'Yankee Doodle' in their very best style."

Fred was off in a jiffy, and soon here came the band, their instruments looking bright and smart and glistening in the June sunlight – playing, however, not "Yankee Doodle," but "Dixie," the musicians appearing to think it important to be entirely impartial in rendering these national airs, and therefore giving us "Dixie" by way of prelude to "Yankee Doodle."

When they got to the head of the column, and struck up "Yankee Doodle," and the Governor, riding alone and bareheaded in front of his staff, began bowing and saluting first one side and then the other, and especially every pretty girl he saw, with that manly, hearty smile which no man or woman ever doubted or resisted – the Yorkers seemed at first astounded, then pleased, and finally, by the time we reached the public square, they had reached the point of ebullition, and broke into enthusiastic cheers as they crowded about the head of the column, actually embarrassing its progress, till the old Governor, - the "Governor-General," we might call him, - nothing loth, acceded to the half suggestion and called a halt, his brigade stacking arms, and constituting, if not formally organizing, themselves and the people of York into a political meeting.

It was a rare scene – the vanguard of an invading army and the invaded and hostile population hobnobbing on the public green in an enthusiastic public gathering. The general did not dismount, but from the saddle he made a rattling, humorous speech, which both the Pennsylvanians and his own brigade applauded to the echo. He said substantially:

"My friends, how do you like this way of coming back into the Union? I hope you like it; I have been in favor of it for a good while. But don't misunderstand us. We are not here with any hostile intent – unless the conduct of your side shall render hostilities unavoidable. You can see for yourselves we are not conducting ourselves like enemies today. We are not burning your houses or butchering your children. On the contrary, we are behaving ourselves like Christian gentlemen, as we are.

"You see, it was getting a little warm down our way. We needed a summer outing and thought we would take it at the North, instead of patronizing the Virginia springs, as we generally do. We are sorry, and apologize that we are not in better guise for a visit of courtesy, but we regret to say our trunks haven't gotten up yet; we were in such a hurry to see you that we could not wait for them. You must really excuse us.

"What we all need, on both sides, is to mingle more with each other, so that we shall learn to know and appreciate each other. Now here's my brigade – I wish you knew them as I do. They are such a hospitable, whole-hearted, fascinating lot of gentlemen. Why, just think of it – of course this part of Pennsylvania is ours to-day; we've got it, we hold it, we can destroy it, or do what we please with it. Yet we sincerely and heartily invite you to stay. You are quite welcome to remain here and to make yourselves entirely at home – so long as you behave yourselves pleasantly and agreeably as you are doing now. Are we not a fine set of fellows? You must admit that we are."

At this point my attention was called to a volley of very heated profanity poured forth in a piping, querulous treble, coming up from the rear, and being mounted and located where I commanded a view of the road, I saw that the second brigade in column, which had been some distance in the rear, had caught up, and was now held up by our public meeting, which filled and obstructed the entire street, and that Old Jube [Major-General Jubal A. Early], who had ridden forward to ascertain the cause of the dead-lock, was fairly blistering the air about him and making furious but for the time futile efforts to get at Extra Billy, who in plain sight, and not far off, yet blissfully unconscious of the presence of the major-general and of his agreeable observations and comments, was still holding forth with great fluency and acceptability.

The jam was solid and impervious. As D. H. Hill's report phrased it, "Not a dog, no, not even a sneaking exempt, could have made his way through" – and at first and for some time, Old Jube couldn't do it, and no one would help him. But at last officers and men were compelled to recognize the division commander, and he made his way so far that, by leaning forward, a long stretch, and a frantic grab, he managed to catch General Smith by the back of his coat collar. Even Jube did not dare curse the old general in an offensive way, but he did jerk him back and around pretty vigorously and half screamed:

"General Smith, what the devil are you about! stopping the head of this column in this cursed town?"

With unruffled composure the old fellow replied:

"Having a little fun, General, which is good for all of us, and at the same time teaching these people something that will be good for them and won't do us any harm."

Suffice it to say the matter was amicably arranged and the brigade and its unique commander moved on, leaving the honest burghers of York wondering what manner of men we were....

Rev. J. William Jones, from his *Personal Reminiscences of General Robert E. Lee*: (3)

When in 1863 the head of the Army of Northern Virginia was turned northward, and it was understood that an invasion of Pennsylvania was contemplated, there resounded through the South a cry for retaliation there for the desolation inflicted by the Federal armies upon our own fair land. The newspapers recounted the outrages that we had endured, painted in vivid colors the devastation of large sections of the South, reprinted the orders of Pope, Butler, and others of like spirit, and called upon the officers and men of the Army of Northern Virginia to remember these things when they reached the rich fields of Pennsylvania, arguing that the best way of bringing the war to a successful termination was to let the people of the North feel it as we had done. Prominent men urged these views on General Lee, and it would not have been surprising if he had so far yielded to the popular clamor as to have at least winked at depredations on the part of his soldiers. But he did not for a single moment forget that he led the army of a people who professed to be governed by the principles of Christian civilization, and that no outrages on the part of others could justify him in departing from these high principles.

Accordingly, as soon as the head of his column crossed the Potomac, he issued a beautiful address, in which he called upon his men to abstain from pillage and depredations of every kind, and enjoined upon his officers to bring to speedy punishment all offenders against this order. If this had been intended for *effect* merely, while the soldiers were to be allowed to plunder at will, nothing further would have been necessary. But we find him publishing the following, which forms one of the brightest pages in the history of that unhappy strife, will go down to coming ages in vivid contrast with the orders of Pope, Butler, Sheridan, and other Federal generals, and will for all time reflect the highest honor alike upon our Christian chieftain and the army he led:

"General Orders No. 73
"Headquarters Army of Northern Virginia,
"Chambersburg, Pa., June 27, 1863.

"The commanding general has observed with marked satisfaction the conduct of the troops on the march, and confidently anticipates results commensurate with the high spirit they have manifested. No troops could have displayed greater fortitude, or better have performed the arduous marches of the past ten days. Their conduct in other respects has, with few exceptions, been in keeping with their character as soldiers, and entitles them to approbation and praise.

"There have been, however, instances of forgetfulness on the part of some that they have in keeping the yet unsullied reputation of the army, and that the duties exacted of us by civilization and Christianity are not less obligatory in the country of the enemy than in our own. The commanding general considers that no greater disgrace could befall the army, and through it our whole people, than the perpetration of the barbarous outrages upon the innocent and defenseless, and the wanton destruction of private property, that have marked the course of the enemy in our own country. Such proceedings not only disgrace the perpetrators and all connected with them, but are subversive of the discipline and efficiency of the army, and destructive of the ends of our present movements. It must be remembered that we make war only upon armed men, and that we cannot take vengeance for the wrongs our people have suffered without lowering ourselves in the eyes of all whose abhorrence has been excited by the atrocities of our enemy and offending against Him to whom vengeance belongeth, and without whose favor and support our efforts must all prove in vain.

"The commanding general, therefore, earnestly exhorts the troops to abstain, with most scrupulous care, from unnecessary or wanton injury to private property; and he enjoins upon all officers to arrest and bring to summary punishment all who shall in any way offend against the orders on this subject.

"R.E. Lee, General."

That these orders were in some instances violated is not denied, but both General Lee and his officers exerted themselves to have them carried out, and with almost perfect success, as even the Northern press abundantly testified at the time.

No blackened ruins, desolate fields, or wanton destruction of private property marked the line of his march. His official dispatches are blotted by no wicked boast of the number of barns burned, and the amount of provisions destroyed, until he had made the country "such a waste that even a crow flying over would be compelled to carry his rations!" But the order above quoted not only expressed the feelings of the commander-in-chief, but was an index to the conduct of his officers and the troops under their command.

When General John B. Gordon, at the head of his splendid brigade of Georgians, entered York, there was great consternation among the people, and he sought to quiet their fears by making the following address to a crowd of women gathered on the street:

"Our Southern homes have been pillaged, sacked, and burned; our mothers, wives, and little ones, driven forth amid the brutal insults of your soldiers. Is it any wonder that we fight with desperation? A natural revenge would prompt us to retaliate in kind, but we scorn to war on women and children. We are fighting for the God-given rights of liberty and independence, as handed down to us in the Constitution by our fathers. So fear not: if a torch is applied to a single dwelling, or an insult offered to a female of your town by a soldier of this command, point me out the man, and you shall have his life"....

Lt. Gen. Jubal A. Early, from his "Lee Memorial Address," January 19, 1872: (4)

The two armies concentrated, and encountered each other at Gettysburg, east of the South Mountain, in a battle extending through three days, from the 1st to the 3d of July, inclusive. On the first day, a portion of our army, composed of two divisions of Hill's corps, and two divisions of Ewell's corps, gained a very decided victory over two of the enemy's corps, which latter were driven back, in great confusion, through Gettysburg, to the heights, immediately south and east of the town, known as Cemetery Hill. On the second and third days, we assaulted the enemy's position at different points, but failed to dislodge his army, now under Meade, from its very strong position on Cemetery and the adjacent hills....

From a Richmond *Enquirer* War Correspondent's report on the battle of Gettysburg: (5)

Friday, the third, preparations were made for a general attack along the enemy's whole line, while a large force was to be concentrated against his centre, with the view of retaking the heights captured and abandoned the day before by Wright. Lieut.-Gen. Longstreet massed a large number of long-range guns – fifty-five in number – upon the crest of a slight eminence just in front of Perry's and Wilcox's brigades, and a little to the left of the heights, upon which they were to open. Lieut.-Gen. Hill massed some sixty guns along the hill in front of Posey's and Mahone's brigades, and almost immediately in front of the heights. At twelve o'clock the signal-gun was fired, and the cannonading commenced....

Our fire drew a most terrific one from the enemy's batteries, posted along the heights from a point near Cemetery Hill to the point in their line opposite to the position of Wilcox. I have never yet heard such tremendous artillery firing. The enemy must have had over one hundred guns, which, in addition to our one hundred and fifteen, made the air hideous with most discordant noise. The very earth shook beneath our feet, and the hills and rocks seemed to reel like a drunken man. For one hour and a half this most terrific fire was continued, during which time the shriek-ing of shells, the crash of falling timber, the fragments of rock flying through the air shattered from the cliffs by solid shot, the heavy mutterings from the valley between the opposing armies, the splash of bursting shrapnel, and the fierce neighing of wound-ed artillery horses, made a picture terribly grand and sublime, but which my pen utterly fails to describe....

But where is that division which is to play so conspicuous a part in this day's tragedy? They are in line of battle, just fronting that frowning hill, from which heavy batteries are belching forth shell and shrapnel with fatal accuracy. The men are lying close to the ground; hours pass, and the deadly missiles come thick and fast on their mission of death. See that shattered arm; that leg shot off; that headless body, and here the mangled form of a young and gallant lieutenant, who had braved the perils of many battles. That hill must be carried to rout the enemy; a terrible chastisement has been inflicted upon him; with immense loss he had been driven from his position two days previous – this is his stronghold. This captured, route is inevitable; exceedingly strong by nature, but rendered more so by the works thrown up the night before. It is a moment of great emergency; if unshrinking valor or human courage can carry those heights, it will be done....

Brig. Gen. A. L. Long, from *Memoirs of Robert E. Lee*: (6)

For more than an hour this fierce artillery conflict contin-ued, when the Federal guns began to slacken their fire under the heavy blows of the Confederate batteries, and ere long sank into silence – an example which was quickly followed by the Confederates.

A deathlike stillness then reigned over the field, and each army remained in breathless expectation of something yet to come still more dreadful. In a few moments the attacking column, consisting of Pickett's division, supported on the left by that of Heth commanded by Pettigrew, and on the right by Wilcox's brigade of Anderson's division, appeared from behind a ridge, and, sweeping over its crest, descended into the depression that separated the two armies. The enemy for a moment seemed lost in admiration of this gallant array as it advanced with the steadiness and precision of a review. Their batteries then opened upon it a spasmodic fire, as if recovering from a stunning blow. The force that moved to the attack numbered about 15,000 men. It had a terrible duty to perform. The distance which it was obliged to traverse was more than half a mile in width, and this an open plain in full front of the enemy, who thickly crowded the crest of the ridge, and within easy range of their artillery.

But the tempest of fire which burst upon the devoted column quickly reduced its strength. The troops of Heth's division, decimated by the storm of deadly hail which tore through their ranks, faltered and fell back in disorder before the withering volleys of the Federal musketry.

This compelled Pender's division, which had marched out to support the movement, to fall back, while Wilcox, on perceiving that the attack had grown hopeless, failed to advance, leaving Pickett's men to continue the charge alone. The other supports, Hood's and McLaws's divisions, which had been expected to advance in support of the charging column, did not move, and were too remote to offer any assistance. The consequence was that Pickett was left entirely unsupported.

Yet the gallant Virginians marched steadily forward, through the storm of shot and shell that burst upon their devoted ranks, with a gallantry that has never been surpassed. As they approached the ridge their lines were torn by incessant volleys of musketry as by a deadly hail. Yet with unfaltering courage the brave fellows broke into the double-quick, and with an irresistible charge burst into the Federal lines and drove everything before them toward the crest of Cemetery Hill, leaping the breastworks and planting their standards on the captured guns with shouts of victory.

The success which General Lee had hoped and expected was gained, but it was a dearly bought and short-lived one. His plan had gone astray through the failure of the supporting columns…. On every side the enemy closed in on Pickett's brigades, concentrating on them the fire of every gun in that part of their lines. It was impossible to long withstand this terrific fusillade. The band of heroes broke and fell back, leaving the greater part of their number dead or wounded upon the field or captive in the hands of their foes….

The Breath of the Night-Wind

The Sea of Faith
Was once, too, at the full, and round earth's shore
Lay like the folds of a bright girdle furl'd.
But now I only hear
Its melancholy, long, withdrawing roar,
Retreating, to the breath
Of the night-wind, down the vast edges drear
And naked shingles of the world....
                    - Matthew Arnold, "Dover Beach" (1)

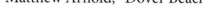

Brig. Gen. John D. Imboden, from "The Confederate Retreat from Gettysburg": (2)

It was a warm summer's night; there were few campfires, and the weary soldiers were lying in groups on the luxuriant grass of the beautiful meadows, discussing the events of the day, speculating on the morrow, or watching that our horses did not straggle off while browsing. About 11 o'clock a horseman came to summon me to General Lee. I promptly mounted and - accompanied by Lieutenant George W. McPhail, an aide on my staff, and guided by the courier who brought the message - rode about two miles toward Gettysburg to where half a dozen small tents were pointed out, a little way from the roadside to our left, as General Lee's headquarters for the night. On inquiry I found that he was not there, but had gone to the headquarters of General A. P. Hill, about half a mile nearer Gettysburg.

When we reached the place indicated, a single flickering candle, visible from the road through the open front of a common wall-tent, exposed to view Generals Lee and Hill seated on camp-stools with a map spread upon their knees. Dismounting, I approached on foot. After exchanging the ordinary salutations General Lee directed me to go back to his headquarters and wait for him. I did so, but he did not make his appearance until about 1 o'clock, when he came riding alone, at a slow walk, and evidently wrapped in profound thought.

When he arrived there was not even a sentinel on duty at his tent, and no one of his staff was awake. The moon was high in the clear sky and the silent scene was unusually vivid. As he approached and saw us lying on the grass under a tree, he spoke, reined in his jaded horse, and essayed to dismount. The effort to do so betrayed so much physical exhaustion that I hurriedly rose and stepped forward to assist him, but before I reached his side he had succeeded in alighting, and threw his arm across the saddle to rest, and fixing his eyes upon the ground leaned in silence and almost motionless upon his equally weary horse, - the two forming a striking and never-to-be-forgotten group. The moon shone full upon his massive features and revealed an expression of sadness that I had never before seen upon his face. Awed by his appearance I waited for him to speak until the silence became embarrassing, when, to break it and change the silent current of his thoughts, I ventured to remark, in a sympathetic tone, and in allusion to his great fatigue:

"General, this has been a hard day on you."

He looked up, and replied mournfully:

"Yes, it has been a sad, sad day to us," and immediately relapsed into his thoughtful mood and attitude. Being unwilling again to intrude upon his reflections, I said no more. After perhaps a minute or two, he suddenly straightened up to his full height, and turning to me with more animation and excitement of manner than I had ever seen in him before, for he was a man of wonderful equanimity, he said in a voice tremulous with emotion:

"I never saw troops behave more magnificently than Pick-ett's division of Virginians did to-day in that grand charge upon the enemy. And if they had been supported as they were to have been, - but, for some reason not yet fully explained to me, were not – we would have held the position and the day would have been ours." After a moment's pause he added in a loud voice, in a tone almost of agony, "Too bad! *Too bad!* OH! TOO BAD!"

I shall never forget his language, his manner, and his ap-pearance of mental suffering. In a few moments all emotion was suppressed, and he spoke feelingly of several of his fallen and trusted officers; among others of Brigadier-Generals Armistead, Garnett, and Kemper of Pickett's division. He invited me into his tent, and as soon as we were seated he remarked:

"We must now return to Virginia. As many of our poor wounded as possible must be taken home. I have sent for you, because your men and horses are fresh and in good condition, to guard and conduct our train back to Virginia. The duty will be arduous, responsible, and dangerous, for I am afraid you will be harassed by the enemy's cavalry. How many men have you?"

"About 2100 effective present, and all well mounted, in-cluding McClanahan's six-gun battery of horse artillery."

"I can spare you as much artillery as you require," he said, "but no other troops, as I shall need all I have to return safely by a different and shorter route than yours. The batteries are gen-erally short of ammunition, but you will probably meet a supply I have ordered from Winchester to Williamsport. Nearly all the transportation and the care of all the wounded will be intrusted to you. You will recross the mountain by the Chambersburg road, and then proceed to Williamsport by any route you deem best, and without a halt till you reach the river. Rest there long enough to feed your animals; then ford the river, and do not halt again till you reach Winchester, where I will again communicate with you."

After a good deal of conversation about roads, and the best disposition of my forces to cover and protect the vast train, he directed that the chiefs of his staff departments should be waked up to receive, in my presence, his orders to collect as early next day as possible all the wagons and ambulances which I was to convoy, and have them in readiness for me to take command of them. His medical director [Dr. Lafayette Guild] was charged to see that all the wounded who could bear the rough journey should be placed in the empty wagons and ambulances. He then remarked to me that his general instructions would be sent to me in writing the following morning....

On the morning of July 4th my written instructions, and a large official envelope addressed to President Davis, were handed to me by a staff officer.

It was apparent by 9 o'clock that the wagons, ambulances, and wounded could not be collected and made ready to move till late in the afternoon. General Lee sent to me eight Napoleon guns of the famous Washington Artillery of New Orleans, under the immediate command of Major Eshleman, one of the best artillery officers in the army, a four-gun battery under Captain Tanner, and a Whitworth under Lieutenant Pegram. Hampton's cavalry brigade, then under command of Colonel P. M. B. Young, with Captain James F. Hart's four-gun battery of horse artillery, was ordered to cover the rear of all trains moving under my convoy on the Chambersburg road. These 17 guns and McClanahan's 6 guns gave us 23 pieces in all for the defense of the trains.

Shortly after noon of the 4th the very windows of heaven seemed to have opened. The rain fell in blinding sheets; the meadows were soon overflowed, and fences gave way before the raging streams. During the storm, wagons, ambulances, and artillery carriages by hundreds – nay, by thousands – were assembling in the fields along the road from Gettysburg to Cashtown, in one confused and apparently inextricable mass. As the afternoon wore on there was no abatement in the storm. Canvas was no protection against its fury, and the wounded men lying upon the naked boards of the wagon-bodies were drenched. Horses and mules were blinded and maddened by the wind and water, and became almost unmanageable. The deafening roar of the mingled sounds of heaven and earth all around us made it almost impossible to communicate orders, and equally difficult to execute them.

About 4 P. M. the head of the column was put in motion near Cashtown, and began the ascent of the mountain in the direction of Chambersburg. I remained at Cashtown giving directions and putting in detachments of guns and troops at what I estimated to be intervals of a quarter or a third of a mile. It was found from the position of the head of the column west of the mountain at dawn of the 5th – the hour at which Young's cavalry and Hart's battery began the ascent of the mountain near Cashtown – that the entire column was seventeen miles long when drawn out on the road and put in motion.

As an advance-guard I had placed the 18th Virginia Cavalry, Colonel George W. Imboden, in front with a section of McClanahan's battery. Next to them, by request, was placed an ambulance carrying, stretched side by side, two of North Carolina's most distinguished soldiers, Generals Pender and Scales, both badly wounded, but resolved to bear the tortures of the journey rather than become prisoners. I shared a little bread and meat with them at noon, and they waited patiently for hours for the head of the column to move. The trip cost poor Pender his life. General Scales appeared to be worse hurt, but stopped at Winchester, recovered, and fought through the war.

After dark I set out from Cashtown to gain the head of the column during the night. My orders had been peremptory that there should be no halt for any cause whatever. If an accident should happen to any vehicle, it was immediately to be put out of the road and abandoned. The column moved rapidly, considering the rough roads and the darkness, and from almost every wagon for many miles issued heart-rending wails of agony. For hours I hurried forward on my way to the front, and in all that time I was never out of hearing of the groans and cries of the wounded and dying.

Scarcely one in a hundred had received adequate surgical aid, owing to the demands on the hard-working surgeons from still worse cases that had to be left behind. Many of the wounded in the wagons had been without food for thirty-six hours. Their torn and bloody clothing, matted and hardened, was rasping the tender, inflamed, and still oozing wounds. Very few of the wagons had even a layer of straw in them, and all were without springs. The road was rough and rocky from the heavy washings of the preceding day. The jolting was enough to have killed strong men, if long exposed to it. From nearly every wagon as the teams trotted on, urged by whip and shout, came such cries and shrieks as these:

"O God! why can't I die?"

"My God! will no one have mercy and kill me?"

"Stop! Oh! for God's sake, stop just for one minute; take me out and leave me to die on the roadside."

"I am dying! I am dying! My poor wife, my dear children, what will become of you?"

Some were simply moaning; some were praying, and others uttering the most fearful oaths and execrations that despair and agony could wring from them; while a majority, with a stoicism sustained by sublime devotion to the cause they fought for, endured without complaint unspeakable tortures, and even spoke words of cheer and comfort to their unhappy comrades of less will or more acute nerves. Occasionally a wagon would be passed from which only low, deep moans could be heard. No help could be rendered to any of the sufferers. No heed could be given to any of their appeals. Mercy and duty to the many forbade the loss of a moment in the vain effort then and there to comply with the prayers of the few. On! On! we *must* move on. The storm continued, and the darkness was appalling. There was no time even to fill a canteen with water for a dying man; for except the drivers and the guards, all were wounded and utterly helpless in that vast procession of misery....

Mrs. Roger A. Pryor, from her *Reminiscences of Peace and War*: (3)

In July, General Lee fought and lost the great battle of Gettysburg, which plunged our state into mourning and lamentation. Never can the world read with dry eyes of the charge of Pickett's brigade and the manner in which it was met. "Decry war as we may and ought," says Rhodes in his *History*, " 'breathes there the man with soul so dead' who would not thrill with emotion to claim for his countrymen the men who made that charge and the men who met it? General Lee bore the disaster magnificently. To an officer attempting to place on the shoulders some portion of the blame, General Lee said solemnly, *'All this has been MY fault –* it is *I* that have lost this fight, and you must all help me out of it in the best way you can.'"

The Federal loss in this battle, killed, wounded, and captured, was 23,003, the Confederate 20,451 – making a total of 43,454 good and true men lost, in one battle, to their country. The emblem of mourning hung at many a door among our friends in Richmond and Petersburg....

Constance Cary Harrison, from her *Recollections Grave and Gay*: (4)

In the middle of the hottest season of the year, Hetty and I went into King William County, far as yet from war's alarms, to stay at an old house surrounded by plantations of sorghum and cotton, by means of which its owners hoped to resist the outside pressure of the blockade. The cotton crop, unfamiliar to our eyes, was a beautiful one, from its blossoms of a delicate lemon tint, to the boll, opening to disclose a fairy fall of snow.

We took our first lessons in spinning from an expert old darky woman in the "quarter," and also in weaving the stuffs required to clothe the small army of blacks on the estate. In her cabin we tasted watermelon molasses, and were regaled with genuine ash-cake, wrapped in cabbage leaves, baked under hickory embers upon the hearth, and served with fresh butter and foaming milk, by way of what she called "des a little snack, honey, to keep yer strength up."

What a pretty scene met our gaze as we stood in the doorway of the spinning-woman's hut! Two rows of whitewashed cabins, bowered in foliage and overgrown with morning-glory and scarlet runner, each having its neat patch of ground with corn, sweet potatoes, tomatoes, and cabbage – (Their vegetables beat mine all hollow!" laughingly said the mistress of the house) – the walks between, like the floors of the cabins, swept as clean as the decks of a man-of-war. In chairs before their doors sat the patriarchs and matriarchs, looking out for numerous little darkies who romped and kicked in the sunshine. No sign here of the horrors for which John Brown had died on the scaffold at Harper's Ferry!

All my observation of the colored folk that summer kept me wondering if they could be happier free. For years after the war I kept coming upon wretched homesick specimens of their class in New York, praying aid and counsel of us Southerners of the old regime, in whom they instinctively trusted more than in their representative abolition friends. One of the best women I ever knew, a lecturer and missionary to her race, said to me once: "Some of these people call me 'Miss' and ask me to sit down in their grand parlors in satin chairs while they tell me how well off my people are. Your kind says, 'You, Susan Jones! you're just wet through, tramping the streets; go straight downstairs to my kitchen and get dry and have your dinner.'"

The maid specially detailed to attend to us at the "gret hus" came one night about nine o'clock to my room on the ground floor in the wing, to conduct me to the quarter where I had promised to read the Bible to a few "church members" in the cabin of our spinning friend. We went down long paths lit by the stars alone and embalmed with the scent of sweet flowers after dark; and to my dismay found the quarter in a state of advanced preparation for an "event." The cabin where I was to read, its inner walls lined with pictures cut from magazines, was brilliant with the glare from pitch-pine torches set in the fireplace, while a couple of tallow candles, in brass candlesticks, illumined the pages of the Holy Book, laid open on a spotless pine table beside a split-bottomed arm-chair. Every available space inside and out of the house was filled with negroes in Sunday best, their black, cream, or chocolate faces looking in at windows and open doors. In the foliage out-side, fire-flies were glancing. Near by, a whippoorwill was calling. Not another sound broke the stillness as I, in great embarrassment, began to read.

Soon my equanimity was disturbed by an old woman who sat in the corner rocking her body to and fro. "That's so! Bress Jesus!" she cried out piercingly, and this was the beginning of a fusillade of pious ejaculations, grunts, and moans, which I could end only by shutting the Book and desiring an ancient elder in their church to lead in prayer. Once I could repeat – I have forgot-ten them now – his words, extraordinarily picturesque, at times vividly eloquent. To my surprise, he prayed for the stricken South-ern country and for "our pore sufferin' soldiers in the camps and on the march." He prayed for their "dear old mistis," for everybody present, some specially mentioned, for their reader, in very flatter-ing and touchingly grateful terms, and, lastly, for that "hoary old sinnah Uncle Si, settin' ober da on his own do'-step this blessed minit, hearin' what was read an' scornin' God's Holy Word, he hade a-whitenin' fur de grabe, he soul a-ripenin' for hell's dark do'."

The climax bringing about a perfect tumult of groans and piously abusive comments upon pagan Uncle Si, I was able to make my escape. Susan told me afterward, that the quarter had "no use for Uncle Si, anyways" and had taken this occasion to administer a public rebuke. The meeting was kept up till nearly morning.

From that time I was always the recipient of smiles, kind words, and little gifts from the quarter. A wooden bowl of luscious peaches, fresh from the tree, would be poked through my open window of a morning; or flowers, a couple of fresh eggs, a bag of chenquapins, and even a fat sweet potato, left upon the sill.

The portly cook (whose price was far above rubies!) lost her husband, and on the following Sunday gave him an imposing funeral: returning from which she was escorted, arm-in-arm, by the deacon who had performed the ceremony, an enterprising fellow with an eye to the rich pickings from the "gret hus" kitchen. The following Sunday they were married amid much rejoicing.

Emily, a trim little housemaid, used to petition me to write letters to her fiance, Tom, a neighbor's "boy," who had followed his young master to war. In one of these epistles I was requested, with many giggles, to tell Tom "yes, please, young mistis." On beseeching her to supply words for this avowal, she threw her apron over her head and, tittering, observed: "Why, don' you know, Miss? Jes' de way you does it yerself!"

When I wound up the epistle by bidding Tom "God speed in his efforts to seek the bubble reputation in the quartermaster's department," and asked if she liked the phrase, Emily smiled rapturously. "Why, laws, Miss, I jes knowed you'd turn it off someway grand." Another year, Emily and Tom waited on me in gratitude for my share in their newly wedded bliss.

We went to a "baptism" in a lovely mill-pond and saw the sable clergyman stand knee deep in water beside a little island, beckoning in one after another of the candidates. One of these, proving obstinate to his appeal, remained goggle-eyed upon the bank, staring toward the preacher, when the latter called out persuasively: "Why does yo' tarry, brother? Why don't yo' come to glory? What is it that yo' fear?"

"I'se afeared o' that darned little moccasin on de lawg 'longside o' you," was the answer, and with one bound, not stopping to look back, the celebrant gathered up his skirts and made for the shore and safety.

When we came to leave our sweet asylum for the stern realities and short commons of Richmond, there was an overhauling of our trunks to find what we could afford to give away to Susan and Emily, and an old crone from the quarter, tottering up to our outer door, looked in longingly at the unpacking. A certain antique petticoat of changeable pigeon's-neck silk, used in some of my theatricals, captured her fancy mightily. (A similar one was offered me recently in the show-room of a fashionable dressmaker in Paris.) Finally, she told me if I would let her have it she would "pay me out" with a turkey sent to Richmond as soon as hers were fit to kill. I gave old Dilsey the garment and forgot it. In the late autumn one day, a quaint old back country wagon stopped at our door in town, and the darky driver brought in a box containing not only a splendid fat turkey, but a fine supply of sweet potatoes, some apples, and a bag of chestnuts, with "Dilsey's sarvice, please mistis, and she hopes you find them good eatin'"....

Upon our return to town that autumn, owing to General Meade's ruminant attitude and the consequent inaction of our troops, the streets and our drawing-rooms were well filled with gray figures wearing stars, bars, scrolls, and other insignia of military rank....

Now was instituted the "Starvation Club," of which, as one of the original founders, I can speak with authority. It was agreed between a number of young women that a place for our soldier visitors to meet with us for dancing and chat, once a week, would be a desirable variation upon evening calls in private homes. The hostesses who successively offered their drawing-rooms were among the leaders in society. It was also decided that we should permit no one to infringe the rule of suppressing all refreshment, save the amber-hued water from the classic James. We began by having piano music for the dances, but the male members of the club made up between them a subscription providing a small but good orchestra. Before our first meeting, a committee of girls waited on General Lee to ask his sanction, with this result to the spokeswoman, who had ended with: "If you say no, general, we won't dance a single step!"

"Why, of course, my dear child. My boys need to be heartened up when they get their furloughs. Go on, look your prettiest, and be just as nice to them as ever you can be!"

We even had cotillions, to which everybody contributed favors. The gatherings were the jolliest imaginable. We had constant demands to admit new members, and all foreigners and general officers who visited Richmond were presented to our club, as a means of viewing the best society of the South.

In summoning "spirits from the vasty deep" to record upon these pages, I had occasion to address a question or two, in writing, to a friend of yore, a Virginian who has identified himself with the best intellectual achievement in his State, since the sword he bore through all the battles delivered by the Army of Northern Virginia was laid aside to gather the rust of peaceful years. If it be a crime to quote a passage from the letter he sent me in return, I cry "Peccavi," swearing that I will never reveal his name. No one else living, perhaps, could have written it, and its insertion here is my best excuse:

"Lord! Lord! What a dazzling, wholesome high-bred little society it was! Night after night, I galloped into town to attend dances, charades, what not? and did not get back to my camp until two – three – what matter the hour? – but was always up, fresh as paint, when the reveille bugles blew, and when, a little later on, my first sergeants reported to me as adjutant with their Battery Reports.

"To you and to me, looking back, it was such a blending of a real 'Heroic Age' and a real 'Golden Age' as could come but once in a million years. Everybody knew everybody (in the highest sense of that phrase), and there was youth, and beauty, and devotion, and splendid daring, a jealous honor and an antique patriotism, an utter self-abnegation and utter defiance of fate, a knightly chastity and beautiful surrender (of the coyest maid when her love was going to certain death). God! what a splendid high society that little handful was! Oh! I never talk of it now. People would only say, 'Why there wasn't one of them worth $100,000'"....

Wonderful were the toilettes concocted that festal winter. Maternal party dresses that had done duty at Newport, Saratoga, the White Sulpher Springs, and in Washington and New Orleans ball-rooms, were already worn to rags. One of them would be made to supply the deficiencies of the other until both passed into thin air. The oft-told stories of damask curtains taken down to fabricate into court trains over petticoats of window curtain lace, and of mosquito nettings made up over pink or blue cambric slips, now took shape. Certain it is that girls never looked prettier or danced with more perfect grace than those shut-in war maidens, trying to obey the great general's behest and look their prettiest for the gallant survivors of his legions....

Maj. Heros von Borcke, from his *Memoirs of the Confederate War for Independence*: (5)

With the heat of the month of June my sufferings commenced, and were greatly aggravated by the conflicting rumours which reached me from Lee's army after the battle of Gettysburg. I could scarcely draw my breath, and coughed continually night and day, bringing up quantities of blood with small fragments of the shattered rings of my windpipe, and pieces of clothing which the bullet had carried along with it. I was frequently attacked with fits of suffocation, which sometimes came upon me while walking in the street, and were so violent that I had to be carried home in a state of insensibility resembling death. At last my doctor, who had but little hope of my recovery, recommended me to try the effects of country air; and having received pressing invitations from my friends at Dundee, in Hanover County, I went there towards the end of August....

I had frequent tidings from General Stuart and my comrades, and received from them letters full of friendship and affection. In one of these the General said: - "My dear Von, my camp seems dull and deserted to me since you left. On the battle-field I do not know how to do without you, and feel as if my right arm had been taken away from me"....

Maj. Robert Stiles, from *Four Years Under Marse Robert*: (6)

Some little time since, in a conversation with Mr. George Cary Eggleston, he remarked that, years ago, perhaps during the war, I mentioned to him an estimate of General Meade which I had heard General Lee express, about the time of Meade's appointment to succeed Hooker in command of the Army of the Potomac. I do not now quite see how I could have overheard the remark precisely at the time indicated, but I have no doubt the story, as far as Lee's estimate of Meade is concerned, is essentially true. As the story goes, someone was congratulating Lee upon having "a mediocre man like Meade" as his opponent, suggesting that he would have an easy time with him. But Lee interrupted the speaker, saying with emphasis that General Meade was the most dangerous man who had as yet been opposed to him; that he was not only a soldier of intelligence and ability, but that he was also a conscientious, careful, thorough and painstaking man; that he would make no such mistake in his [Lee's] front as some of his predecessors had made, and that if he made any mistake in Meade's front he would be certain to take advantage of it.

It is noteworthy how exactly this estimate was fulfilled and confirmed, not only at Gettysburg, but in the campaign of the succeeding autumn upon Virginia soil, in which Meade showed himself to be able and cautious, wary and lithe; incomparably superior to Pope or Burnside, or even Hooker. In October, at Bristoe Station, when we were attempting to outflank him, as we had done Pope, he not only escaped by giving such attention to his "lines of retreat" as the latter had boasted he would not give, but he actually inflicted upon us a decided defeat, accentuated by the almost unparalleled capture of five pieces of artillery; and that, when his force engaged was inferior to ours. In November, at the *tete-de-pont* at Rappahannock Bridge, he wrote for us what Colonel Taylor calls "the saddest chapter in the history of this army," by snapping up two brigades, of twelve or fifteen hundred men, and four pieces of artillery, which had been exposed, by an arrangement of his lines more nearly questionable perhaps than any other General Lee was ever known to make. In December, at Mine Run, while he failed in his main design of turning our flank and forcing us to abandon our fortified line on the Rapidan, and so pushing us back on Hanover Junction, and while he got decidedly the worst of the fighting, yet he succeeded in getting away without the overwhelming defeat we hoped to have inflicted upon him; and, upon the whole, no preceding Federal commander of the Army of the Potomac had made anything like as good a showing in an equal number of moves against their great Confederate opponent.

Apropos of the time and the region in which the operations just commented upon occurred, - being the great battlefield of central Virginia, threshed over for three years by the iron flail of war, - Billy sends me what he very justly terms "the most pathetic and harrowing incident of my service in the Army of Northern Virginia." I give it substantially in his own words:

"One day while we were encamped in the Poison Fields of Spottsylvania County, Tom Armistead and I were summoned to Captain McCarthy's quarters. We found him talking to a woman very poorly but cleanly dressed, who seemed in bitter distress. The captain ordered us to go with the woman and bury her child. We went with her to her home, a small house with but two rooms. There we found her mother, an aged woman, and the child, a boy of ten, who had just died of a most virulent case of diphtheria. The father, a soldier in some Virginia regiment, was of course absent, and of neighbors there were none in that war-stricken country.

"Armistead and I bathed and dressed the little body and then had to rip planks off part of the shed room of the house to make something to bury it in, tearing off the palings of the garden to get nails, having no saw and being compelled to cut and break the planks with an axe. Before we had finished the box the battery bugle sounded '*Harness and hitch up'*. We stayed long enough to finish the box and place the body in it, but could not stay to dig the grave. We had to leave these two poor women alone with the unburied child.

"There was not a farm animal, not even a fowl, on the place. How these women and many others in the track of both those great armies lived was then, and always has been, a mystery to me"....

… Ah, love, let us be true
To one another! for the world, which seems
To lie before us like a land of dreams,
So various, so beautiful, so new,
Hath really neither joy, nor love, nor light,
Nor certitude, nor peace, nor help for pain;
And we are hear as on a darkling plain
Swept with confused alarms of struggle and flight,
Where ignorant armies clash by night.
       - Matthew Arnold, Dover Beach (7)

BOOK IV

WINTER (1864)

Waken, lords and ladies gay,
To the greenwood haste away;
We can show you where he lies,
Fleet of foot and tall of size;
We can show the marks he made
When 'gainst the oak his antlers fray'd;
You shall see him brought to bay;
'Waken, lords and ladies gay'....
                    - Sir Walter Scott, "Hunting Song" (1)

RIGHT *Lt. Gen. Jubal A. Early* – Courtesy of Library of Congress

BOOK IV - CHAPTER ONE

The Hammer

Constance Cary Harrison, from her *Recollections Grave and Gay*: (1)

Now came the winter's lull before the new fury of the storm should break forth with the spring. It was evident to all older and graver people that the iron belt surrounding the Southern country was being gradually drawn closer and her vitality in mortal peril of exhaustion. Our armies were dwindling, those of the North increasing with every draft and the payment of liberal bounties. Starved, nearly bankrupt, thousand of our best soldiers killed in battle, their places filled by boys and old men, the Federal Government refusing to exchange prisoners; our exports useless because of armed ships closing in our ports all along the coast, our prospects were of the gloomiest, even though Lee had won victory for our banners in the East. We young ones, who knew nothing and refused to believe in "croakers," kept on with our valiant boasting about our invincible army and the like; but the end was beginning to be in sight....

Edward A. Pollard, from his *Southern History of the War*: (2)

We must take the reader's attention from military campaigns to certain political movements, which, in the fall of 1863, apparently involved more or less distinctly the fortunes of the war.... The Democratic party in the North went into the fall elections of 1863, on the issue of a general opposition to the Lincoln

Administration.... But even on its moderate issues, with reference to the war, which ... proposed only certain constitutional limitations, the Democratic party in the North was badly beaten in the fall elections. From Minnesota to Maine, the Democrats were defeated. In the latter, which was supposed to be the least fanatical of the New England States, the Republicans carried the election by an overwhelming majority. In Ohio, Vallandigham was defeated. He was still in exile. Voorhies, who had proclaimed doctrines somewhat similar to his, in a neighboring State, narrowly escaped being lynched by the soldiers. The elections were followed by a remarkable period of political quiet in the North. Those who had the courage to confront the administration of Lincoln, had either been suppressed by the strong hand of lawless power, or had supinely sought safety in silence. The overthrow of free government in the North was complete....

The North had yet shown no real disposition to abandon the war. The Yankees were still busy with the game of self-glorification.... Their favorite generals were all Napoleons; in the cities mobs of admirers chased them from hotel to hotel; in the New England towns, deputations of school-girls kissed them in public.... These childish displays and vain glory had culminated in an immense banquet given to a Russian fleet in the harbor of New York, at which distinguished Yankee orators declared that the time had come when Russia and the United States were to be taken as twins in civilization and power, to hold in subjugation all others of Christendom, and accomplish the "destiny" of the nineteenth century.

And really this festive fervor but gave insolent expression to an idea that had long occupied thoughtful minds in distant quarters of the world. Christendom was called upon to witness two political murders. While twenty millions of Yankees sought to strangle the Southern Confederacy, fifty millions of Muscovites combined to keep ten or twelve millions of Poles under a detested yoke. In their infamous attempt upon Poland, Russians tried to pass themselves off as the defenders of liberal ideas against Polish aristocracy; and it was declared that the Polish nobility was in rebellion in order not to be forced to emancipate the serfs. "Russia and the United States," said a French writer of the time, "proclaim the liberty of the serf and the emancipation of the slave, but in return both seek to reduce to slavery all who defend liberty and independence."

Liberty of the press, of speech, of public meetings, even the venerable privilege of *habeas corpus*, inherited from England, had already been put under the feet of Abraham Lincoln....

Lt. Gen. Jubal A. Early, from his "Lee Memorial Address," January 19, 1872: (3)

At the close of the year 1863 the enemy was no farther advanced in his oft-repeated effort to capture the Confederate capital, than when Manassas was evacuated, early in the spring of 1862; but, in the Southwest, the fall of Vicksburg, the disaster of Missionary Ridge, and the failure of the campaign in Eastern Tennessee, had not only severed the trans-Mississippi region from the remainder of the Confederacy, but had left all Kentucky and Tennessee firmly in the power of the enemy, and rendered all the lower basin of the Mississippi practically useless to us.

The main army of the West had been compelled to retire to Dalton, in the northwestern corner of Georgia, and, for all useful purposes, the Confederacy was confined to Georgia, North and South Carolina, and the portion of Virginia held by us. It is true that we held posts and had troops in Alabama, Florida, and Mississippi, but they could contribute nothing to the general defense, and the resources of those States were substantially lost to us, at least so far as operations in Virginia were concerned.

This state of things left the enemy at liberty to concentrate his resources against the two principal armies of the Confederacy. Grant was made commander-in-chief of all the armies of the enemy in the spring of 1864, and took his position with the Army of the Potomac in the field, while Sherman was assigned to the command of the army at Chattanooga, which was to operate against ours at Dalton.

By the 1st of May Grant had accumulated an army of more than one hundred and forty-one thousand men on the north of the Rapidan; and General Lee's army on the south bank, including two of Longstreet's divisions, which had returned from Tennessee, was under fifty thousand [Lt. Col. Walter H. Taylor, p. 125, says sixty-four thousand] men of all arms.

Grant's theory was to accumulate the largest numbers practicable against us, so as, by constant 'hammering,' to destroy our army 'by mere attrition if in no other way.' Besides the army under Grant, in Culpepper, there was near fifty thousand men in Washington and Baltimore, and the military control of the railroads and the telegraph, as well as an immense number of steam transports, rendered it an easy matter to reinforce him indefinitely.

On the 4th of May he crossed the Rapidan on our right to the Wilderness, to get between us and Richmond. General Lee advanced promptly to attack him and thwart his purpose; and then ensued that most wonderful campaign from the Rapidan to the James, in which the ever-glorious Army of Northern Virginia grappled its gigantic antagonist in a death-struggle, which continued until the latter was thrown off, crippled and bleeding, to the cover of the James and Appomattox Rivers, where it was enabled to recruit and renew its strength for another effort.

Two days of fierce battle were had in the Wilderness, and our little army never struck more rapid and vigorous blows. Grant was compelled to move off from our front, and attempt to accomplish his purpose by another flank movement, but General Lee promptly intercepted him at Spottsylvania Court-House; where again occurred a series of desperate engagements, in which, though a portion of our line was temporarily broken, and we sustained a loss which we could ill afford, yet Grant's army was so crippled that it was unable to resume the offensive until it had been reinforced from Washington and Baltimore to the full extent of forty thousand men. But General Lee received no reinforcements; and yet Grant, after waiting six days for his, when they did arrive, was again compelled to move off from us, and attempt another flank-movement, under cover of the network of difficult water-courses around and east of Spottsylvania Court-House.

Never had the wonderful powers of our great chief, and the unflinching courage of his small army, been more conspicuously displayed than during the thirteen days at this place. One of his three corps commanders had been disabled by wounds at the Wilderness, and another was too sick to command his corps, while he himself was suffering from a most annoying and weakening disease. In fact, nothing but his own determined will enabled him to keep the field at all; and it was there rendered more manifest than ever that he was the head and front, the very life and soul, of his army....

Maj. Heros von Borcke, from his *Memoirs of the Confederate War for Independence*: (4)

As my health grew stronger I tried repeatedly, after the opening of the spring campaign, to take the field again, but each time I was severely punished for my imprudence by being thrown upon a sick-bed for weeks, and I had to confine my ambition to the discharge of office duty in Richmond, while General Lee was fighting the grand battles of the Wilderness and Spottsylvania....

On the morning of the 11th May 1864, Richmond was thrown once more into a state of excitement by the rapid advance against it of the Federal cavalry under General Sheridan, who had managed to march around our lines. Several brigades of infantry hastened from the south side of the James River to the defense of the city; the militia was called out, and all expected that the outer lines of fortifications would every moment become the scene of a serious combat. Everything continued quiet, however, in that direction until about eleven o'clock, when a sudden cannonade sounded in the rear of the enemy – the indefatigable Stuart having followed in their track, and with the small force, which was all he had been able, owing to the rapid marching, to take with him, being now enabled to cut off the Federal line of retreat.

The sound of our light guns, which I recognized so well, did not fail to rouse me into a state of excitement; and as an old war-horse prances and curvets at the shrill ringing of the trumpet, I felt the blood pour like electric fire through my veins, and rushed about in feverish uneasiness. I fancied I heard my sword rattling in its scabbard to summon me to the scene of conflict by my General's side; but, as I was separated from my own chargers, I tried to borrow a horse for the occasion from one of my many friends. All my endeavors to this effect, however, were vain; everybody had already hastened to the front, and, unable to bear the suspense any longer, I impressed by force one of the horses from the first Government team I came across, and, throwing my saddle on its back, I hurried off to the scene of action.

The animal I had laid hold of was a miserable little pony, but I managed to spur him forward at a tolerably swift pace; and rapidly passing our double line of intrenchments, I soon reached our last infantry pickets, where I endeavored to ascertain the exact position of our own troops and of the enemy. As the hostile force lay immediately between ours, it was not easy to get this information; but a road was pointed out to me with such assurance that it would take me to General Stuart without bringing me into collision with the Yankees, that I galloped along it with very little precaution, and had just crossed over a bridge, when, from the woods on the right and left, a scattered band of Federal cavalry bore down upon me with loud shouts, firing their revolvers at me, and demanding my surrender. I immediately turned my pony's head round, and galloped off to the rear with all the speed I could, and an exciting chase now ensued for several miles, till it was put a stop to by the fire of our pickets....

It was sufficiently evident, by the sound of the firing, that Stuart was hardly pressed, and I hastened at once to General Bragg, commanding our infantry, which, from a succession of reinforcements, was now of considerable strength, begging him at once to advance several brigades to the assistance of Stuart. The cautiousness characteristic of that general, however, induced him to resist my appeals, and finding further effort useless, I slowly retraced my steps to Richmond. The rapid run and the excitement of my pursuit had proved too much for my strength, and I had scarcely reached the outskirts of the town, when, as I approached a friend's house, the blood began to stream from my mouth, and I was carried, half fainting, to my temporary domicile at Mr. P.'s, where I was immediately put to bed.

After a long and refreshing sleep, I was awakened suddenly about daybreak by the voice of Dr. Brewer, Stuart's brother-in-law, who informed me that my General had been wounded severely, and carried during the night to his place, where he was anxious to see me. Forgetting my own condition at these sad tidings, I dressed myself in a few minutes and hastened to the bedside of my dear friend, whom I found in a small room of the Doctor's house, surrounded by most of the members of his Staff. He received me with a smile, saying, "I'm glad you've come, my dear Von; you see they've got me at last, but don't feel uneasy. I don't think I'm so badly wounded as you were, and I hope I shall get over it as you did." He then recounted to me all the incidents of the combat, and the manner in which he had been wounded.

Hoping every hour to hear of General Bragg's attack, which in all probability would have resulted in the annihilation of the whole force of the enemy, he had successfully resisted their efforts to break through his lines, and for more than six hours had fought with eleven hundred men against eight thousand. At about four o'clock, the Federals succeeded by a general charge in breaking and driving back one of our regiments which General Stuart was rallying in an open field. When continuing their advance the enemy were met by the 1st Virginia and driven back again in confusion. Seeing near him some of the dismounted Federal cavalry, who were running off on the opposite side of a high fence, Stuart rode up to them calling on them to surrender, and firing at them as they continued their flight. He had just discharged the last barrel of his revolver when the hindmost of the fugitives, coming close up to the fence, fired his revolver at him, the ball taking effect in the lower part of the stomach and traversing the whole body. Stuart, finding himself severely wounded, and the enemy at the same time renewing their attack, turned his charger quickly round and galloped half a mile further to the rear, where he was taken from his horse nearly insensible from loss of blood, and sent in an ambulance to Richmond.

During the early part of the morning the General felt comparatively easy, and the physician entertained great hope that the wound might not prove fatal. Towards noon, however, a change took place for the worse…. As evening approached mortification set in, and no hopes could any longer be entertained…. I had been sitting on his bed, holding his hand in mine, and handing him the ice, which he ate in great abundance, and which was applied to his burning hot wounds to cool them. Drawing me towards him, and grasping my hand firmly, he said, "My dear Von, I am sinking fast now, but before I die I want you to know that I never loved a man as much as yourself. I pray your life may be long and happy; look after my family after I'm gone, and be the same true friend to my wife and children that you have been to me." These were the last connected words he spoke; during the next few hours the paroxysms of pain became more frequent and violent, until at about seven o'clock death relieved the suffering hero from his agonies….

On the evening of the 13th, in the midst of the roaring of the enemy's cannon, which reached us from Drewry's Bluff, we carried Stuart's remains to the beautiful cemetery at Hollywood, near Richmond, where he lies in a simple grave by the side of his beloved little daughter Flora….

The Anvil

Lt. Col. Walter Taylor, from *Four Years with General Lee*: (1)

The army under General Grant was at this time heavily reinforced from Washington. In his official report of this campaign he says, "The 13th, 14th, 15th, 16th, 17th, and 18th (of May), were consumed in maneuvering and awaiting the arrival of reinforcements from Washington." In numerical strength his army so much exceeded that under General Lee that, after covering the entire Confederate front with double lines of battle, he had in reserve a large force with which to extend his flank, and compel a corresponding movement on the part of his adversary, in order to keep between him and his coveted prize – the capital of the Confederacy.

On the 18th another assault was directed against the Confederate lines, but it produced no impression. No effort was made after this – the task was a hopeless one, and was reluctantly relinquished.

On the night of the 20th, General Grant started on another flank movement in the direction of Bowling Green. General Lee in order to intercept him moved to Hanover Junction.... The gage of battle proffered by General Lee at Hanover Junction was declined by General Grant, who, in order to extricate his army from a position of some embarrassment, about the 26th of May, recrossed to the north side of the North Anna River, and made another *detour* to the east. General Lee moved upon a parallel line....

On the 30th of May General Lee was in line of battle, with his left at Atlee's Station.... After feeling the Confederate position, attack was declined by the enemy. By another gyratory movement of the kind so persistently pursued by General Grant in this campaign, the two armies again gravitated east, and were soon (June 3d) face to face on the historic field of Cold Harbor.

Here, gallant but fruitless efforts were made by General Grant to pierce or drive back the army under General Lee. The Confederates were protected by temporary earthworks, and while under cover of these were gallantly assailed by the Federals. But in vain: the assault was repulsed along the whole line, and the carnage on the Federal side was frightful. I well recall having received a report after the assault from General Hoke – whose division reached the army just previous to this battle – to the effect that the ground in his entire front, over which the enemy had charged, was literally covered with their dead and wounded; and that up to that time he had not had a single man killed. No wonder that, when the command was given to renew the assault, the Federal soldiers sullenly and silently declined to advance. After some disingenuous proposals, General Grant finally asked a truce to enable him to bury his dead. Soon after this he abandoned his chosen line of operations, and moved his army to the south side of the James River.

The struggle from the Wilderness to this point covered a period of over one month; during which time there had been an almost daily encounter of hostile arms, and the Army of Northern Virginia had placed *hors de combat* of the army under General Grant a number equal to its entire numerical strength at the commencement of the campaign, and, notwithstanding its own heavy losses and the reinforcements received by the enemy, still presented an impregnable front to its opponent, and constituted an insuperable barrier to General Grant's "On to Richmond!"

After an unsuccessful effort to surprise and capture Petersburg – which was prevented by the skill of Generals Beauregard and Wise, and the bravery of the troops, consisting in part of militia and home-guards – and a futile endeavor to seize the Richmond & Petersburg Railroad, General Grant concentrated his army south of the Appomattox River. General Lee, whom he had not been able to defeat in the open field, was still in his way, and the siege of Petersburg was begun....

Mrs. Roger A. Pryor, from *Reminiscences of Peace and War*: (2)

As soon as the enemy brought up their siege guns of heavy artillery, they opened on the city with shell without the slightest notice, or without giving opportunity for the removal of non-combatants, the sick, the wounded, or the women and chil- dren. The fire was at first directed toward the Old Market, pre- sumably because of the railroad depot situated there, about which soldiers might be supposed to collect. But the guns soon enlarged their operations, sweeping all the streets in the business part of the city, and then invading the residential region....

To persons unfamiliar with the infernal noise made by the screaming, ricocheting, and bursting of shells, it is impossible to describe the terror and demoralization which ensued. Some families who could not leave the besieged city dug holes in the ground, five or six feet deep, covered with heavy timbers banked over with earth, the entrance facing opposite the batteries from which the shells were fired. They made these bomb-proofs safe, at least, and thither the family repaired when heavy shelling com- menced. General Lee seemed to recognize that no part of the city was safe, for he immediately ordered the removal of all the hospitals.... There were three thousand sick and wounded, many of them too ill to be moved. A long, never-ending line of wagons, carts, everything that could run on wheels, passed my door, until there were no more to pass....

Lt. Col. Walter Taylor, from *Four Years with General Lee*: (3)

Having failed to obtain possession of Petersburg by surprise, and General Lee being now well established in his line of defense, General Grant determined upon the method of slow approaches, and proceeded to invest the city and its brave defenders by a line of earthworks and mines. While with his constantly-increasing numbers General Grant undertook to tighten the ligature thus applied to the carotid artery of the Confederacy, General Sherman was sent upon his desolating expedition through the States of Georgia and South Carolina to add the policy of *starvation* to that of *attrition* inaugurated a few months previous. After this manner it was proposed to exhaust and wear out the people who could not be beaten in a trial of arms....

John S. Wise, from *The End of an Era*: (4)

Much of the month of July we passed in the trenches. Father was in command of Petersburg, and Colonel J. Thomas Goode commanded the brigade, but we visited it almost daily. It was assigned to Bushrod Johnson's division, and our position was next to the South Carolinians under Elliot. Our left was about a hundred yards south of a bastion known as Elliott's salient.

Life in the trenches was indescribably monotonous and uncomfortable. In time of sunshine, the reflected heat from the new red-clay embankments was intense, and unrelieved by shade or breeze; and in wet weather one was ankle-deep in tough, clinging mud. The incessant shelling and picket-firing made extreme caution necessary in moving about; and each day, almost each hour, added to the list of casualties. The opposing lines were not over two hundred yards apart, and the distance between the rifle-pits was about one hundred yards. Both sides had attained accurate marksmanship, which they practiced with merciless activity in picking off men. One may fancy the state of mind of soldiers thus confined, who knew that even the act of going to a spring for water involved risk of life or limb....

All during the month of July, the fact that the enemy was mining in our front was discussed and accepted by the troops. How soldiers get their information is one of the mysteries of the service, yet they are often in possession of more accurate knowledge than those high in authority. For some time the reports about the mine were exceedingly vague. More than one Union picket had hinted at a purpose to "send you to Heaven soon," or threatened that they were "going to blow you up next week." For some time, no less than three salients were discussed as the possible points. Our engineers had some sort of information, for countermining was begun at all these salients.... Whatever doubts the engineers may have felt, the privates knew where the works were being mined. Elliott's men told the fellows on the left of our brigade all about it long before the explosion. Our men would go down there, and, lying on the ground with Elliott's men, would listen to the work going on below, and come back and tell all about it.

About daybreak, July 30, the mine was exploded.... The ground trembled for an instant; an immense mass of earth, cannon, timbers, human beings, and smoke shot skyward, paused for an instant in mid-air, illuminated by the flash of the explosion; and; bursting asunder, fell back into and around the smoking pit. The dense cloud of smoke drifted off, tinged by the faint rays of sunrise; a silence like that of death succeeded the tremendous report. Nearly three hundred Confederates were buried in the debris of the crater; their comrades on either side adjacent to the fatal spot fled from a sight so much resembling the day of judgment. To the south of the crater, our lines were unmanned even as far as our brigade, and a similar condition existed on its northern side; at least three hundred yards of our lines were deserted by their defenders, and left at the mercy of the assaulting columns. Beyond that breach not a Confederate infantryman stood to dispute their passage into the heart of Petersburg....

The Union troops designated for the assault, instead of drawing inspiration from the sight of the breach they had effected, actually appeared to recoil from the havoc. For some time no demonstration followed the explosion; when they finally advanced, it was not with the eagerness of grenadiers or guardsmen, but with rushes and pauses of uncertainty; and when they reached our lines, instead of treating the opening as a mere passageway to their objective point beyond, they halted, peeped, and gaped into the pit, and then, with the stupidity of sheep, *followed their bell-wethers into the crater itself*, where, huddled together, all semblance of organization vanished....

General Elliott promptly disposed the portion of his brigade left to him in the traverses commanding the crater; Colonel Goode, commanding our brigade, concentrated on his left flank, and with the fragment of Elliott's brigade, which was driven into ours by the explosion, opened a brisk fire upon the assailants. From our ten-inch and eight-inch mortars in the rear of the line, a most accurate fire was opened upon the troops in the breach; and our batteries to north and south began to pour a deadly storm of shell and canister upon their crowded masses. The situation looked desperate for us, nevertheless, for it was all our infantry could do to hold their lines, and not a man could be spared to meet an advance upon Blandford cemetery heights, which lay before the Union troops. At this juncture, heroic John Haskell, of South Carolina, came dashing up the plank road with two light batteries, and from a position near the cemetery began the most effective work of the day.... Haskell, almost superhuman in the energy of his defense, "flamed amazement" upon the foe....

General Lee immediately sent Colonel Venable, of his staff, direct to Mahone, with instructions to come with two brigades of his division to Blandford cemetery to support the artillery.... For the first time during the day, a line of infantry was between our guns and the enemy....

Mahone formed his troops for battle.... At the command "Forward!" the men sprang to their feet; advanced at a run in perfect alignment; absolutely refrained from firing until within a few feet of the enemy; then, with their guns almost upon the bodies of their foes, delivered a deadly fire, and, rushing upon them with bayonets and clubbed muskets, drove them pell-mell back into the intrenchments which they had just left.... Our fellows seized the muskets abandoned by the retreating enemy, and threw them like pitchforks into the huddled troops over the ramparts. Screams, groans, and explosions throwing up human limbs made it a scene of awful carnage....

About one o'clock, the Alabama brigade of Mahone's division, under Saunders, arrived upon the scene, formed and charged, and the white flag went up from the crater. Out of it into our lines filed as prisoners eleven hundred and one Union troops, including two brigade commanders, and we captured twenty-one standards and several thousand of small arms. Over a thousand of the enemy's dead were in and about the breach, and his losses exceeded five thousand effective troops, while our lines were re-established just where they were when the battle began.

The crater fight was not only one of the bloodiest, but one of the most brutal of the war. It was the first time Lee's army had encountered negroes, and their presence excited in the troops indignant malice such as had characterized no former conflict. To the credit of the blacks be it said that they advanced in better order and pushed forward farther than the whites, on that day so unfortunate for the Union cause.... On the other hand, our men, inflamed to relentless vengeance by their presence, disregarded the rules of warfare which restrained them in battle with their own race, and brained and butchered the blacks until the slaughter was sickening....

The prisoners were corralled at Poplar Lawn, in Petersburg. It was soon discovered that nearly all the negroes were from eastern Virginia, many of them owned by the men they were fighting. A notice was posted permitting owners to reclaim their property, and the negroes were delighted at the prospect of being treated as slaves, instead of being put to death or sent to a Confederate military prison….

It seems fitting to close this ghastly narrative with one ludicrous incident, which shows that no situation is so bloody or so tragic that it has not some episode to relieve its horrors. In our brigade was a young fellow who, while fighting gallantly at the traverse near the crater, received a bullet in the forearm. His wound was dressed, and he was given a ten days' furlough. He was from eastern Virginia, and his home was in the Union lines. He had no friends, no money, and nowhere to go. In this condition, he was wandering about the streets of Petersburg the day after the crater fight, when his eye fell upon the notice to owners that they might reclaim their slaves from the prisoners. Thinking that possibly he might find one of his father's slaves among them, he wandered down to Poplar Lawn. In vain he sought for a familiar face, and was turning away, when an attractive, smiling young darkey caught his eye and said, "Boss, fur God sake, claim me fur yo' nigger."

"What do you mean, you rascal? I never saw you before," was the reply.

"I know it, sah," said the darkey; "but ef I says I belongs to you, who gwine to dispute it, if you don't?"

"If I had you, I'd sell you to-morrow," was the quick reply of the young fellow, whose eye brightened with a happy thought.

"I doan' keer ef you does sell me, sah," said the darkey. "Dat's a heap better dan goin' to a Confederick prison pen."

"Done!" said the soldier; "when I come back here, you speak to me and call me 'Mars' Ben,' and I'll attend to the rest."

So out he went, and soon came back; and, as he went searching for his slaves, accompanied by an officer in charge, the darkey greeted him with "How you do, Mars' Ben?" Then Ben swore at him, and denounced him for his ingratitude and desire to kill his master and benefactor, and they carried it off so well that no one suspected the ruse, and the darkey was delivered to "Mars'

Ben" as his owner, and "Mars' Ben" took him to Richmond and sold him for $5000 in Confederate money. "Mars' Ben" had a great furlough with that $5000. At the end of ten days, he returned to duty with a new suit of clothes and fed like a fighting-cock, but without a dollar in his pocket. The darkey went to some plantation and never saw a prison pen, and a year afterward was a free citizen of the United States, and probably wound up his career in some scalawag legislature, or even as a member of Congress - who knows? Such things were possible in those days.

A short while ago, I met Ben. He is gray-headed now. I asked him where he was going. He said to a protracted meeting. He told me he had become religious, and said he wished I would reform.

"Is it an experience meeting, Ben?" said I.

"Yes," said he.

"Have you ever told them about that darkey you sold after the crater fight?" said I.

"Now, look here, old fellow," said he, growing confidential, and with a genuine touch of pitiful pleading in his voice, "I wish you would not give me away about that thing. I have prayed for forgiveness for that many a night. But I don't believe the Lord wants me to expose myself before my neighbors, and I hope you will not." I agreed to spare him, and so I will; but, if necessity should demand it, I can put my hand upon him now, within eight hours' ride from the spot on which I write....

BOOK IV - CHAPTER THREE

Fire and Sword

Senator John Warwick Daniel, from *Speeches and Orations of John Warwick Daniel*: (1)

The valley campaign of 1864 had its beginning yonder at Cold Harbor, in sight of the spires of Richmond…. Soon after Cold Harbor, Lee communicated to [Lt. Gen. Jubal A.] Early that he was maturing plans for offensive operations against Grant, and desired him to take the initiative with his corps. "We must destroy," he said, "this army of Grant's before he gets to James River. If he gets there it will become a siege, and then it will become a mere question of time." But while Grant was slipping off to Petersburg a new danger now threatened Lee in his rear; for war in the Valley again lifted its angry head.

On the 15th of May Breckenridge had sharply repulsed Sigel's column at New Market, the cadets of the Virginia Military Institute making a gallant charge, to the admiration of both armies, and capturing guns from veterans, at a loss to themselves of one to every five killed or wounded. Breckenridge had hastened with his slender division to join Lee at Cold Harbor, and after that battle had been fought, wheeled right about to meet the same force which, reinforced, and now commanded by Major-General David Hunter, was marching up the Valley from Harrisonburg, with 8,500 men. On June 5th Hunter had defeated and slain the gallant cavalry General, W. E. Jones, at Piedmont, in Augusta. Three days later, June 8th, Crook and Averill had joined him at Staunton with 10,000 men, and now with this united force, 18,500 strong, he … on June 12th was within forty miles of Lynchburg, at Lexington, Virginia, where he burned the Virginia Military Institute and Governor Letcher's home, and sacked Washington College.

General Lee on that day ordered Lieutenant-General Early, commanding the Second Corps, to be ready to move at 3 a. m. on the morrow.... Their orders were to move to the Valley, strike Hunter, destroy him if possible, and threaten Washington.... The battle-scarred and battle-worn veterans destined for this under-taking contained the men who, under "Stonewall" Jackson, had won the name of the "Foot Cavalry of the Valley." During the month of May ... the rank and file of the corps was now reduced to 8,000 muskets....

On the 16th Early was at the Rivanna, near Charlottesville, having marched over eighty miles in four days, and there he re-ceived a telegram from General Breckenridge, at Lynchburg, that Hunter was at Liberty, in Bedford county, about twenty-five miles from that place....

At 1 o'clock, June 17th, Early reached Lynchburg. Not a moment was to spare, for as Ramseur's and Gordon's troops went at quick time through the streets of the town, Hunter was in sight advancing in line of battle on its southern border, and McCaus-land's and Imboden's brave but weary cavalrymen were being driven back. The few troops of Breckinridge, under Wharton - in-valids from the hospitals, the old men of the town in an extempo-re battalion of silver grays, with five or six guns of horse artillery and the reduced cavalry brigades of Imboden and McCausland, and the battalion of cadets from the Virginia Military Institute - constituted our whole force....

As Hunter's skirmishers were pushing close to the town, and as the cavalry were falling back before them, a few pieces of artillery near the toll-gate, under Lieutenant Carter Berkley, were doing their best to stop the oncomers. In this condition Tinsley, the bugler of the Stonewall Brigade, came trotting up the road, sounding the advance, and behind him came the skirmishers of Ramseur's Division with rapid strides. Just then the artillerists saw through the smoke the broad, white slouch hat and the black feather of "Old Jube," who rode amongst them and, looking to-ward the enemy, exclaimed: "No buttermilk rangers after you now, damn you!" ... Poor Tinsley! his last bugle call, like the bagpipes of Lucknow, foretold the rescue of Lynchburg; but on that field he found in a soldier's duty and with a soldier's glory, a soldier's death.

On the afternoon of the 18th, Hunter, with his cavalry on each wing, his two infantry divisions and his artillery in the center, advanced to the assault, but the attack was feeble and quickly repulsed.... Early was hot upon his heels, McCausland leading, with his cavalry. The night of the 19th Ramseur drove his rear guard through Liberty, twenty-five miles away. On the 21st, McCausland, always enterprising, struck him again at Hanging Rock, in Roanoke county, capturing some guns and prisoners, and Hunter passed on through Craig county to West Virginia....

While Hunter's men were reposing under the great oaks at White Sulpher Springs [West Virginia], Early's men were moving to Staunton, where he arrived June 25th.... On the 28th of June this force started up the Valley; July 3rd it was at Winchester; July 4th at Shepherdstown; July 6th it drove the enemy into his works at Harper's Ferry and Maryland Heights.... Early passed swiftly on through the gaps of the South Mountain, and on the 9th confronted General Lew Wallace, strongly posted ... on the banks of the Monocacy, between six and seven thousand strong. Right at this force Early hurled his men, and after a fierce, decisive fight that reddened the river for a hundred yards with blood, he drove it from the field....

While the alarm-bells were ringing in Baltimore that Sunday morning, July 10th, Harvey Gilmore struck the Philadelphia and Wilmington railroad at Magnolia, and captured Major-General Franklin, while Bradley Johnson, with his brigade, occupied Towsontown, Westminster, and Reistertown, and tore up the Northern Central railroad at Cockeysville, and Early pushed on to Rockville.

At 11 o'clock, July 11th, Early's head of column ... appeared in front of Fort Stevens, on the edge of Washington, the National Capitol looming up in full view. At half-past 1 o'clock Rodes' skirmishers were deployed and the big guns of Fort Stevens sent them a loud reception. While the sturdy infantry that had trudged from Cold Harbor came struggling forward on the dusty, sun-baked roads, Generals Early and Rodes rode upon the field.

Very different scenes were transpiring in the Federal lines. Down at the wharf President Lincoln was receiving the Sixth Corps and a part of the Nineteenth Corps, which was arriving by transports coming up the Potomac River. As Generals Early and Rodes, on horseback, surveyed the situation, a cloud of dust beyond the earthworks denoted the coming lines. Presently a line leaped over the works, and as their skirmishers deployed in the open field, General Rodes exclaimed, "They are no hundred-days men, General."

A council of war was held that night between Early, Breckinridge, Gordon, Rodes, and Ramseur, and it was resolved to storm the lines at daybreak, unless the revelations of the night should lead to a change of conclusion. Before dawn a message came from that enterprising [cavalry] officer, General Bradley T. Johnson, who had pushed on to the suburbs of Baltimore, that two corps of Grant's army had arrived at Washington, and, reluctantly, Early determined to withdraw.

As he retreated a portion of the Sixth Corps advanced to attack, while President Lincoln and some members of his Cabinet looked on from Fort Stevens. This affair lost to General Bidwell, the United States officer in command, 280 men, with a slight loss to Early, who now turned towards Virginia....

The "foot cavalry" paused near Leesburg, July 14th and 15th, and soon "march and fight" is again the watchword. Their situation is perilous, for a column, commanded by General H. G. Wright, consisting of the Sixth and Nineteenth corps, is moving on their rear from Washington, while Hunter's army, which had returned from the Ohio river by railroad, has united with Sigel at Harper's Ferry, and this force has moved under Major-General Crook, down into Loudoun county. To slip between them is the problem. Early solved it....

Grant now wrote to Halleck to send back to him the Sixth and Nineteenth corps, before Early could get back to Lee; but Early was too quick for him. On the 22nd Early posted himself across Cedar Creek near Strasburg. On the 23d news came which proved to be correct, that Wright's column had returned to Washington, where transports were ready to convey them to Grant at Petersburg and that Crook and Averill had united at Kernstown.

Quick as an eagle swoops upon its prey, Early leaped upon Crook, who commanded the Army of West Virginia, consisting of Hunter's and Sigel's forces and Averill's cavalry, and there where Jackson and Shields had such rough work, he rolled up Crook's flanks [and] drove him from the field…. This flying and broken army six weeks before had defeated and killed General Jones. It had now had a second defeat from Early's hands; and when Grant heard the news he sent another division of the Nineteenth Corps to Washington, instead of the troops there continuing their movements to return to him.

The 29th finds Early on the Potomac and McCausland at Chambersburg, where, in default of payment of $100,000 levied upon the town, in retaliation for Hunter's excesses in Virginia, he, under Early's orders, put it to the flames….

Lt. Gen. Jubal A. Early, from his *Memoir of the Last Year of the War for Independence*: (2)

The scenes on Hunter's route from Lynchburg had been truly heart-rending. Houses had been burned, and helpless women and children left without shelter. The country had been stripped of provisions and many families left without a morsel to eat. Furniture and bedding had been cut to pieces, and old men and women and children robbed of all the clothing they had except that on their backs. Ladies trunks had been rifled and their dresses torn to pieces in mere wantonness. Even the negro girls had lost their little finery. We now had renewed evidences of the outrages committed by Hunter's orders in burning and plundering private houses. We saw the ruins of a number of houses to which the torch had been applied by his orders. At Lexington he had burned the Military Institute, with all of its contents, including its library and scientific apparatus; and Washington College had been plundered and the statue of Washington stolen. The residence of Ex-Governor Letcher at that place had been burned by orders, and but a few minutes given Mrs. Letcher and her family to leave the house. In the same county a most excellent Christian gentleman, a Mr. Creigh, had been hung, because, on a former occasion, he had killed a straggling and marauding Federal soldier while in the act of insulting and outraging the ladies of his family. These are but some of the outrages committed by Hunter or his orders, and I will not insult the memory of the ancient barbarians of the North by calling them "acts of Vandalism." If those old barbarians were savage and cruel, they at least had the manliness and daring of rude soldiers, with occasional traits of magnanimity. Hunter's deeds were those of a malignant and cowardly fanatic, who was better qualified to make war upon helpless women and children than upon armed soldiers....

On [July 2nd] we passed through Newtown where several houses, including that of a Methodist minister, had been burned by Hunter's orders, because a part of [Col. John S.] Mosby's command had attacked a train of supplies for Sigel's force, at this place. The original order was to burn the whole town, but the officer sent to execute it had revolted at the cruel mandate of his superior, and another had been sent who but partially executed it, after having forced the people to take an oath of allegiance to the United States to save their houses. Mosby's Battalion, though called "guerillas" by the enemy, was a regular organization in the Confederate Army, and was merely serving on detached duty under General Lee's orders. The attack on the train was an act of legitimate warfare, and the order to burn Newtown, and the burning of the houses mentioned were most wanton, cruel, unjustifiable, and cowardly....

On the 26th we moved to Martinsburg.... While at Martinsburg, it was ascertained, beyond all doubt, that Hunter had been
again indulging in his favorite mode of warfare, and that, after his
return to the Valley, while we were near Washington, among other
outrages, the private residences of Mr. Andrew Hunter, a member
of the Virginia Senate, Mr. Alexander R. Boteler, an ex-member of
the Confederate Congress, as well as of the United States Congress, and Edmund I. Lee, a distant relative of General Lee, all
in Jefferson County, with their contents, had been burned by his
orders, only time enough being given for the ladies to get out of
the houses. A number of towns in the South, as well as private
country houses, had been burned by the Federal troops, and the
accounts had been heralded forth in some of the Northern papers
in terms of exultation, and gloated over by their readers, while
they were received with apathy by others. I now came to the conclusion that we had stood this mode of warfare long enough, and
that it was time to open the eyes of the people of the North to its
enormity, by an example in the way of retaliation....

I had often seen delicate ladies, who had been plundered,
insulted and rendered desolate by the acts of our most atrocious
enemies, and while they did not call for it, yet in the anguished
expressions of their features while narrating their misfortunes,
there was a mute appeal to every manly sentiment of my bosom
for retribution which I could no longer withstand....

The town of Chambersburg in Pennsylvania was selected
as the one on which retaliation should be made, and McCausland
was ordered to proceed with his brigade and that of Johnson and
a battery of artillery to that place, and demand of the municipal
authorities the sum of $100,000 in gold, or $500,000 in United
States currency, as a compensation for the destruction of the
houses named and their contents; and, in default of payment, to
lay the town in ashes, in retaliation for the burning of those houses and others in Virginia, as well as for the towns which had been
burned in other Southern States. A written demand to that effect
was sent to the municipal authorities, and they were informed
what would be the result of a failure or refusal to comply with it.

I desired to give the people of Chambersburg an opportunity of saving their town, by making compensation for part of the injury done, and hoped that the payment of such a sum would have the desired effect, and open the eyes of the people of other towns at the North, to the necessity of urging upon their government the adoption of a different policy....

On the 30th of July McCausland reached Chambersburg, and made the demand as directed, reading to such of the authorities as presented themselves the paper sent by me. The demand was not complied with, the people stating that they were not afraid of having their town burned, and that a Federal force was approaching. The policy pursued by our army on former occasions had been so lenient, that they did not suppose the threat was in earnest this time, and they hoped for speedy relief. McCausland, however, proceeded to carry out his orders, and the greater part of the town was laid in ashes.

For this act I, alone, am responsible, as the officers engaged in it were simply executing my orders, and had no discretion left them. Notwithstanding the lapse of time which has occurred, and the result of the war, I am perfectly satisfied with my conduct on this occasion, and see no reason to regret it....

Maj. John Warwick Daniel, from *Speeches and Orations of John Warwick Daniel*: (3)

Grant had been greatly stirred up by Early's movements, and Hunter infinitely mystified, just as Early calculated they would be. On the 4th of August Grant jumped upon the train for City Point, took a steamer, and posted direct through Washington for Monocacy. There he found Hunter, who had started to Richmond and landed at White Sulphur Springs, the Ohio River, and finally at Monocacy.

He asked Hunter an embarrassing question: "Where is the enemy?" He replied that he did not know, and was so embarrassed with orders from Washington that he had lost all trace of the enemy. Grant told him that Sheridan was in Washington with one cavalry division and another on the way, and suggested that he (Hunter) should make his headquarters at Cumberland, Baltimore, or elsewhere and give Sheridan command in the Valley. Hunter asked to be relieved, and was relieved, to the equal relief of his foot-sore excursionists. The upshot was that Sheridan was placed in command....

Lt. Gen. John B. Gordon, from *Reminiscences of the Civil War*: (4)

Thenceforward to the end of July, through the entire month of August, and during more than half of September, 1864, Early's little army was marching and countermarching toward every point of the compass in the Shenandoah Valley, with scarcely a day of rest, skirmishing, fighting, rushing hither and thither to meet and drive back cavalry raids, while General Sheridan gathered his army of more than double our numbers for his general advance up the Valley....

Maj. Jed Hotchkiss, from *Confederate Military History*: (5)

The battle of Winchester, of September 19th, was opened by an advance of the enemy along the Berryville road toward Winchester, and across the Opequon, at 3 a.m. Ramseur, on the west bank of the Opequon, with Johnson's and Jackson's cavalry on his right, opposed and delayed this advance. Rodes came up from Stephenson's at 10 o'clock and formed on Ramseur's left, and Gordon, arriving about noon from Bunker Hill, formed on Rodes' left....

The Federal infantry, about midday, made a furious attack all along the line; but its advances were all repulsed, with great slaughter, by the Confederate infantry and artillery. At 1 p.m. Sheridan massed his large body of cavalry and attempted to turn the Confederate left, but this attack was also repulsed. At 4 p.m. this attempt was renewed, and this great force, consisting of two divisions of cavalry backed by a fresh corps of infantry, turned and got in the rear of Early's left, when the whole line gave way and the army retreated, near sundown, some of it in confusion and disorder, but most of it in an orderly way, followed by the enemy's cavalry to Kernstown, where they were gallantly repulsed by Ramseur, who brought up the rear....

Lt. Gen. John B. Gordon, from *Reminiscences of the Civil War*: (6)

General Sheridan graciously granted us two days and a part of the third to sleep and rest and pull ourselves together for the struggle of September 22. The battle, or, to speak more accurately, the bout at Fisher's Hill, was so quickly ended that it may be described in a few words. Indeed, to all experienced soldiers the whole story is told in one word – "flanked."

We had again halted and spread our banners on the ramparts which nature built along the Shenandoah's banks. Our stay was short, however, and our leaving hurried, without ceremony or concert. It is the old story of failure to protect flanks. Although the Union forces more than doubled Early's army, our position was such that in our stronghold we could have whipped General Sheridan had the weak point on our left been sufficiently protected. Sheridan demonstrated in front while he slipped his infantry around our left and completely enveloped that flank. An effort was made to move Battle and Wharton to the enveloped flank in order to protect it, but the effort was made too late. The Federals saw their advantage, and seized and pressed it. The Confederates saw the hopelessness of their situation, and realized that they had only the option of retreat or capture. They were not long in deciding.

The retreat (it is always so) was at first stubborn and slow, then rapid, then – a rout....

Nearly a month – twenty-six days, to be exact – of comparative rest and recuperation ensued after Fisher's Hill. General Sheridan followed our retreat very languidly.... This was all very fine for Early's battered little army; and it seemed that Sheridan's victories of the 19th and 22nd had been so costly, notwithstanding his great preponderance in numbers, that he sympathized with our desire for a few weeks of dallying. He appeared to be anxious to do just enough to keep us reminded that he was still there. So he decided upon a season of burning, instead of battling....

The arrival of reinforcements under Kershaw not only revived the hopes of our high-mettled men, but enabled General Early and his division commanders to await with confidence General Sheridan's advance, which was daily expected. He did not come, however. Our rations were nearly exhausted, and after holding a council of war, General Early decided to advance upon the Union forces strongly intrenched on the left bank of Cedar Creek....

George M. Neese, from *Three Years in the Confederate Horse Artillery*: (7)

October 4 – This morning we received orders to move down the Valley. We left camp early in the day and marched once more for the Valley turnpike....

October 6 – .... We will soon strike some sort of game, though it may be ignoble, as I saw some fresh tracks in its slimy trail in the way of recently burnt barns and a few houses in ruins. These highly civilized and pious Yankees have at last gallantly and patriotically resorted to the torch as a glorious means through which to strangle the great rebellion, by trying to starve women and children of this Southland.

October 7 – .... The Yankees are burning all the mills and barns in this part of the Shenandoah Valley; I saw a hundred barns burning to-day....

October 8 – We renewed our march this morning, in pursuit of the Yankee barn-burners, down the Valley.... General Sheridan is the boss burner of this continent, so far as destroying barns is concerned. It is estimated that his troops have burned two thousand barns in Rockingham and Shenandoah counties, and I have no idea how many mills; all that they could find, I suppose.

The principal object in this highly civilized warfare is the wanton destruction of hay and grain, and nearly all the wheat that was in the Shenandoah Valley for a distance of thirty miles is in ashes this evening. If the destruction of wheat is considered to be a military necessity by the powers that be at Washington, then it is an open acknowledgment that the United States feels itself too weak and incompetent to crush the great rebellion by the fair and simple force of arms and has resorted to the torch, a mode of warfare down level with savagery, for this destruction of bread means almost and perhaps actual starvation to hundreds, yes, thousands of women, children, and old men throughout the burnt district.

It is true, General Sheridan, that you are now in the land of the swarthy captive; but if you will lift the curtain of the past and look well in the sands of time you will see the footprints of a Washington and a Jefferson who dwelt in this same land that held the dusky captive in bondage. And, moreover, these same mountain peaks that now silently look down on your hellish work of destruction once echoed the inspiring drum-tap that summoned our grandsires to the plains of Boston, where they willingly, voluntarily, and patriotically rushed to assist their New England brethren in tearing the claws of the British lion from the bleeding flesh of the young American eagle. Ah, but you scornfully say that we are Rebels. That is the same ugly word that George the Third's red-coated Britishers used on the field of Concord and Lexington, and applied it also to General Washington, Putnam, Patrick Henry, and the whole host of American patriots; that epithet of itself surely puts us in no mean company, and surely not so as to deserve the cursed calamity that you are now heaping on the women and children in the Shenandoah Valley.

In 1775 in yonder little town of Woodstock the Rev. Peter Muhlenberg, whose patriotism called him from the pulpit to the field, cast aside his clergyman's gown after pronouncing the benediction to his last sermon, and stepped from the pulpit in the full uniform of an American soldier. And as he moved through the aisle toward the door, distinctly and impressively uttering the stirring words, "There is a time to pray and a time to fight," and proceeded to the church door and ordered drums to be beaten, from his congregation on that memorable Sunday a large company of faithful men volunteered as recruits for the American army that was then struggling for independence. Colonel Muhlenberg marched his men north, and subsequently the crash of the rifles in the hands of Muhlenberg's sturdy and valiant Virginians on the fields of Brandywine, Germantown, Monmouth, and Stony Point unmistakably proclaimed the gallant and unselfish patriotism and true fealty of the Virginians in the cause of American freedom and independence, and without the least trace of sectional hatred, envious jealousy, or mock philanthropy.

But now all these recollections of past little favors lie buried in the ruins and wreck of two thousand barns and their valuable contents, and somebody is trying to crawl to fame through the ashes....

Maj. Jed Hotchkiss, from *Confederate Military History*: (8)

Early remained at Fisher's Hill during the 15th, having some skirmishing with the enemy on Hupp's hill, as he reconnoitered, and found them busily fortifying the north bank of Cedar creek and the camp which they had reoccupied....

On the 17th of October, Early's troops were advanced a mile or more, to between Tumbling run and Strasburg … while General Gordon and Captain Hotchkiss of the engineers went to the signal station, on the end of Three-top [Massanutten] Mountain, to reconnoiter the enemy's position… From the reports of General Gordon and Captain Hotchkiss, and the remarkable location of Sheridan's camps … General Early became convinced that, notwithstanding the great disparity of the opposing forces … an unexpected and successful attack could be made on Sheridan's camps….

Early's plan assigned to each division its place and time of attack, almost precisely as it was subsequently carried into execution. Gordon, with the Second Corps … was to march, after dark, from the Fisher's Hill encampment to a crossing of the North Fork of the Shenandoah, near its right, which the pioneer corps was to bridge for it, then along and around the base of the Three-top Mountain, by a blind and concealed pathway, to its northeastern end, and then, by fording the North Fork of the Shenandoah at Bowman's Ford, with a squadron of Payne's cavalry in advance, to capture the enemy's pickets and turn his flank. Kershaw was to march to Strasburg at a later hour, then by a country road to Bowman's mill, on Cedar Creek, and attack the enemy; Wharton, at a still later hour, was to move along the Valley Turnpike … past Strasburg to Hupp's Hill … and be ready to second the other attacks…. The marches were so arranged that each of the attacking forces should be in position and ready to begin the assault at precisely 5 o'clock, about daylight of the morning of the 19th….

[W]ith remarkable precision, the three prearranged simultaneous attacks began. Payne's cavalry dashed across the river, in front of Gordon, and captured the outer pickets; Gordon followed with the bold rush characteristic of the famous Stonewall Brigade, which was in his advance, and soon fell on the rear of the encampment of the Nineteenth Corps…. At the same time Kershaw's division fairly sprang down the steep slope of the south bank of Cedar Creek, rushed across that stream, … charged rapidly up the long slope north of the creek, captured the battery that crowned its summit, turned its guns upon the as yet profoundly sleeping Eighth Corps, rushed upon its flank, then bore to the left, and crossing the Valley Turnpike fell upon the flank of the Nineteenth Corps, there encamped on the Belle Grove farm.

By these rapid and nearly simultaneous advances Kershaw's command and that of Gordon were, practically, brought into line of battle, with Gordon on the right and Kershaw on the left, that swept like wildfire through the camps of the Eighth and Nineteenth Corps, routed the sleeping soldiers from their tents, and drove them, some half-dressed and all dazed, to retreat in wild confusion or to promptly surrender, and giving little opportunity for any rally except by some of those in the more distant parts of the encampment, who were quickly aroused and formed by their officers, and who, with desperate courage, vainly strove to check the onrushing tide of the victorious Confederates.

When the sun rose and tempered the sharp air of that frosty October morning, it beheld Kershaw and Gordon in full possession of the camps and earthworks of the Eighth and Nineteenth Corps of Sheridan's army and the captors of a large number of prisoners, many pieces of artillery, most of the camp equipage and the trains belonging to these two large bodies of infantry, and preparing to attack the Sixth Corps, which was encamped farthest to the enemy's right and on high ground beyond Meadow Branch....

The infantry attack on the Sixth Corps, especially by Wharton's division on the [enemy's] right, was but partially successful, as the swampy character of the ground along Meadow Run prevented it from getting across, and the furious fire of the enemy drove it back; but the Confederate artillery, formidable in the number and character of its guns and in the magnificent handling of these by its officers and men, soon forced the Sixth Corps from its position, so that before noon the entire infantry command of the Federal army had been routed and driven nearly two miles beyond Middletown, and Early had halted in the pursuit, apprehensive that the 10,000 Federal cavalry, which Rosser had merely routed from their camps on Sheridan's right, might cross over and fall upon his little army....

This inexcusable delay, although abundant excuses have been offered for it, enabled the commanders of the Federal regiments, brigades and corps to rally and reform their men, so that when Sheridan, who had been absent, reached them from Winchester not long before noon - after a ride, not of 20 miles at headlong speed, but of 10 miles in about two hours – he found his army reformed by Crook and ready to advance, with all arms of the service, overlapping, on either flank, the little band of Confederate heroes that, from his position, he could plainly see stretched out in a thin line not far in front.

When all was ready, at about 4 p.m., with a great mass of cavalry upon his flanks, and especially upon his right, Sheridan ordered an advance and attacked Early's line, turning his left; and the mere weight of numbers, especially of cavalry, forced the whole line to give way....

Lt. Gen. John B. Gordon, from *Reminiscences of the Civil War*: (9)

Regiment after regiment, brigade after brigade, in rapid succession was crushed, and, like hard clods of clay under a pelting rain, the superb commands crumbled to pieces. The sun was sinking, but the spasmodic battle still raged. Wrapped in clouds of smoke and gathering darkness, the overpowered Confederates stubbornly yielded before the advancing Federals.

There was no yelling on the one side, nor huzzahs on the other. The gleaming blazes from hot muzzles made the murky twilight lurid. The line of light from Confederate guns grew shorter and resistance fainter. The steady roll of musketry, punctuated now and then by peals of thunder from retreating or advancing batteries, suddenly ceased; and resistance ended as the last organized regiment of Early's literally overwhelmed army broke and fled in the darkness....

BOOK IV - CHAPTER FOUR

Famine and Pestilence

The Rev. Joseph B. Traywick, from his "Prison Life at Point Lookout": (1)

I was captured at Fisher's Gap, near Strasburg, on September 22, 1864. After some delay at Winchester, Harper's Ferry and Baltimore, I was carried by steamer to Point Lookout, Maryland, arriving on October 3, 1864. On entering the prison we were divested of everything except personal wear and blankets. Not long after our arrival an inspection was held, and in every case where prisoners had more than one blanket, they were all taken except one to each man, and then those who did not have any were supplied with blankets that had been taken from their fellow prisoners. Barefooted prisoners were supplied with shoes, and a scant quantity of clothing was given to the most destitute.

The tents were mostly bell or round-shaped. They had been refused for use in the Federal army and generally leaked. The rations as to quality were, as a rule, good. Pork two out of three days, the third day beef, but occasionally the ribs of beef were round, which showed that it was mule-beef. Hungry prisoners ate it all the same. The bread was served in pound loaves daily, one loaf to be divided between two prisoners – it was short weight. A pint cup of soup went with each loaf of bread. Two days' rations were issued on Saturday, and so small was the quantity that men frequently ate all given at one time.

The ration for a day was about sufficient for a well man one meal. It was said by the prison authorities to be one-half ration, allowing three meals per day. I would consider it one-third ration a day. The pork was very fat, and always boiled. The prisoners never got the lard that came out of the pork, and it was commonly reported that the provost marshal and other officers there realized a vast amount from the sale of this grease to soap-makers and lard-refiners. The water used by the prisoners was mineral, giving the sharpest of appetites with so little to eat. Our suffering from hunger was indescribable.

I have heard men pray to be made sick that the appetite might be taken away. The prisoners being so poorly clad, and the Point so much exposed to cold, it caused them great suffering. Every intensely cold night from four to seven prisoners would freeze to death. Almost no wood was furnished. About a cord of green pine to one thousand men for five days. It was a mockery.

The post was commanded by General Barnes. His nephew, Captain Barnes, was assistant provost marshal. These were kind and considerate officers, but the former never was brought in contact with the prisoners. They were under the immediate charge of the provost marshal, Major Brady, of New York State. He was a shrewd man, of powerful administrative abilities, but withal a cruel, heartless man. His whole conduct toward the prisoners impressed me that he enjoyed two things immensely – first, the suffering and humiliation of the prisoners; secondly, the fact that he was their despot.

The prison was enclosed by a strong stockade of heavy plank fourteen feet high. Four feet from the top on the outside was a parapet extending all around. On this the guards walked by day and night. They were all negroes, commanded by white officers. The night police inside the prison were negroes, but their barbarity was so great that through the earnest entreaties of the prisoners they were removed some time in January, 1865. I recollect one sick man who had not been carried to the hospital. His complaint caused him to leave his tent about 3 o'clock a.m. While out he was set on by a large negro guard, who double-quicked him, in his night clothes and weak condition, up and down the streets between the tents for an hour. When the brute ordered the sick man back to his tent he made fifteen other prisoners come out in their night clothes and run up and down like a heard of cattle.

The greatest cruelty perpetrated while I was in prison was on thirty-two inmates of one of the cook-houses. At the side of the prison, next to the gate, was located a number of long cook and eating-houses, where all the cooking except baking was done. There was only a street or roadway between these houses and the stockade where the guards walked continually. Between two of these houses, a little nearer one than the other, one of the ne-gro guards fell from the parapet and was found dead. A contusion was on his head and a piece of brick near him. This discovery took place about sunset. No one saw him when he fell. No one saw who hit him.

The following night after taps, when every prisoner was in bed, a file of soldiers rushed into the nearest cook-house to the scene and hurried the thirty-two inmates out in the night. The weather was intensely cold — thermometer below zero. They had on nothing but shirt and drawers — two of them had on socks. They were placed in a block-house which had a door and a hole a few inches wide, without food, water or fire. They were told that one of them killed the negro guard, possibly all of them knew of it, and when the fact was so made known, then all the oth-ers could go back to their quarters, but if they did not come out and confess who killed the guard that the day following the next had been fixed as the time when all thirty-two of them would be shot. So in that bitter weather these innocent helpless men (not all men, for two of them were boys) passed that fearful night and next day in the block building, where they were continually jeered at through the little window by the negro guards who were off duty, they telling the suffering prisoners how delighted they would be to see them shot.

The awful hours rolled on, another night of indescribable suffering passed away, and the day of execution has come. To many of these men a quick death was to be preferred to the slow and cruel death they were then passing. The hour for the execution arrives. All the troops, mostly negroes, off guard on the Point were formed into the hollow square. The thirty-two almost naked, freezing, starving men were marched out in line into the hollow square. Major Brady, with the audacity of the wolf before eating the lamb, proceeded to ask each man if he knew who killed the guard. As he proceeded he received a very positive no from the heroic boys first, and then from the brave men. He had not gone far, however, when an alarm was heard in the direction of the gate. Four or five men were seen coming on horseback at full speed and yelling at the top of their voices. It was an officer who had found a young man, a prisoner and employ in the next cook-house, who could tell them something about who killed the guard.

But we must go back one day in the narrative. During that day of cruel mocking there was one kind man who visited the suffering prisoners. He was a commissioned officer and a Mason. Among the thirty-two prisoners there was but one Mason, and he gave a signal which will stir the deepest emotions of a brother. This officer lost no time, but set to work to ferret out the cause of the death of the guard. Major Brady, unfeeling monster as he was, attempted to find out the cause by torturing innocent men.

Of course the proceedings were stayed until the young man was heard from. He was placed on a box to testify, but he could not do this until Major Brady had indulged in some silly, irrelevant questions. He, however, stated that on the evening the guard was killed he was at the wood-pile gathering some chips for the fire when he was hit on the leg by the brick. Smarting with pain he threw the brick back and hit the guard on the head, and he fell off the parapet. Whether, said the young man, the brick or the whiskey in the guard caused the fall and death he could not say; for, said he, the guard was drunk that afternoon. Then the young man added, I am sorry that I did not know that you were bestowing this cruelty on these men, for I should have come forward and made known these things.

The thirty-two were immediately sent back to their quarters, where they were clothed and fed, but three of them died soon after from this exposure....

George M. Neese, from *Three Years in the Confederate Horse Artillery*: (2)

Just when the severe weather set in, some time about the last of November, all the prisoners were formed in line for the especial purpose of holding a blanket show. We were told to be sure and have all our blankets on exhibition, good, bad, and indifferent. When the parade was ready for the judges a Yankee squad passed along the line and, without much ceremony, took every blanket from us, save one to each man throughout the whole camp. I have often read and heard about the inhumanity of man to man and the cold charity of this world, but on shell-out blanket day was the first time that I ever saw the priceless virtue frozen up in solid chunks.

I never heard of any plausible reason assigned for the cruel performance, but I suppose that it was done in the true spirit of might makes right; or perhaps such inhuman treatment is what some of the pure and pious psalm-singing Puritans call freezing out the fires of rebellion....

Many of the prisoners are thinly clad and all of them are scantily fed. I slept on the damp sand for two months without any sign of a blanket or bedding under me, and nothing but my shoe for a pillow. Old Boreas fiercely sweeps and howls across the prison walls, with his front, center and rear whetted to a keen edge by gliding across the icy waves of Chesapeake Bay, and the searching blast with frosty needles creeps through every crack and crevice in the habiliments of a shivering prisoner and chills to the very marrow in the bone. Every cold morning I see hundreds of prisoners walking briskly back and forth through the streets and along the edge of the Bay trying to warm themselves by active exercise in the rays of the rising sun.

Every cold night some few men freeze to death in bed, one of the direful effects of robbing us of our blankets when the cold weather set in. Even wood seems to be a scarce commodity in Uncle Sam's vast realm, as we get a very scanty supply, and that is mostly green pine, which never fails to make more smoke than fire. The wood allowed each tent is not enough to keep a little fire more than a day in a week, and actually I have not seen nor felt a good fire this whole winter, and I have become so inured to the cold that I can endure it like a horse or dog.

There are about ten thousand prisoners in our pen, and in that vast crowd I have not seen one man smile or heard a hearty laugh since I have been here. Everyone moves around in almost sullen silence, with a sad countenance, and the whole crew looks as if they had just returned from a big funeral. No more does rollicking song or laughing merriment cheerfully ring with gleeful mood among the tents of the camping host, like it does around the bright evening camp-fires that blaze and dance on the leas of Dixie's fair land, but all is hushed in grievous silence, for the austere discipline and rigid rules that govern this dismal prison life has dried up the very fountain of song; hunger, cold, and privations, in connection with bullets in the bottom of negro sentinels' guns, have thoroughly quenched the spirit of merriment and laughter. Oh, had I the wings of a seagull I would fly and speed away from this wretched existence, to new feeding grounds, and once more gather around a happy camp-fire where Rebels rule the ranch.

January 1, 1865 – This is Happy New Year. A cold northwest wind is sweeping through camp in a regular hurricane style, with all the fierceness and chilliness of a midwinter tempest.

To commence the new year with an inauspicious outlook we drew but half rations to-day. All of us in our tent went to bed at noon to keep from freezing; at sunset we got up and stood out in ranks and shiveringly answered evening roll-call, then went back to bed to spend the remainder of this Happy New Year in trying to have pleasant dreams of some warm, steaming, delicious New Year dinner somewhere far, far away....

January 13 – This far in the new year the weather has been very disagreeable, windy, and cold. Last night about nine o'clock a man died, frozen to death or starved in bed, in the next tent to mine. The orderly sergeant of our company called for four volunteers to bear the corpse to the dead house; I volunteered for one.

The night was bitter cold, with a full moon in a clear, wintry sky which rendered the night almost as bright as day. As we bore the body of our comrade through the silent street the pale silvery moonbeams with kindly light played softly over the cold thin white face of the dead. The moonlit wavelets of the Bay, as they kissed the pebbly strand, whispered a soft vesper hymn, a fitting requiem, as we moved away with our silent burden toward the house of the dead.

When we arrived at the dead house, which is a large Sibley tent, the Great Reaper had already harvested seven sheaves garnered in silent waiting for the morrow's interment. The burial hour here is daily at four o'clock in the afternoon, and the man that we carried to the dead house made the eighth one that died from four o'clock until nine. Death with its fatal shears clips a brittle thread of life here, and with insatiable greed calls for "next" every hour of the day and night and gathers on an average twenty-five passengers for the daily train to the Silent City....

Rev. J. William Jones, from *Personal Reminiscences of General Robert E. Lee*: (3)

As [the] charge of cruelty to Federal prisoners has been again and again reiterated ... the following facts, which can be proved before any fair tribunal, should go on the record:

1. The Confederate authorities gave to prisoners in their hands *the same rations which they issued to their own soldiers, and gave them the very best accommodations which their scant means afforded.*

2. *They were always anxious to exchange prisoners, man for man, and, when this was rejected by the Federal authorities, they offered to send home the prisoners in their hands without any equivalent.*

3. *By refusing all propositions to exchange prisoners, and declining even to receive their own men without equivalent, the Federal authorities made themselves responsible for all the suffering, of both Federal and Confederate prisoners, that ensued.*

4. And yet, notwithstanding these facts, it is susceptible of proof, from the official records of the Federal Department, that *the suffering of Confederate prisoners in Federal prisons was much greater than that of Federal prisoners in Confederate prisons.* Without going more fully into the question, the following figures from the report of Mr. Stanton, Secretary of War, in response to a resolution of the House of Representatives calling for the number of prisoners on both sides and their mortality, are triumphantly submitted:

	In Prison	Died
U. S. soldiers	260,940	22,526
Confederates	200,000	26,500

That is, the Confederate States held as prisoners sixty-one thousand men more than the Federals held of the Confederates; and yet the deaths of Federal prisoners fell below those of Confederates *four thousand.*

Two Federal prisoners died out of every twenty-three; while two out of every fifteen Confederates died in Federal prisons....

John M. Daniel, from the Richmond *Examiner*, 25 November 1863: (4)

The Yankee policy with respect to the exchange of prisoners has been clearly exposed. It is based upon the simple principle that our men are intrinsically worth more than theirs, and that if they continue to hold our prisoners and to allow their own to remain in our hands they will be the gainers. Such, in fact, is the whole scheme of the war. If, by dint of superior numbers and a lavish expenditure of blood, they can inflict such losses upon the South as to render it incapable of further resistance, their point, they think, is gained....

While this savage and cold-blooded idea is at the bottom of their reasoning, they are aware that it is necessary to cloak their purposes under as decent a veil as they can find. It will not do to tell their soldiers, or the classes from which they expect to recruit their armies, that they regard them merely as fighting animals, to be used sparingly, or sacrificed wantonly, according to the varying necessities of the case. It would be ruinous frankly to avow that they are delighted to retain a certain number of Confederates in prison at the expense of an equal or even greater number of their own men. An excuse must be found which will throw the odium of refusing exchange upon the Confederacy. Yankee ingenuity, unhampered by the restraints of an adherence to truth, can easily accomplish this....

We have sought to carry out the cartel of exchange in good faith. Let us not allow the Yankees to take advantage of their own wrong, and, while they avoid the odium attaching to the desertion of their prisoners, retain the advantage of neutralizing thousands of our soldiers.

That such is their object there can be no doubt. [This] unwilling tribute of an enemy's praise belongs, in the fullest measure, to our gallant soldiers. Gladly would the Yankee Government, in order to deprive us of their services, agree to lodge [our soldiers] at the Fifth Avenue or the Metropolitan, and to feed them upon turtle soup and champagne. It would be a vastly cheaper way of disposing of them than maintaining armies of hirelings to oppose them in the field....

Abraham Lincoln, from his *Fourth Annual Message to Congress*, December 6, 1864: (5)

The war continues. Since the last annual message all the important lines and positions then occupied by our forces have been maintained and our arms have steadily advanced, thus liberating the regions left in rear, so that Missouri, Kentucky, Tennessee, and parts of other States have again produced reasonably fair crops.

The most remarkable feature in the military operations of the year is General Sherman's attempted march of 300 miles directly through the insurgent region. It tends to show a great increase of our relative strength that our General in chief should feel able to confront and hold in check every active force of the enemy, and yet to detach a well-appointed large army to move on such an expedition. The result not yet being known, conjecture in regard to it is not here indulged.

Important movements have also occurred during the year to the effect of molding society for durability in the Union. Although short of complete success, it is much in the right direction that 12,000 citizens in each of the States of Arkansas and Louisiana have organized loyal State governments, with free constitutions, and are earnestly struggling to maintain and administer them. The movements in the same direction, more extensive though less definite, in Missouri, Kentucky, and Tennessee should not be overlooked. But Maryland presents the example of complete success. Maryland is secure to liberty and union for all the future. The genius of rebellion will no more claim Maryland. Like another foul spirit being driven out, it may seek to tear her, but it will woo her no more....

The most reliable indication of public purpose in this country is derived through our popular elections. Judging by the recent canvass and its result, the purpose of the people within the loyal States to maintain the integrity of the Union was never more firm nor more nearly unanimous than now....

The election has exhibited another fact not less valuable to be known – the fact that we do not approach exhaustion in the most important branch of national resources, that of living men.... The important fact remains demonstrated that we have *more* men *now* than we had when the war *began*; that we are not exhausted nor in the process of exhaustion; that we are *gaining* strength and may if need be maintain the contest indefinitely. This as to men. Material resources are now more complete and abundant than ever.

The national resources, then, are unexhausted, and, as we believe, inexhaustible. The public purpose to reestablish and maintain the national authority is unchanged, and, as we believe, unchangeable. The manner of continuing the effort remains to choose....

Maj. John Scott, from his *Partisan Life With Col. John S. Mosby*: (6)

In obedience to orders issued by the military authorities, all the granaries, stack-yards, stables, and mills in the Valley of Virginia had been burned by General Sheridan's army, and General Merritt, toward the latter part of November, crossed the Blue Ridge at Ashby's and Snicker's Gaps, to carry the work of destruction into Loudoun and Upper Fauquier. This total departure from the usages of modern warfare, to be paralleled only by the example of a Tilly or a Geneseric, originated in the conviction that, in addition to European mercenaries and insurrectionary negroes, the alliance of Famine, too, was necessary to subdue the stubborn spirit of resistance which animated the Southern people.

The policy of devastation as a material agent is one of vast power, but its efficacy in restoring affection for the government that invokes it may well be doubted. But this is a question for politicians to ponder. It is mine to give an account, however imperfect, of this act of incendiarism in the most fruitful part of "Mosby's Confederacy." From Paris and Snickersville, as central points, strong detachments were sent through the devoted region upon their destructive mission. In this way, Merritt's army of five thousand men was expanded like a fan from the Blue Ridge to the Bull Run Mountain, and each soldier being armed with a torch, that terrible implement of war, this beautiful and productive region was soon reduced to a waste. In order more certainly to enlist the starving cohorts of hunger on the side of the Constitution and the laws, all farm-cattle, including milch-cows with their "white abundance," were carried off and collected in one vast drove at Snickersville.

As soon as night invested the scene, blazing fires were visible in all directions, lighting up with their lucid glare the whole of the vast circumference, while columns of dense black smoke mounted up from the burning piles as though some demons of conflagration, rejoicing in the mischief they had wrought, had assumed those terrible forms in which to manifest themselves.

Various were the emotions displayed by the agents of destruction as they would approach a smiling homestead. The most, animated by the spirit which dictated the inhuman orders, would laugh at the despair and wretchedness of the forlorn family; while others, with whom no political object could justify crime, invoked divine vengeance on the men who thus deliberately prepared for the helpless and innocent members of society – the old men, the women, the children, and the young maidens of this once happy land – death in its most revolting, lingering, and painful forms.

As I gazed horror-struck upon the awful spectacle, I was carried back to the dark and savage period when Attila, with his fierce barbarians, burst over the Alps and ravaged the plains of Italy – adorned with vineyards and villas – and cities which in magnificence and population were hardly secondary to Rome herself.

When I remembered the ties of consanguinity which united the hostile peoples, the startling theory of my friend the Philosopher forced itself into my mind:

"That republican institutions are imbued with an uncontrollable tendency to barbarize and degrade the human character, and that, instead of mounting higher in the ascending circles of civilization, society, from the relaxation of the imposed and wholesome discipline of well-ordered states, sinks lower and lower in the moral scale, till Anarchy, with its devouring jaws, engulfs all things, returning man, the pride of the creation, for a season at least, to his savage state.

"Under its malign influence," continued my friend, "the nicer shades of personal honor first disappear; then follows morality, the substance of all things; and, finally, the spirit of humanity flies from the accursed land."

As the different corps of incendiaries proceeded through the country, Mosby's men, with orders to take no prisoners, hounded their tracks....

BOOK IV - CHAPTER FIVE

The Waste Land

John S. Wise, from *The End of an Era*: (1)

Hints from home indicated that by this time visitors to the Confederate capital were most welcome when they brought their rations…. The city, in its chill winter garb, showed signs of desperate depletion. The problem of sustenance had become serious, even with the rich. The clothing of the most prosperous was simple, domestic, even rough. The poorer classes were scantily clad in every kind of makeshift garment, oft times in rags. People without overcoats met one another upon the streets, and talked over the prospects of peace, with their teeth chattering, their thin garments buttoned over their chests, their shoulders drawn up, their gloveless hands sunk deep into their pockets for warmth. At meals, the dishes were few and simple, procured at prices which sound fabulous. Many a family existed upon little else than bacon and cornfield peas….

The town was filled with hospitals. Several of them took their names from the people whose houses had been devoted to these uses. Many ladies had volunteered as matrons, and even as attendants. It was part of the daily life of Richmond for women to save something from their scant sustenance, and take or send it to the sick and wounded. One devoted woman so distinguished and endeared herself to everybody by her self-sacrifice that the name of Sally Tompkins is known to the Confederates as well as Florence Nightingale to the British, or Clara Barton to Americans. She was commissioned a captain, and the boys all call her, even now, "Captain Sally." God will make her an officer of higher grade.

My father had long since rejoined his brigade. They were now transferred to the right of our army at Hatcher's Run. The privations and sufferings which officers and men were undergoing were very fearful. They were huddled in snow and mud, without adequate supplies of food or fuel or clothing. I went out to the camp, but had not heart to remain long. The struggle was no longer a test of valor in excitement: it had become one of inactive endurance.

The Confederate authorities had adopted the policy of enlisting negro troops. One sunny afternoon, I visited the Capitol Square, and witnessed the parade and drill of a battalion of Confederate darkies. The sight was in strange contrast with other parades I had witnessed there - that, for example, of the New York Seventh in 1858, or of the [Virginia Military Institute] cadets, even, in the preceding May.

"Ah!" I thought, "this is but the beginning of the end."

Yet there were thousands – many of them old, many of them actually pale from insufficient nutriment, many of them without money or employment to provide for present or future – who still believed that the Confederacy would achieve its independence.

The Confederate Congress passed resolutions of hope, and sent orators to the trenches and camps to tell the soldiers that "the darkest hour was just before day." One of these blatant fellows I recall particularly. He had been a fire-eater, a nullifier, a secessionist, a blood-and-thunder orator, foremost in urging that we "fight for our rights in the Territories." He was a young man, an able-bodied man, and a man of decided ability. But never for one moment was his precious carcass exposed to danger. There was something inexpressibly repulsive to me, and irritating beyond expression, when I saw men like this, from their safe places, in a lull in hostilities, ride down to the Confederate lines during that awful winter, and counsel our poor soldiers to fight on. Even if it was right to fight on, they had no right to advise it. Old Jubal Early had opposed the war until it actually came upon him, but when it was inevitable, he fought. Things were turning out just as he had predicted they would. When these people, whose extravagant oratory had done so much to bring on the fight, and who had then contributed nothing of personal service to sustain it, came among his starving men to urge them to sacrifices which they themselves had never made, he treated them with undisguised scorn. He refused to attend their meetings. From the door of his hut he blistered them with his biting satire: -

"Well – well ----!" he shouted; "still sicking them on, are ye?" "Before you leave, tell them what you think of your rights in the Territories now." "One day out here with a musket would help the cause more than all your talk." "Don't talk the men to death. You can't talk the Yankees to death. Fighting is the only thing that talks now."

"Old Jubal" had his faults, but skulking in bomb-proofs was not one of them. The men had implicit faith in his unflinching courage. He punctured and embalmed the lip-service of these "last ditchers," as he called them; and his soldiers, taking the cue from him, hooted and derided them, and long resented their unwelcome intrusion….

Lt. Gen. Jubal A. Early, from his "Lee Memorial Address," January 19, 1872: (2)

For nine long months was the unequal contest protracted by the genius of one man, aided by the valor of his little force, occupying a line of more than thirty miles, with scarcely more than a respectable skirmish line. During this time there were many daring achievements and heroic deeds performed by the constantly-diminishing survivors of those who had rendered the Army of Northern Virginia so illustrious; but, finally, constant attrition and lingering starvation did their work.

General Lee had been unable to attack Grant in his stronghold, south of the James and east of the Appomattox, where alone such a movement was practicable, because a concentration for that purpose, on the east of the latter river, would have left the way to Richmond open to the enemy. When - by the unsuccessful expedition into Tennessee, the march of Sherman through the center of Georgia to the Atlantic, his subsequent expedition north through South Carolina into North Carolina, and the consequent fall of Charleston and Wilmington – the Confederacy had been practically reduced to Richmond City, the remnant of the Army of Northern Virginia, and the very narrow slips of country bordering on the three railroads and the canal running out of that city into the Valley, Southwestern Virginia, and North Carolina, the struggle in Virginia, maintained so long by the consummate ability of our leader, began to draw to a close. To add to his embarrassments, he had been compelled to detach a large portion of his cavalry to the aid of the troops falling back before Sherman in his march northward, and a portion of his infantry to the defense of Wilmington; and at the close of March, 1865, Sherman had approached as far north as Goldsborough, North Carolina, on his movement to unite with Grant.

It was not till then that Grant, to whose aid an immense force of superbly-equipped cavalry had swept down from the Valley, was able to turn General Lee's flank and break his attenuated line....

Capt. Clement Sulivane, from "The Fall of Richmond": (3)

About 11:30 a.m. on Sunday, April 2nd, a strange agitation was perceptible on the streets of Richmond, and within half an hour it was known on all sides that Lee's lines had been broken below Petersburg; that he was in full retreat on Danville; that the troops covering the city at Chaffin's and Drewry's Bluffs were on the point of being withdrawn, and that the city was forthwith to be abandoned. A singular security had been felt by the citizens of

Richmond, so the news fell like a bomb-shell in a peaceful camp, and dismay reigned supreme.

All that Sabbath day the trains came and went, wagons, vehicles, and horsemen rumbled and dashed to and fro, and, in the evening, ominous groups of ruffians – more or less in liquor – began to make their appearance on the principal thoroughfares of the city. As night came on pillage and rioting and robbing took place. The police and a few soldiers were at hand, and, after the arrest of a few ringleaders and the more riotous of their followers, a fair degree of order was restored. But Richmond saw few sleeping eyes during the pandemonium of that night....

Upon receipt of the news from Petersburg I reported to General Ewell (then in Richmond) for instructions, and was ordered to assemble and command the Local Brigade, cause it to be well supplied with ammunition and provisions, and await further orders. All that day and night I was engaged in this duty, but with small result, as the battalions melted away as fast as they were formed, mainly under orders from the heads of departments who needed all their employees in the transportation and guarding of the archives, etc., but partly, no doubt, from desertions. When morning dawned fewer than 200 men remained, under command of Captain Edward Mayo.

Shortly before day General Ewell rode in person to my headquarters and informed me that General G. W. C. Lee was then crossing the pontoon at Drewry's; that he would destroy it and press on to join the main army; that all the bridges over the river had been destroyed, except Mayo's, between Richmond and Manchester, and that the wagon bridge over the canal in front of Mayo's had already been burned by Union emissaries. My command was to hasten to Mayo's bridge and protect it, and the one remaining foot-bridge over the canal leading to it, until General Gary, of South Carolina, should arrive.

I hurried to my command, and fifteen minutes later occupied Mayo's bridge, at the foot of 14th street, and made military dispositions to protect it to the last extremity. This done, I had nothing to do but listen for sounds and gaze on the terrible splendor of the scene. And such a scene probably the world has seldom witnessed. Either incendiaries, or (more probably) fragments of bombs from the arsenals, had fired various buildings, and the two cities, Richmond and Manchester, were like a blaze of day amid the surrounding darkness. Three high arched bridges were in flames; beneath them the waters sparkled and dashed and rushed on by the burning city. Every now and then, as a magazine exploded, a column of white smoke rose up as high as the eye could reach, instantaneously followed by a deafening sound. The earth seemed to rock and tremble as with the shock of an earthquake, and immediately afterward hundreds of shells would explode in air and send their iron spray down far below the bridge. As the immense magazines of cartridges ignited the rattle as of thousands of musketry would follow, and then all was still for the moment, except the dull roar and crackle of the fast-spreading fires. At dawn we heard terrific explosions about "The Rocketts," from the unfinished iron-clads down the river.

By daylight, on the 3rd, a mob of men, women, and children, to the number of several thousands, had gathered at the corner of 14th and Cary streets and other outlets, in front of the bridge, attracted by the vast commissary depot at that point; for it must be remembered that in 1865 Richmond was a half-starved city, and the Confederate Government had that morning removed its guards and abandoned the removal of the provisions, which was impossible for the want of transportation. The depot doors were forced open and a demoniacal struggle for the countless barrels of hams, bacon, whiskey, flour, sugar, coffee, etc., etc., raged about the buildings among the hungry mob. The gutters ran whiskey, and it was lapped as it flowed down the streets, while all fought for a share of the plunder. The flames came nearer and nearer, and at last caught in the commissariat itself.

At daylight the approach of the Union forces could be plainly discerned. After a little came the clatter of horses' hoofs galloping up Main Street. My infantry guard stood to arms, the picket across the canal was withdrawn, and the engineer officer lighted a torch of fat pine. By direction of the Engineer Department barrels of tar, surrounded by pine-knots, had been placed at intervals on the bridge, with kerosene at hand, and a lieutenant of engineers had reported for the duty of firing them at my order. The noisy train proved to be Gary's ambulances, sent forward preparatory to his final rush for the bridge. The muleteers galloped their animals about half-way down, when they were stopped by the dense mass of human beings. Rapidly communicating to Captain Mayo my instructions from General Ewell, I ordered that officer to stand firm at his post until Gary got up. I rode forward into the mob and cleared a lane. The ambulances were galloped down to the bridge, I retired to my post, and the mob closed in after me and resumed its wild struggle for plunder.

A few minutes later a long line of cavalry in gray turned into 14th Street, and sword in hand galloped straight down to the river; Gary had come. The mob scattered right and left before the armed horsemen, who reigned up at the canal. Presently a single company of cavalry appeared in sight, and rode at headlong speed to the bridge. "My rear-guard," explained Gary. Touching his hat to me he called out, "All over, good-bye; blow her to h-ll," and trotted over the bridge….

BOOK V

SPRING (1865)

Louder, louder chant the lay,
Waken, lords and ladies gay!
Tell them youth and mirth and glee
Run a course as well as we,
Time, stern huntsman! Who can balk,
Staunch as hound and fleet as hawk;
Think of this, and rise with day
Gentle lords and ladies gay!
- Sir Walter Scott, "Hunting Song" (1)

RIGHT *General Robert E. Lee* – Courtesy of Library of Congress

BOOK V - CHAPTER ONE

The Stirrup Cup

John S. Wise, from *The End of an Era*: (1)

At the time of the evacuation of Richmond, in 1865, I had been in the Confederate army for about ten months, had reached the mature age of eighteen, and had attained the rank of lieutenant. I was for the time at Clover Station, on the Richmond and Danville Railroad, south of the fallen capital. A light glimmered in headquarters and at the telegraph station. Suspecting that news of importance had been received, and knowing the telegraph operator well, I repaired to his office. He was sitting at his instrument, closely attentive to its busy clicking.

"Any news, Tom?" inquired I.

Holding up his hand he said, "Yes! hush!" and continued to listen. Then, seizing his pad and pencil, he wrote rapidly. Again the clicking of the instrument began, and he resumed his attitude of intent listening. He was catching messages passing over the lines to Danville. During the lull, he informed me that heavy fighting on the right of the army at Five Forks had been going on all day, in which the slaughter on both sides had been very great, and that there were reports of the evacuation of Petersburg. Repairing to the quarters of General Walker, I found that he had substantially the same advices. Vainly and despondently we waited until late at night for more particulars.

Sunday morning broke clear and calm. It was one of the first of those heavenly spring days which to me seem brighter in Virginia than elsewhere. Sitting in a sunny spot near the telegraph station, a party of staff officers waited for telegrams until nearly eleven o'clock. Then a storm of news broke upon us, every word of which was freighted with deep import to our cause.

Click – click – click. "Our lines in front of Petersburg were broken this morning. General Lee is retiring from the city."

Click – click – click. "General A. P. Hill was killed."

Click – click – click. "Colonel William Pegram of the artillery also killed."

Click – click – click. "In the battle of Five Forks, which continued until long after dark last night, Pickett was overwhelmed by Sheridan with a greatly superior force of cavalry and infantry, and the enemy is now endeavoring to turn our right, which is retiring toward the Appomattox, to make a stand there."

Click – click – click. "Petersburg is evacuated. Our army in full retreat toward Burkeville."

Click – click – click. "General Lee has notified the President that he can no longer hold Richmond, and orders have been issued for the immediate evacuation of the city. The town is the scene of the utmost turmoil and confusion."

General Walker issued the necessary commands to place our own house in order. There was not much to be done. Such government stores and provisions as were at our post were promptly put on freight cars, and every preparation was made for an orderly departure, if necessary. We expected that Lee would make a stand at or near Burkeville, forty miles distant, and that, if he must, he would retreat along the line of the Richmond and Danville Railroad. From the accounts of the fighting, I felt sure that my father's command was in the thick of it; and this fear gave an added trouble to the gloomy reflections of those sad hours....

A few hours later, train after train, all loaded to their utmost capacity with whatever could be transported from the doomed capital, came puffing past Clover Station on the way southward. These trains bore many men who, in the excitement, were unwilling to admit that all was lost. They frankly deplored the necessity of giving up the Confederate capital, but insisted that the army was not beaten or demoralized, and was retreating in good order. They argued that Lee, relieved of the burden of defending his long lines from Richmond to Petersburg, and of the hard task of maintaining his communications, would draw Grant away from his base of supplies, and might now, with that generalship of which we all knew him to be master, be free to administer a stunning if not a crushing blow to Grant in the open, where strategy might overcome force. These arguments cheered and revived me. I hoped it might so turn out. I dared not ask myself if I believed that it would.

Monday morning, April 3, a train passed Clover bearing the President, his Cabinet and chief advisors, to Danville. They had left Richmond after the midnight of that last Sunday when Mr. Davis was notified, while attending St. Paul's Church, that the immediate evacuation of the city was unavoidable. Mr. Davis sat at a car window. The crowd at the station cheered. He smiled and acknowledged their compliment, but his expression showed physical and mental exhaustion. Near him sat General Bragg, whose shaggy eyebrows and piercing eyes made him look like a much greater man than he ever proved himself to be. In this car was my brother-in-law, Dr. Garnett, family physician to Mr. Davis. I entered, and sat with him a few minutes, to learn what I could about the home folk. His own family had been left at his Richmond residence, to the mercy of the conqueror. The presidential train was followed by many others. One bore the archives and employees of the Treasury Department, another those of the Post Office Department, another those of the War Department. I knew many in all these departments, and they told me the startling incidents of their sudden flight.

I saw a government on wheels. It was the marvelous and incongruous debris of the wreck of the Confederate capital. There were very few women on these trains, but among the last in the long procession were trains bearing indiscriminate cargoes of men and things. In one car was a cage with an African Parrot, and a box of tame squirrels, and a hunchback! Everybody, not excepting the parrot, was wrought up to a pitch of intense excitement. The last arrivals brought the sad news that Richmond was in flames. Our departing troops had set fire to the tobacco warehouses. The heat, as it reached the hogsheads, caused the tobacco leaves to expand and burst their fastenings, and the wind, catching up the burning tobacco, spread it in a shower of fire upon the doomed city.

It was after dark on Monday when the last train from Richmond passed Clover Station bound southward. We were now the northern outpost of the Confederacy. Nothing was between us and the enemy except Lee's army, which was retreating towards us, - if indeed it were coming in this direction. All day Tuesday, and until midday Wednesday, we waited, expecting to hear of the arrival of our army at Burkeville, or some tidings of its whereabouts. But the railroad stretching northward was as silent as the grave.

The cessation of all traffic gave our place a Sabbath stillness. Until now, there had been the constant rumble of trains on this main line of supplies to the army. After the intense excitement of Monday, when the whole Confederate government came rushing past at intervals of a few minutes, the unbroken silence reminded one of death after violent convulsions.

We still maintained telegraphic communication with Burkeville, but we could get no definite information concerning the whereabouts of Lee. Telegrams received Tuesday informed us he was near Amelia Court House. Wednesday morning we tried in vain to call up Amelia Court House. A little later, Burkeville reported the wires cut at Jetersville, ten miles to the north, between Burkeville and Amelia Court House. When General Walker heard this, he quietly remarked, "They are pressing him off the line of this road, and forcing him to retreat by the Southside Road to Lynchburg." I knew the topography of the country well enough to realize that if the army passed Burkeville Junction, moving westward, our position would be on the left flank and rear of the Union army, and that we must retire or be captured.

Many messages came from Mr. Davis at Danville, inquiring for news from General Lee. Shortly after General Walker reported that the wires were cut at Jetersville, another message came from Mr. Davis. He asked if General Walker had a trusted man or officer who, if supplied with an engine, would venture down the road toward Burkeville, endeavor to communicate with General Lee, ascertain from him his situation and future plans, and report to the President. I was present when this telegram arrived. By good luck, other and older officers were absent. The suspense and inactivity of the past three days had been unendurable, and I volunteered gladly for the service. At first, General Walker said that I was too young; but after considering the matter, he ordered me to hold myself in readiness, and notified Mr. Davis that he had the man he wanted, and requested him to send the engine. The engine, with tender and a baggage car, arrived about eight p.m.

General Walker summoned me to headquarters, and gave me my final instructions. Taking the map, he showed me that in all probability the enemy had forced General Lee westward from Burkeville, and that there was danger of finding the Union troops already there. I was to proceed very slowly and cautiously. If the enemy was not in Burkeville, I must use my judgement whether to switch my train on the Southside Road and run westward, or to leave the car and take a horse. If the enemy had reached Burkeville, as he feared, I was to run back to a station called Meherrin, return the engine, secure a horse, and endeavor to reach General Lee. "The reason that I suspect the presence of the enemy at Burkeville," said he, "is that this evening, after a long silence, we have received several telegrams purporting to come from General Lee, urging the forwarding of stores to that point. From the language used, I am satisfied that it is a trick to capture the trains. But I may be mistaken. You must be careful to ascertain the facts before you get too close to the place. Do not allow yourself to be captured."

The general was not a demonstrative man. He gave me an order which Mr. Davis had signed in blank, in which my name was inserted by General Walker, setting forth that, as special messenger of the President, I was authorized to impress all necessary men, horses, and provisions to carry out my instructions. He accompanied me to the train, and remarked that he had determined to try me, as I seemed so anxious to go; that it was a delicate and dangerous mission, and that its success depended upon my quickness, ability to judge of situations as they arose, and powers of endurance. He ordered the engineer, a young, strong fellow, to place himself implicitly under my command. I threw a pair of blankets into the car, shook hands cordially with the general, buttoned my papers in my breast pocket, and told the engineer to start. I did not see General Walker again for more than twenty years.

I carried no arms except a navy revolver at my hip, with some loose cartridges in my haversack. The night was chilly, still, and overcast. The moon struggled out now and then from watery clouds. We had no headlight, nor any light in the car. It seemed to me that our train was the noisiest I had ever heard. The track was badly worn and very rough. In many places it had been bolstered up with beams of wood faced with strap iron, and we were compelled to move slowly. The stations were deserted. We had to put on our own wood and water. I lay down to rest, but nervousness banished sleep. The solitude of the car became unbearable. When we stopped at a water-tank, I swung down from the car and clambered up to the engine. Knowing that we might have to reverse it suddenly, I ordered the engineer to cut loose the baggage car and leave it behind. This proved to be a wise precaution.

About two o'clock, we reached Meherrin Station, twelve miles south of Burkeville. It was dark, and the station was deserted. I succeeded in getting an answer from an old man in a house near by, after hammering a long time upon the door. He had heard us, but he was afraid to reply.

"Have you heard anything from Lee's army?" I asked.

"Naw, nothin' at all. I heerd he was at Amelia Cote House yisterday."

"Have you heard of or seen any Yankees hereabouts?"

"None here yit. I heerd there was some at Green Bay yisterday, but they had done gone back."

"Back where?"

"I dunno. Back to Grant's army, I reckin."

"Where is Grant's army?"

"Gord knows. It 'pears to me like it's everywhar."

"Are there any Yankees at Burkeville?"

"I dunno. I see a man come by here late last evenin', and he said he come from Burkeville; so I reckin there weren't none thar when he lef', but whether they is come sence, I can't say."

I determined to push on. When we reached Green Bay, eight miles from Burkeville, the place was dark and deserted. There was nobody from whom we could get information. A whip-poorwill in the swamp added to the oppressive silence all about. Moving onward, we discovered, as we cautiously approached a turn in the road near Burkeville, the reflection of lights against the low-hanging clouds. Evidently, somebody was ahead, and somebody was building fires. Were these reflections from the camp-fires of Lee's or of Grant's army, or of any army at all? On our right, concealing us from the village and the village from us, was a body of pine woods. Not until we turned the angle of these woods could we see anything. I was standing by the engineer. We were both uncertain what to do. At first, I thought I would get down and investigate; but I reflected that I should lose much time in getting back to the engine, whereas, if I pushed boldly forward until we were discovered, I should be safe if those who saw us were friends, and able to retreat rapidly if they were enemies.

"Go ahead!" I said to the engineer.

"What, lieutenant? Ain't you afraid they are Yankees? If they are, we're goners," said he hesitatingly.

"Go ahead!" I repeated; and in two minutes more we were at the curve, with the strong glare of many fires lighting up our engine. What a sight! Lines of men were heaving at the rails by the light of fires built for working. The fires and working parties crossed our route to westward, showing that the latter were devoting their attention to the Southside Railroad. In the excitement of the moment, I thought they were destroying the track. In fact, as I afterward learned, they were merely changing the gauge of the rails. Grant, with that wonderful power he possessed of doing everything at once, was already altering the railroad gauge so as to fetch provisions up to his army. The enemy was not only in Burkeville, but he had been there all day, and was thus following up his occupation of the place. Lee must be to the north or to the west of him, pushed away from Danville Road, and either upon or trying to reach the Southside Railroad, which led to Lynchburg. All these things I thought out a little later, but not just at that moment. A blazing meteor would not have astonished our foes more than the sight of our locomotive. They had not heard our approach, amid the noise and confusion of their own work. They had no picket out in our direction, for this was their rear. In an instant, a number of troopers rushed for their horses and came galloping down upon us. They were but two or three hundred yards away.

"Reverse the engine!" I said to the engineer. He seemed paralyzed. I drew my pistol.

"It's no use, lieutenant. They'll kill us before we get under way," and he fumbled with his lever.

"Reverse, or you're a dead man!" I shouted, clapping the muzzle of my pistol behind his ear. He heaved at the lever; the engine began to move, but how slowly! The troopers were coming on. We heard them cry, "Surrender!" The engine was quickening her beats. They saw that we were running, and they opened fire on us. We lay down flat, and let the locomotive go.

The fireman on the tender was in an exposed position, and seemed to be endeavoring to burrow in the coal. A shot broke a window above us. Presently the firing ceased. Two or three of the foremost of the cavalrymen had tumbled into a cattle-guard, in their reckless pursuit. We were safe now, except that the engine and tender were in momentary danger of jumping the rotten track.

When we were well out of harm's way, the engineer, with whom I had been on very friendly terms till this last episode, turned to me and asked, with a grieved look, "Lieutenant, would you have blowed my brains out sure 'nuff, if I hadn't done what you tole me?"

"I would that," I replied, not much disposed to talk; for I was thinking, and thinking hard, what next to do.

"Well," said he, with a sigh, as with a greasy rag he gave a fresh rub to a piece of machinery, "all I've got to say is, I don't want to travel with you no mo'."

"You'll not have to travel far," I rejoined. "I'll get off at Meherrin, and you can go back."

"What!" exclaimed he. "You goin' to get off there in the dark by yourself, with no hoss, and right in the middle of the Yankees? Durn my skin if I'd do it for Jeff Davis hisself!"

Upon our arrival at Meherrin, I wrote a few lines to General Walker, describing the position of the enemy, and telling him that I hoped to reach General Lee near High Bridge by traveling across the base of a triangle formed by the two railroads from Burkeville and my route, and that I would communicate with him further when I could.

It was a lonesome feeling that came over me when the engine went southward, leaving me alone and in the dark at Meherrin. The chill of daybreak was coming on, when I stepped out briskly upon a road leading northward. I knew that every minute counted, and that there was no hope of securing a horse in that vicinity. I think that I walked three or four miles. Day broke and the sun rose before I came to an opening. A kind Providence must have guided my steps, for at the very first house I reached, a pretty mare stood at the horse-rack saddled and bridled, as if waiting for me.

The house was in a grove by the roadside. I found a hospitable reception, and was invited to breakfast. My night's work had made me ravenous. My host was past military age, but he seemed dazed at the prospect of falling into the hands of the enemy. I learned from him that Sheridan's cavalry had advanced nearly to his place the day before. We ate breakfast almost in silence.

At the table I found Sergeant Wilkins, of the Black Walnut Troop, from Halifax County. He had been on "horse furlough." Confederate cavalrymen supplied their own horses, and his horse furlough meant that his horse had broken down, that he had been home to replace it, and that he was now returning to duty with another beast. His mare was beautiful and fresh, - the very animal that I needed. When I told him that I must take his horse, he laughed, as if I were joking; then he positively refused; but finally, when I showed the sign manual of Jefferson Davis, he yielded, very reluctantly. It was perhaps fortunate for Sergeant Wilkins that he was obliged to go home again, for his cavalry command was engaged heavily that day, and every day thereafter, until the surrender at Appomattox.

On the morning of April 6, mounted upon as fine a mare as there was in the Confederacy, I sallied forth in search of General Lee. I started northward for the Southside Railroad. It was not long before I heard cannon to the northeast. Thinking that the sounds came from the enemy in the rear of Lee, I endeavored to bear sufficiently westward to avoid the Union forces. Seeing no sign of either army, I was going along leisurely, when a noise behind me attracted my attention. Turning in my saddle, I saw at a distance of several hundred yards the head of a cavalry command coming from the east, and turning out of a cross-road that I had passed into the road that I was traveling. They saw me, and pretended to give chase; but their horses were jaded, and my mare was fresh and swift. The few shots they fired went wide of us, and I galloped out of range quickly and safely. My filly, after her spin, was mettlesome, and as I held her in hand, I chuckled to think how easy it was to keep out of harm's way on such a beast.

But this was not to be my easy day. I was rapidly approaching another road, which came into my road from the east. I saw another column of Union cavalry filing into my road, and going in the same direction that I was going. Here was a pretty pickle! We were in the woods. Did they see me? To be sure they did. Of course they knew of the parallel column of their own troops which I had passed, and I think they first mistook me for a friend. But I could not ride forward: I should have come upon the rear of their column. I could not turn back: the cavalry force behind was not a quarter of a mile away. I stopped, thus disclosing who I was. Several of them made a dart for me; several more took shots with their carbines; and once more the little mare and I were dashing off, this time through the woods to the west.

What a bird she was, that little mare! At a low fence in the woods she did not make a pause or blunder, but cleared it without turning a hair. I resolved now to get out of the way, for it was very evident that I was trying to reach General Lee by riding across the advance columns of Sheridan, who was on Lee's flank. Going at a merry pace, just when my heart was ceasing to jump and I was congratulating myself upon a lucky escape, I was "struck flat aback," as the sailors say. From behind a large oak a keen, racy-looking fellow stepped forth, and, leveling his cavalry carbine, called, "Halt!" He was not ten feet away.

Halt I did. It is all over now, thought I, for I did not doubt that he was a Jesse scout. (That was the name applied by us to Union scouts who disguised themselves in our uniform.) He looked too neat and clean for one of our men. The words "I surrender" were on my lips, when he asked, "Who are you?" I had half a mind to lie about it, but I gave my true name and rank. "What the devil are you doing here, then?" he exclaimed, his whole manner changing. I told him. "If that is so," said he, lowering his gun, to my great relief, "I must help get you out. The Yankees are all around us. Come on." He led the way rapidly to where his own horse was tied behind some cedar bushes, and, mounting, bade me follow him. He knew the woods well. As we rode along, I ventured to inquire who he was. "Curtis," said he, - "one of General Rooney Lee's scouts. I have been hanging on the flank of this cavalry for several days. They are evidently pushing for the High Bridge, to cut the army off from crossing there."

After telling him of my adventure, I added: "You gave me a great fright. I thought you were a Yankee, sure, and came near telling you that I was one."

"It is well you did not. I am taking no prisoners on this trip," he rejoined, tapping the butt of his carbine significantly.

"There they go," said he, as we came to an opening and saw the Union cavalry winding down a red-clay road to the north of us, traveling parallel with our own route. "We must hurry, or they'll reach the Flat Creek ford ahead of us. Fitz Lee is somewhere near here, and there'll be fun when he sees them. There are not many of them, and they are pressing too far ahead of their main column."

After a sharp ride through the forest, we came to a wooded hill overlooking the ford of Flat Creek, a stream which runs northward, entering the Appomattox near High Bridge.

"Wait here a moment," said Curtis. "Let me ride out and see if we are safe." Going on to a point where he could reconnoitre, he turned back, rose in his stirrups, waved his hand, and crying, "Come on, quick!" galloped down the hill to the ford.

I followed; but he had not accurately calculated the distance. The head of the column of Union cavalry was in sight when he beckoned to me and made his dash. They saw him and started toward him. As I was considerably behind him, they were much nearer to me than to him. He crossed safely; but the stream was deep, and by the time I was in the middle, my little mare doing her best with the water up to her chest, the Yankees were in easy range, making it uncomfortable for me. The bullets were splashing in the water all around me. I threw myself off the saddle, and, nestling close under the mare's shoulder, I reached the other side unharmed. Curtis and a number of pickets stationed at the ford stood by me manfully. The road beyond the ford ran into a deep gully and made a turn. Behind the protection of this turn, Curtis and the pickets opened fire upon the advancing cavalry, and held them in check until I was safely over. When my horse trotted up with me, wet as a drowned rat, it was time for us all to move on rapidly. In the afternoon, I heard Fitz Lee pouring hot shot into that venturesome body of cavalry, and I was delighted to learn afterward that he had given them severe punishment.

Curtis advised me to go to Farmville, where I would be beyond the chance of encountering more Union cavalry, and then to work eastward toward General Lee. I had been upset by the morning's adventures, and I was somewhat demoralized. About a mile from Farmville, I found myself to the west of a line of battle of infantry, formed on a line running north and south, moving toward the town. Not doubting they were Union troops, I galloped off again, and when I entered Farmville I did not hesitate to inform the commandant that the Yankees were approaching. The news created quite a panic. Artillery was put in position and preparations were made to resist, when it was discovered that the troops I had seen were a reserve regiment of our own, falling back in line of battle to a position near the town. I kept very quiet when I heard men all about me swearing that any cowardly, panic-stricken fool who would set such a report afloat ought to be lynched.

I had now very nearly joined our army, which was coming directly toward me. Early in the afternoon, the advance of our troops appeared. How they straggled, and how demoralized they seemed! Eastward, not far from the Flat Creek ford, a heavy fire opened, and continued for an hour or more. As I afterward learned, Fitz Lee had collided with my cavalry friends of the morning, and, seeing his advantage, had availed himself of it by attacking them fiercely. To the north, about four o'clock, a tremendous fire of artillery and musketry began, and continued until dark. I was riding towards this firing, with my back to Farmville. Very heavy detonations of artillery were followed time and again by crashes of musketry. It was the battle of Sailor's Creek, the most important of those last struggles of which Grant said, "There was as much gallantry displayed by some of the Confederates in these little engagements as was displayed at any time during the war, notwithstanding the sad defeats of the past weeks."

My father's command was doing the best fighting of that day. When Ewell and Custis Lee had been captured, when Pickett's division broke and fled, when Bushrod Johnson, his division commander, left the field ingloriously, my fearless father, bareheaded and desperate, led his brigade into action at Sailor's Creek, and, though completely surrounded, cut his way out, and reached Farmville at daylight with the fragments of his command.

It was long after nightfall when the firing ceased. We had not then learned the particulars, but it was easy to see that the contest had gone against us. The enemy had, in fact, at Sailor's Creek, stampeded the remnant of Pickett's division, broken our lines, captured six general officers, including Generals Ewell and Custis Lee, and burned a large part of our wagon trains. As evening came on, the road was filled with wagons, artillery, and bodies of men, hurrying without organization and in a state of panic toward Farmville. I met two general officers, of high rank and great distinction, who seemed utterly demoralized, and they declared that all was lost. That portion of the army which was still unconquered was falling back with its face to the foe, and bivouacked with its right and left flanks resting upon the Appomattox to cover the crossings to the north side, near Farmville.

Upon reaching our lines, I found the divisions of Field and Mahone presenting an unbroken and defiant front. Passing from camp to camp in search of General Lee, I encountered General Mahone, who told me where to find General Lee. He said that the enemy had "knocked hell out of Pickett." "But," he added savagely, "my fellows are all right. We are just waiting for 'em." And so they were. When the army surrendered, three days later, Mahone's division was in better fighting trim and surrendered more muskets than any other division of Lee's army.

It was past midnight when I found General Lee. He was in an open field north of Rice's Station and east of the High Bridge. A camp-fire of fence-rails was burning low. Colonel Charles Marshall sat in an ambulance, with a lantern and a lap-desk. He was preparing orders at the dictation of General Lee, who stood near, with one hand resting on a wheel and one foot upon the end of a log, watching intently the dying embers as he spoke in a low tone to his amanuensis.

Touching my cap as I rode up, I inquired, "General Lee?"

"Yes," he replied quietly, and I dismounted and explained my mission. He examined my autograph order from Mr. Davis, and questioned me closely concerning the route by which I had come. He seemed especially interested in my report of the position of the enemy at Burkeville and westward, to the south of his army. Then, with a long sigh, he said: "I hardly think it is necessary to prepare written dispatches in reply. They may be captured. The enemy's cavalry is already flanking us to the south and west. You seem capable of bearing a verbal response. You may say to Mr. Davis that, as he knows, my original purpose was to adhere to the line of the Danville Road. I have been unable to do so, and am now endeavoring to hold the Southside Road as I retire in the direction of Lynchburg."

"Have you any objective point, General, - any place where you contemplate making a stand?" I ventured timidly.

"No," said he slowly and sadly, "no; I shall have to be governed by each day's developments." Then, with a touch of resentment, and raising his voice, he added, "A few more Sailor's Creeks and it will all be over – ended – just as I have expected it would end from the first."

I was astonished at the frankness of this avowal to one so insignificant as I. It made a deep and lasting impression on me. It gave me an insight into the character of General Lee which all the books ever written about him could never give. It elevated him in my opinion more than anything else he ever said or did. It revealed him as a man who had sacrificed everything to perform a conscientious duty against his judgement. He had loved the Union. He had believed secession was unnecessary; he had looked upon it as hopeless folly. Yet at the call of his State he had laid his life and fame and fortune at her feet, and served her faithfully to the last.

After another pause, during which, although he spoke not a word and gave not a sign, I could discern a great struggle within him, he turned to me and said: "You must be very tired, my son. You have had an exciting day. Go rest yourself, and report to me at Farmville at sunrise. I may determine to send a written dispatch." The way in which he called me "my son" made me feel as if I would die for him.

Hesitating a moment, I inquired, "General, can you give me any tidings of my father?"

"Your father?" he asked. "Who is your father?"

"General Wise."

"Ah!" said he, with another pause. "No, no. At nightfall, his command was fighting obstinately at Sailor's Creek, surrounded by the enemy. I have heard nothing from them since. I fear they were captured, or – or – worse." To these words, spoken with genuine sympathy, he added: "Your father's command has borne itself nobly throughout this retreat. You may well feel proud of him and of it."

My father was not dead. At the very moment when we were talking, he and the remnant of his brigade were tramping across the High Bridge, feeling like victors, and he, bareheaded and with an old blanket pinned around him, was chewing tobacco and cursing Bushrod Johnson for running off and leaving him to fight his own way out.

I found a little pile of leaves in a pine thicket, and lay down in the rear of Field's division for a nap. Fearing that somebody would steal my horse, I looped the reins around my wrist, and the mare stood by my side. We were already good friends. Just before daylight, she gave a snort and a jerk which nearly dislocated my arm, and I awoke to find her alarmed at Field's division, which was withdrawing silently and had come suddenly upon her. Warned by this incident, I mounted, and proceeded toward Farmville, to report, as directed, to General Lee for further orders.

North of the stream at Farmville, in the forks of the road, was the house then occupied by General Lee. On the hill behind the house, to the left of the road, was a grove. Seeing troops in this grove, I rode in, inquiring for General Lee's headquarters. The troops were lying there more like dead men than live ones. They did not move, and they had no sentries out. The sun was shining upon them as they slept. I did not recognize them. Dismounting, and shaking an officer, I awoke him with difficulty. He rolled over, sat up, and began rubbing his eyes, which were bloodshot and showed great fatigue.

"Hello, John!" said he. "In the name of all that is wonderful, where did you come from?" It was Lieutenant Edmund R. Bagwell, of the 46th. The men, a few hundred in all, were the pitiful remnant of my father's brigade.

"Have you seen the old general?" asked Ned. "He's over there. Oh, we have had a week of it! Yes, this is all that is left of us. John, the old man will give you thunder when he sees you. When we were coming on last night in the dark, he said, 'Thank God, John is out of this!' Dick? Why, Dick was captured yesterday at Sailor's Creek. He was riding the general's old mare, Maggie, and she squatted like a rabbit with him when the shells began to fly. She always had that trick. He could not make her go forward or backward. You ought to have seen Dick belaboring her with his sword. But the Yanks got him!" and Ned burst into a laugh as he led me where my father was.

Nearly sixty years old, he lay, like a common soldier, sleeping on the ground among his men. We aroused him, and when he saw me, he exclaimed: "Well, by great Jehoshaphat, what are you doing here? I thought you, at least, were safe." I hugged him, and almost laughed and cried at the sight of him safe and sound, for General Lee had made me very uneasy. I told him why I was there.

"Where is General Lee?" he asked earnestly, springing to his feet. "I want to see him again. I saw him this morning about daybreak. I had washed my face in a mud-puddle, and the red mud was all over it and in the roots of my hair. I looked like a Comanche Indian; and when I was telling him how we cut our way out last night, he broke into a smile and said, 'General, go wash your face!'" The incident pleased him immensely, for at the same time General Lee made him a division commander, - a promotion he had long deserved for gallantry, if not for military knowledge.

"No, Dick is not captured. He got out, I'm sure," said he, as we walked down the hill together. "He was separated from me when the enemy broke our line. He was not riding Maggie. I lent her to Frank Johnson. He was wounded, and, remembering his kindness to your brother Jennings the day he was killed, I tried to save the poor fellow, and told him to ride Maggie to the rear. Dick was riding his black horse, I know it. When the Yankees advanced, a flock of wild turkeys flushed before them and came sailing into our lines. I saw Dick gallop after a gobbler and shoot him and tie him to his saddle-bow. He was coming back toward us when the line broke, and, mounted as he was, he no doubt escaped, but is cut off from us by the enemy.

"Yes, the Yanks got the bay horse, and my servants Joshua and Smith, and all my baggage, overcoats, and plunder. A private soldier pinned this blanket around me last night, and I found this hat when I was coming off the field."

He laughed heartily at his own plight. I have never since seen a catch-pin half so large as that with which his blanket was gathered at the throat. As we passed down the road to General Lee's headquarters, the roads and the fields were filled with stragglers. They moved looking behind them, as if they expected to be attacked and harried by a pursuing foe. Demoralization, panic, abandonment of all hope, appeared on every hand. Wagons were rolling along without any order or system. Caissons and limber-chests, without commanding officers, seemed to be floating aimlessly upon a tide of disorganization. Rising to his full height, casting a glance around him like that of an eagle, and sweeping the horizon with his long arm and bony forefinger, my father exclaimed, "This is the end!" It is impossible to convey an idea of the agony and the bitterness of his words and gestures.

We found General Lee on the rear portico of the house that I have mentioned. He had washed his face in a tin basin, and stood drying his beard with a coarse towel as we approached. "General Lee," exclaimed my father, "my poor, brave men are lying on yonder hill more dead than alive. For more than a week they have been fighting day and night, without food, and, by God, sir, they shall not move another step until *somebody* gives them something to eat!"

"Come in, General," said General Lee soothingly. "They deserve something to eat, and they shall have it; meanwhile you shall share my breakfast." He disarmed everything like defiance by his kindness.

It was but a few moments, however, before my father launched forth in fresh denunciation of the conduct of General Bushrod Johnson in the engagement of the 6th. I am satisfied that General Lee felt as he did; but, assuming an air of mock severity, he said, "General, are you aware that you are liable to court-martial and execution for insubordination and disrespect toward your commanding officer?"

My father looked at him with lifted eyebrows and flashing eyes, and exclaimed: "Shot! You can't afford to shoot the men who fight for cursing those who run away. Shot! I wish you would shoot me. If you don't, some Yankee probably will within the next twenty-four hours."

Growing more serious, General Lee inquired what he thought of the situation.

"Situation?" said the bold old man. "There is no situation! Nothing remains, General Lee, but to put your poor men on your poor mules and send them home in time for spring ploughing. This army is hopelessly whipped, and is fast becoming demoralized. These men have already endured more than I believed flesh and blood could stand, and I say to you, sir, emphatically, that to prolong the struggle is murder, and the blood of every man who is killed from this time forth is on your head, General Lee."

This last expression seemed to cause General Lee great pain. With a gesture of remonstrance, and even of impatience, he protested: "Oh, General, do not talk so wildly. My burdens are heavy enough. What would the country think of me, if I did what you suggest?"

"Country be d----d!" was the quick reply. "There is no country. There has been no country, General, for a year or more. You are the country to these men. They have fought for you. They have shivered through a long winter for you. Without pay or clothes, or care of any sort, their devotion to you and faith in you have been the only things which have held this army together. If you demand the sacrifice, there are still left thousands of us who will die for you. You know the game is desperate beyond redemption, and that, if you so announce, no man or government or people will gainsay your decision. That is why I repeat that the blood of any man killed hereafter is upon your head."

General Lee stood for some time at an open window, looking out at the throng now surging by upon the roads and in the fields, and made no response. Then, turning his attention to me, he said cheerfully that he was glad my father's plight was not so bad as he had thought it might be, at the time of our conversation the night before. After a pause, he wrote upon a piece of paper a few words to the effect that he had talked with me, and that I would make a verbal report. If occasion arose, he would give further advices. "This," said he, "you will deliver to the President. I fear to write, lest you be captured, for those people are already several miles above Farmville. You must keep on the north side to a ford eight miles above here, and be careful about crossing even there." He always referred to the enemy as "those people." Then he bade me adieu, and asked my father to come in and share his breakfast.

I hugged my father in the presence of General Lee, and I saw a kindly look in his eyes as he watched us. Remembering that my father had no horse, I said, "Take my mare. I can easily get another."

"What!" said he, laughing, "a dispatch-bearer giving away his horse! No, sir. That is too pretty a little animal to make a present to a Yankee. I know they will bag us all, horse, foot, and dragoons, before long. No. I can walk as well as anybody. Have you any chewing tobacco?"

I was immensely flattered at this request, and gave him a plug of excellent tobacco. It was the first time that he had recognized me as entitled to the possession of all the "modern improvements" of a soldier.

And so I left them. As I rode along in search of the ford to which General Lee had directed me, I felt that I was in the midst of the wreck of that immortal army which, until now, I had believed to be invincible....

BOOK V - CHAPTER TWO

The Passing of Arthur

In yon bright track that fires the western skies
They melt, they vanish from my eyes.
But O! What solemn scenes on Snowdon's height
Descending slow their glittering skirts unroll?
Visions of glory, spare my aching sight,
Ye unborn ages, crowd not on my soul!
No more our long-lost Arthur we bewail: -
All hail, ye genuine kings! Britannia's issue, hail! ….
- Thomas Gray, "The Bard" (1)

Rev. J. William Jones, from *Personal Reminiscences of General Robert E. Lee*: (2)

General Lee was pressing on toward Lynchburg, and, on the evening of the 8th, his vanguard reached Appomattox Station, where rations for the army had been ordered to be sent from Lynchburg. Four loaded trains were in sight, and the famished army about to be supplied, when the head of Sheridan's column dashed upon the scene, captured the provisions, and drove the vanguard back to Appomattox Court-House, four miles off. Sheridan's impetuous troopers met a sudden and bloody check in the streets of the village, the colonel commanding the advance being killed.

That morning General Lee had divided the remnant of his army into two wings, under Gordon and Longstreet – Gordon having the advance, and Longstreet the rear. Upon the repulse of the cavalry, Gordon's corps advanced through the village and spent another night of sleepless vigilance and anxiety, while Longstreet, four miles in the rear, had to intrench against the army of the Potomac under Meade.

That night General Lee held a council of war with Longstreet, Gordon, and Fitz Lee, at which it was determined that Gordon should advance early the next morning to "feel" the enemy in his front; that, if there was nothing but cavalry, he should press on, followed by Longstreet; but that, if Grant's infantry had gotten up in too large force to be driven, he should halt and notify General Lee....

Col. Charles Marshall, an Aide-de-Camp of General Lee, from his address on the observance of the anniversary of the birthday of General R. E. Lee, delivered at Baltimore, Maryland, January 19, 1894: (3)

When the army halted on the night of the 8th, General Lee and his staff turned out of the road into a dense woods to seek some rest.... We lay upon the ground, near the road, with our saddles for pillows, our horses picketed near by, and eating the bark from the trees for want of better provender....

Soon after one o'clock I was aroused by the sound of a column of infantry marching along the road. We were so completely surrounded by the swarming forces of General Grant that at first, when I awoke, I thought the passing column might be Federal soldiers. I raised my head and listened intently. My doubts were quickly dispelled.... I soon knew that the command that was passing consisted, in part, at least, of Hood's old Texas brigade.... On this occasion I recognized these troops ... by hearing one of them repeat the Texas version of a passage of Scripture....

"The race is not to them that's got
The longest legs to run,

> Nor the battle to that people
> That shoots the biggest gun."

Soon after the Texans passed we were all astir and our bivouac was at an end. We made our simple toilets, consisting mainly of putting on our hats and saddling our horses. We then proceeded to look for something to satisfy our now ravenous appetites.

Somebody had a little corn meal, and somebody else had a tin can, such as is used to hold hot water for shaving. A fire was kindled, and each man in his turn, according to rank and seniority, made a can of corn-meal gruel, and was allowed to keep the can until the gruel became cool enough to drink. General Lee, who reposed as we had done, not far from us, did not, as I remember, have even such a refreshment as I have described.

This was our last meal in the Confederacy....

As soon as we had all had our turn at the shaving can we rode towards Appomattox Courthouse, when the sound of guns announced that Gordon had already begun the attempt to open the way. He forced his way through the cavalry of the enemy, only to encounter a force of infantry far superior to his own weary and starving command....

Col. Charles S. Venable, of General Lee's Staff, from his address at the *Lee Memorial Meeting* in Richmond, November 3, 1870: (4)

General Lee rode forward, still hoping that we might break through the countless hordes of the enemy which hemmed us in. Halting a short distance in rear of our vanguard, he sent me on to General Gordon to ask him if he could break through the enemy. I found General Gordon and General Fitz Lee on their front line in the dim light of the morning, arranging an attack. Gordon's reply to the message (I give the expressive phrase of the gallant

Georgian) was this: "Tell General Lee I have fought my corps to a frazzle, and I fear I can do nothing unless I am heavily supported by Longstreet's corps." When I bore this message back to General Lee, he said: "Then there is nothing left me but to go and see General Grant, and I would rather die a thousand deaths"....

Behold, the hour cometh, yea, is now come, that ye shall be scattered, every man to his own....
- St. John 16:32

Lee's *General Order No. 9*: (5)

Headquarters, Army of Northern Virginia.
April 10, 1865.

After four years of arduous service, marked by unsurpassed courage and fortitude, the Army of Northern Virginia has been compelled to yield to overwhelming numbers and resources. I need not tell the survivors of so many hard-fought battles, who have remained steadfast to the last, that I have consented to this result from no distrust of them; but, feeling that valour and devotion could accomplish nothing that could compensate for the loss that would have attended the continuation of the contest, I have determined to avoid the useless sacrifice of those whose past services have endeared them to their countrymen. By the terms of the agreement, officers and men can return to their homes and remain there until exchanged. You will take with you the satisfaction that proceeds from the consciousness of duty faithfully performed; and I earnestly pray that a merciful God will extend to you His blessing and protection. With an increasing admiration of your constancy and devotion to your country, and a grateful remembrance of your kind and generous consideration of myself, I bid you an affectionate farewell.

R. E. Lee, General

… and from them rose
A cry that shiver'd to the tingling stars,
And, as it were one voice, an agony
Of lamentation, like a wind that shrills
All night in a waste land, where no one comes,
Or hath come, since the making of the world….
- Tennyson, *Idylls of the King* (6)

BOOK V – CHAPTER THREE

The Death of a Nation

Lt. E. M. Boykin, 7th South Carolina Cavalry, from *The Falling Flag*: (1)

We stacked eight thousand stands of arms, all told; artillery, cavalry, infantry stragglers, wagon-rats, and all the rest, from twelve to fifteen thousand men. The United States troops, by their own estimate, were 150,000 men, with a railroad connecting their rear with Washington, New York, Germany, France, Belgium, Africa, "all the world and the rest of mankind," as General Taylor comprehensively remarked, for their recruiting stations were all over the world, and the crusade against the South, and its peculiar manners and civilization, under the pressure of the "almighty American dollar," was as absolute and varied in its nationality as was that of "Peter the Hermit," under the pressure of religious zeal, upon Jerusalem....

Those who took serious consideration of the state of affairs, felt that with our defeat we had as absolutely lost our country – the one we held under the Constitution – as though we had been conquered and made a colony of by France or Russia. The right of the strongest – the law of the sword – was as absolute at "Appomattox" that day as when Brennus, the Gaul, threw it in the scale at the ransom of Rome.

So far, it was all according to the order of things, and we stood on the bare hills men without a country. General Grant offered us, it was said, rations and transportation - each man to his native State, now a conquered province, or to Halifax, Nova Scotia. Many would not have hesitated to accept the offer for Halifax and rations; but, in distant Southern homes were old men, helpless women and children, whose cry for help it was not hard to hear. So, in good faith, accepting our fate, we took allegiance to this, our new country, which is now called the "United States", as we would have done to France or Russia.

With all that was around us – the destruction of the "Army of Northern Virginia" and certain defeat of the Confederacy as the result – no one dreamed of what has followed. The fanaticism that has influenced the policy of the Government to treat subject States – whose citizens had been permitted to take an oath of allegiance, accepted them as such, and promised to give them the benefits of laws protecting person, property and religion - as the dominant party in the United States has done, exceeds belief.

To place the government of the States absolutely in the hands of its former slaves, and call their "acts" "laws;" to denounce the slightest effort to assert the white vote, even under the laws, treason; and, finally, force the unwilling United States soldier to use his bayonet to sustain the grossest outrages of law and decency against men of his own color and race! - this has gone on until, lost in wonder as to what is to come next, the southern white man watches events as a tide that is gradually rising and spreading, and from which he sees no avenue of escape, and must, unless an intervention almost miraculous takes place, soon sweep him away....

Joseph A. Waddell, from *Annals of Augusta County, Virginia, from 1726 to 1871*: (2)

The war closed when General Lee surrendered at Appomattox Courthouse. For many days afterwards all the roads in the State were full of weary men wending their ways homeward. Many homes were devastated and poverty-stricken. The army of the Confederate States had wasted away, and not only so, but the people were impoverished. Some food was left in the county, - more, indeed, than was generally known of a few weeks before, - and the pressing need was for articles of clothing. Railroads had been torn up, factories destroyed, farms laid waste, towns wrecked, the banks were all broken, and there was literally no currency in the county. Farmers set to work to do what they could, and a few other people found employment. Most white people were idle from necessity, and the negroes asserted and proved their newly acquired freedom by leaving the farms and flocking to town. The recuperation of the country, which began at once and has so far been consummated, is one of the marvels of the age.

It was not anticipated at the close of the war that the Southern people generally would be subjected to pains and penalties. Edmund Burke said: "It is impossible to frame an indictment against a whole people." But the fate of many regarded as leaders was for some time in suspense.

We continue our extracts from the diary:

April 19 – No rumors to-day of any consequence. Yesterday there was a report that Lincoln had been assassinated....

Friday night, April 21 – I hear that a lady arrived this evening from Washington with a newspaper giving an account of Lincoln's assassination. Seward was assailed in his chamber at the same time and wounded.

April 22 – The assassin was an actor, named John Wilkes Booth. He and twenty or thirty others associated with him escaped down the Potomac on the Maryland side. He was not considered a Southern sympathizer, having left Richmond early in the war to go North. Rumor says that some persons at the North attribute the murder to the ultra abolitionists, who are disaffected on account of Lincoln's supposed leniency to the South....

William Gilmore Simms, from his *History of South Carolina*: (3)

It was President Lincoln's idea that the seceding States should be restored to the Union under terms dictated by the President; that is, that they should declare the freedom of the negro, should cease resistance, appoint provisional governors, and take the oath of amnesty, which was to be offered to all but men who had been prominent in the war. On the 14th of April, 1865, Lincoln was assassinated. Andrew Johnson, Vice-president of the United States, became President. Johnson set himself to carrying out the restoration plans of Lincoln.

On May 29, 1865, President Johnson issued a proclamation granting amnesty to the Confederates upon stated terms and conditions. The proclamation granted full pardon and restoration of civil rights except as to slaves. Pardon, however, was denied to thirteen classes of men, among whom were all who had held rank above colonel in the Confederate army, all officers who had received their education at West Point or at the United States Naval Academy, all who had left seats in Congress to aid their States in the war, and all who had voluntarily participated in the war whose taxable property was over $20,000. Upon the issuance of this proclamation, meetings were held in South Carolina, at which resolutions were adopted expressing a desire for a place in the Union and for the re-establishment of civil government....

Walter Lynwood Fleming, from *The Sequel of Appomattox*: (4)

[General Ulysses S.] Grant's opinion was short and direct: "I am satisfied that the mass of thinking men of the South accept the present situation of affairs in good faith.... The citizens of the Southern States are anxious to return to self-government within the Union as soon as possible"....

The point of view of the Confederate military leaders was exhibited by General Wade Hampton in a letter to President Johnson....: "The South unequivocally 'accepts the situation' in which she is placed. Everything that she has done has been done in perfect faith, and in the true and highest sense of the word, she is loyal. By this I mean that she intends to abide by the laws of the land honestly, to fulfill all her obligations faithfully and to keep her word sacredly, and I assert that the North has no right to demand more of her. You have no right to ask, or expect that she will at once profess unbounded love to that Union from which for four years she tried to escape at the cost of her best blood and all her treasures"....

Joseph A. Waddell, from his *Annals of Augusta County, Virginia, from 1726 to 1871*: (5)

At the close of 1865, our people flattered themselves that they would be left to attend to their own affairs, under the Constitution of the United States, without further molestation. They had in good faith "accepted the situation," and had no thought of future resistance to Federal authority. We shall see how far they were disappointed.

Congress and the [Virginia] Legislature met in December, on the same day. Mr. Stuart could not take the prescribed oath, and he and all Southern men were excluded from the halls of Congress. This was a strange spectacle. The war was waged for four years to compel the Southern people to return to the Union, and now their representatives, although prepared to swear allegiance, were denied all participation in the government....

Representative Thaddeus Stevens, leader of the Radicals in control of the U. S. Congress, December 18, 1865: (6)

The future condition of the conquered power depends on the will of the conqueror. They must come in as new states or remain as conquered provinces. Congress … is the only power that can act in the matter…. Congress must create States and declare when they are entitled to be represented. Then each House must judge whether the members presenting themselves from a recognized State possess the requisite qualifications of age, residence, and citizenship; and whether the election and returns are according to law…. It is obvious from all this that the first duty of Congress is to pass a law declaring the condition of these outside or defunct States, and providing proper civil governments for them. Since the conquest they have been governed by martial law. Military rule is necessarily despotic, and ought not to exist longer than is absolutely necessary. As there are no symptoms that the people of these provinces will be prepared to participate in constitutional government for some years, I know of no arrangement so proper for them as territorial governments. There they can learn the principles of freedom and eat the fruit of foul rebellion…. They ought never to be recognized as capable of acting in the Union, or of being counted as valid States, until the Constitution shall have been so amended as to make it what its framers intended; and so as to secure perpetual ascendancy to the party of the Union….

For rebellion is as the sin of witchcraft….
- I Samuel 15: 23

First Reconstruction Act, passed by Congress March 2, 1867: (7)

WHEREAS no legal State governments or adequate protection for life or property now exists in the rebel States of Virginia, North Carolina, South Carolina, Georgia, Mississippi, Alabama, Louisiana, Florida, Texas, and Arkansas; and whereas it is necessary that peace and good order should be enforced in said States until loyalty and republican State governments can be legally established: Therefore

Be it enacted ... That said rebel States shall be divided into military districts and made subject to the military authority of the United States, as hereinafter prescribed, and for that purpose Virginia shall constitute the first district; North Carolina and South Carolina the second district; Georgia, Alabama and Florida, the third district; Mississippi and Arkansas the fourth district; and Louisiana and Texas the fifth district....

When the people of any one of said rebel States shall have formed a constitution of government in conformity with the Constitution of the United States in all respects, framed by a convention of delegates elected by the male citizens of said State twenty-one years old and upward, of whatever race, color, or previous condition, who have been resident of that State for one year previous to the day of such election, except such as may be disfranchised for participation in the rebellion ... and when said State, by a vote of its legislature elected under said constitution, shall have adopted the amendment to the Constitution of the United States, proposed by the thirty-ninth Congress, and known as article fourteen, and when said article shall have become a part of the Constitution of the United States, said State shall be declared entitled to representation in Congress....

William A. Dunning, PhD, from his *Essays on the Civil War and Reconstruction and Related Topics*: (8)

The reconstruction of the Southern states, by the process which we have followed above, is one of the most remarkable achievements in the history of government. As a demonstration of political and administrative capacity, it is no less convincing than the subjugation of the Confederate armies as an evidence of military capacity. The Congressional leaders – Trumbull, Fessenden, Stevens, Bingham and others – who practically directed the process of reconstruction, were men of as rugged a moral and intellectual fibre as Grant, Sherman and the other officers who crushed the material power of the South. The obstacles to success were as great for the one set of men as for the other. In the path of reconstruction lay a hostile white population in the South, a hostile executive at Washington, a doubtful if not decidedly hostile Supreme Court, a divided Northern sentiment in respect to negro suffrage, and an active and skillfully directed Democratic Party. Yet the process as laid out in 1867 was carried through to its completion.

With much the feelings of the prisoner of tradition who watched the walls of his cell close slowly in from day to day to crush him, the Southern whites saw in the successive developments of Congress' policy the remorseless approach of negro rule. The fate of the Southern whites, like that of the prisoner of tradition, may excite our commiseration; but the mechanism by which the end was achieved must command an appreciation on its merits.

From a constitutional point of view, the actual conduct of the reconstruction has no particular interest. The power of the national government to impose its will upon the rebel states, irrespective of any restriction as to means, was assumed when the first Reconstruction Act was passed, and this assumption was acted upon to the end. Only in connection with the relations between legislature and executive were important issues raised during the process, and these are not within the scope of this essay.

It is from the political point of view that the process of reconstruction is most interesting to the historical observer. Given the end, there is something refreshingly efficient in the means employed to achieve it. Wide and deep divergences of opinion there were in the Republican majority in Congress; but they were fought out and settled in the party caucus; the capacity for discipline, which is the surest evidence of political wisdom under party government, manifested itself in a high degree; and the measures that determined the fate of the South rolled inexorable as the decrees of Providence from the two-thirds votes of House and Senate.

Was a restrictive construction of a law devised by clever lawyers, new legislation promptly overruled it. Was the authority of the attorney-general invoked on the side of tradition and legalism, Congress ordered the commanders to disregard him. Were the ordinary methods of political campaigning resorted to by the whites to profit by the ignorance or stupidity of the blacks, general orders from headquarters nullified them. Did the Conservatives win a success, as in Alabama, by exact conformity to the law, Congress ignored its own law and gave victory to the other side. Was an assurance embodied in law that admission of a state should follow ratification of one constitutional amendment, no hesitation was felt about postponing admission till the ratification of another. Such methods as these were not the methods common to political practice in republican governments. But no more were the circumstances under which they were employed common in republics. The methods were well adapted to the end, and the end was a huge social and political revolution under the forms of law.

Another way of attaining the end would have been a simple decree by the majority in Congress to the effect that the freedmen and white Unionists in the rebel states should organize governments, and control those states indefinitely thereafter. Essentially that was the conscious practical purpose of reconstruction, and everything beyond that in the content and execution of the Reconstruction Acts was incidental....

The enfranchisement of the freedmen and their enthrone-
ment in political power … was not determined to any great extent
by abstract theories of equality. Though Charles Sumner and the
lesser lights of his school solemnly proclaimed, in season and out,
the trite generalities of the Rights of Man, it was a very practical dilemma that played the chief part in giving the ballot to the
blacks.

By 1867 it seemed clear that there were three ways available for settling the issues of the war in the South: first, to leave
the Johnson governments in control and permit the Southern
whites themselves, through the Democratic Party, to determine
either chiefly or wholly the solution of existing problems; second,
to maintain Northern and Republican control through military government; and third, to maintain Northern and Republican control
through negro suffrage.

The first expedient, however defensible as to social and
economic readjustment in the South itself, was from the stand-
point of the great national issues demanding settlement gro-
tesquely impossible. The choice had to be made between indefi-
nite military rule and negro suffrage. It was a cruel dilemma. The
traditional antipathy of the English race toward military power
determined resort to the second alternative. It was proved by the
sequel that the choice was unwise.

The enfranchisement of the blacks, so far from removing,
only increased the necessity for military power. The two expedi-
ents were not alternative, but indissolubly united. Months before
the final restoration of Georgia this truth had begun to make itself
manifest.…

Robert Somers, an English visitor to the South,
from *The Southern States since the War 1870-1.* (9)

The negroes, after the Confederate surrender, were dis-
orderly. Many of them would not settle down to labour on any

terms, but roamed about with arms in their hands and hunger in their bellies; and the governing power, with the usual blind deter- mination of a victorious party, was thinking only all the while of every device of suffrage and reconstruction by which "the freed- men" might be strengthened, and made, under Northern dictation, the ruling power in the country. Agitators of the loosest fibre came down among the towns and plantations, and, organizing a Union league, held midnight meetings with the negroes in the woods, and went about uttering sentiments which, to say the least, in all the circumstances were anti-social and destructive. Crimes and outrages increased. The law, which must be always more or less weak in all thinly populated countries, was all but powerless; and the new Governments in the South, supposing them to have been most willing, were certainly unable to repress disorder, or to spread a general sense of security throughout the community. A real terror reigned for a time among the white people; and in this situation the "Ku-Klux" started into being. It was one of those secret organizations which spring up in disordered states of soci- ety, when the bonds of law and government are all but dissolved, and when no confidence is felt in the regular public administra- tion of justice. But the power with which the "Ku-Klux" moved in many parts of the South, the knowledge it displayed of all that was going on, the fidelity with which its secret was kept, and the complacency with which it was regarded by the general com- munity, gave this mysterious body a prominence and importance seldom attained by such illegal and deplorable associations. Nearly every respectable man in the Southern States was not only dis- franchised, but under fear of arrest or confiscation; the old foun- dations of authority were utterly razed before any new ones had yet been laid, and in the dark and benighted interval the remains of the Confederate armies – swept, after a long and heroic day of fair fight, from the field – flitted before the eye of the people in this weird and midnight shape of a "Ku-Klux-Klan."

Walter Lynwood Fleming, from *The Sequel of Appomattox*: (10)

The Ku Klux movement, it is to be noted in retrospect, originated as an effort to restore order in the war-stricken Southern States. The secrecy of its methods appealed to the imagination and caused its rapid expansion, and secrecy was inevitable because opposition to reconstruction was not lawful. As the reconstruction policies were put into operation, the movement became political and used violence when appeals to superstitious fears ceased to be effective....

The Ku Klux system of regulating society is as old as history; it had often been used before; it may even be used again. When a people find themselves persecuted by aliens under legal forms, they will invent some means outside the law for protecting themselves; and such experiences will inevitably result in a weakening of respect for law and in a return to more primitive methods of justice.

William A. Dunning, PhD, from his *Essays on the Civil War and Reconstruction and Related Topics*: (11)

On March 30, 1870, the ratification of the Fifteenth Amendment had been proclaimed, and just two months later the first enforcement act became law....

The Birth of an Empire

Booker T. Washington, educator, author, Civil Rights leader, head of Tuskegee Institute in Alabama, born a slave on a Virginia plantation, from his *Up from Slavery*: (1)

Freedom was in the air, and had been for months. Deserting soldiers returning to their homes were to be seen every day. Others who had been discharged, or whose regiments had been paroled, were constantly passing near our place. The "grape-vine telegraph" was kept busy night and day. The news and mutterings of great events were swiftly carried from one plantation to another. In the fear of "Yankee" invasions, the silverware and other valuables were taken from the "big house," buried in the woods, and guarded by trusted slaves. Woe be to any one who would have attempted to disturb the buried treasure. The slaves would give the Yankee soldiers food, drink, clothing – anything but that which had been specifically intrusted to their care and honour. As the great day drew nearer, there was more singing in the slave quarters than usual. It was bolder, had more ring, and lasted later into the night. Most of the verses of the plantation songs had some reference to freedom. True, they had sung those same verses before, but they had been careful to explain that the "freedom" in those songs referred to the next world, and had no connection with life in this world. Now they gradually threw off the mask, and were not afraid to let it be known that the "freedom" in their songs meant freedom of the body in this world.

The night before the eventful day, word was sent to the slave quarters to the effect that something unusual was going to take place at the "big house" the next morning. There was little, if any, sleep that night. All was excitement and expectancy. Early the next morning word was sent to all the slaves, old and young, to gather at the house. In company with my mother, brother, and sister, and a large number of other slaves, I went to the master's house. All of our master's family were either standing or seated on the veranda of the house, where they could see what was to take place and hear what was said. There was a feeling of deep interest, or perhaps sadness, on their faces, but not bitterness. As I now recall the impression they made upon me, they did not at the moment seem to be sad because of the loss of property, but rather because of parting with those whom they had reared and who were in many ways very close to them. The most distinct thing that I now recall in connection with the scene was that some man who seemed to be a stranger (a United States officer, I presume) made a little speech and then read a rather long paper – the Emancipation Proclamation, I think. After the reading we were told that we were all free, and could go when and where we pleased. My mother, who was standing by my side, leaned over and kissed her children, while tears of joy ran down her cheeks. She explained to us what it all meant, that this was the day for which she had been so long praying, but fearing that she would never live to see.

For some minutes there was great rejoicing, and thanksgiving, and wild scenes of ecstasy. But there was no feeling of bitterness. In fact, there was pity among the slaves for our former owners. The wild rejoicing on the part of the emancipated coloured people lasted but a brief period, for I noticed that by the time they returned to their cabins there was a change in their feelings. The great responsibility of being free, of having charge of themselves, of having to think and plan for themselves and their children, seemed to take possession of them. It was very much like suddenly turning a youth of ten or twelve years out into the world to provide for himself. In a few hours the great questions with which the Anglo-Saxon race had been grappling for centuries had been thrown upon these people to be solved. These were the questions of a home, a living, the rearing of children, education, citizenship, and the establishment and support of churches. Was it any wonder that within a few hours the wild rejoicing ceased and a feeling of deep gloom seemed to pervade the slave quarters?

To some it seemed that, now that they were in actual possession of it, freedom was a more serious thing than they had expected to find it. Some of the slaves were seventy or eighty years old; their best days were gone. They had no strength with which to earn a living in a strange place and among strange people, even if they had been sure where to find a new place of abode. To this class the problem seemed especially hard. Besides, deep down in their hearts there was a strange and peculiar attachment to "old Marster" and "old Missus," and to their children, which they found it hard to think of breaking off. With these they had spent in some cases nearly a half-century, and it was no light thing to think of parting. Gradually, one by one, stealthily at first, the older slaves began to wander from the slave quarters back to the "big house" to have a whispered conversation with their former owners as to the future....

Lt. Gen. Richard Taylor, from *Destruction and Reconstruction*: (2)

In their dealings with the negro the white men of the South should ever remember that no instance of outrage occurred during the war. Their wives and little ones remained safe at home, surrounded by thousands of faithful slaves, who worked quietly in the fields until removed by the Federals. This is the highest testimony to the kindness of the master and the gentleness of the servant; and all the dramatic talent prostituted to the dissemination of falsehood in "Uncle Tom's Cabin" and similar productions can not rebut it....

Extinction of slavery was expected by all and regretted by none, although the loss of slaves destroyed the value of land.

Existing since the earliest colonization of the Southern States, the institution was interwoven with the thoughts, habits, and daily lives of both races, and both suffered by the sudden disruption of the accustomed tie. Bank stocks, bonds, all personal property, all accumulated wealth, had disappeared. Thousands of houses, farm-buildings, work-animals, flocks and herds, had been wantonly burned, killed, or carried off. The land was filled with widows and orphans crying for aid, which the universal destitution prevented them from receiving. Humanitarians shuddered with horror and wept with grief for the imaginary woes of Africans; but their hearts were as adamant to people of their own race and blood. These had committed the unpardonable sin, had wickedly rebelled against the Lord's anointed, the majority....

Famine and pestilence have ever followed war, as if our Mother Earth resented the defilement of her fair bosom by blood, and generated fatal diseases to punish humanity for its crimes. But here there fell upon the South a calamity surpassing any recorded in the annals or traditions of man. An article in the "North American Review," from the pen of Judge Black, well describes the new curse, the carpet-baggers, as worse than Attila, scourge of God. He could only destroy existing fruits, while, by the modern invention of public credit, these caterans stole the labor of unborn generations. Divines, moralists, orators, and poets throughout the North commended their thefts and bade them God-speed in spoiling the Egyptians; and the reign of these harpies is not yet over.... Greed of office, curse of democracies, will impel demagogues to grovel deeper and deeper in the mire in pursuit of ignorant votes....

Booker T. Washington, from *Up from Slavery*: (3)

Though I was but little more than a youth during the period of Reconstruction, I had the feeling that mistakes were being made, and that things could not remain in the condition that they were in then very long. I felt that the Reconstruction policy, so far as it related to my race, was in a large measure on a false foundation, was artificial and forced. In many cases it seemed to me that the ignorance of my race was being used as a tool with which to help white men into office, and that there was an element in the North which wanted to punish the Southern white men by forcing the Negro into positions over the heads of the Southern whites. I felt that the Negro would be the one to suffer for this in the end....

Walter Lynwood Fleming, from *The Sequel of Appomattox*: (4)

The elections of 1867-68 showed that the negroes were well organized under the control of the radical Republican leaders.... Until 1867 the principal agency in bringing about the separation of the races had been the Freedmen's Bureau which, with its authority, its courts, its rations, clothes, and its "forty acres and a mule," did effective work in breaking down the influence of the master. But to understand fully the almost absolute control exercised over the blacks in 1867-68 by alien adventurers one must examine the workings of an oath-bound society known as the Union or Loyal League. It was this order, dominated by a few radical whites, which organized, disciplined, and controlled the ignorant negro masses and paralyzed the influence of the conservative whites.

The Union League of America had its origin in Ohio in the fall of 1862, when the outlook for the Union cause was gloomy.... The members were pledged to uncompromising and unconditional loyalty to the Union, to complete subordination of political views to this loyalty, and to the repudiation of any belief in state rights.... With the close of the Civil War the League did not cease its active interest in things political. It was one of the first organizations to declare for negro suffrage and the disfranchisement of Confederates; it held steadily to this declaration during the four years following the war; and it continued as a sort of bureau in the radical Republican party for the purpose of controlling the negro vote in the South....

From the beginning the [Freedmen's] Bureau agents, the teachers, and the preachers had been holding meetings of negroes, to whom they gave advice about the problems of freedom. Very early these advisers of the blacks grasped the possibilities inherent in their control of the schools, the rationing system, and the churches. By the spring of 1866 the negroes were widely organized under this leadership, and it needed but slight change to convert the negro meetings into local councils of the Union League. As soon as it seemed likely that Congress would win in its struggle with the President the guardians of the negro planned their campaign for the control of the race. Negro leaders were organized into councils of the League or into Union Republican Clubs. Over the South went the organizers, until by 1868 the last negroes were gathered into the fold....

The influence of the League over the negro was due in large degree to the mysterious secrecy of the meetings, the weird initiation ceremony that made him feel fearfully good from his head to his heels, the imposing ritual, and the songs. The ritual, it is said, was not used in the North; it was probably adopted for the particular benefit of the African. The would-be Leaguer was informed that the emblems of the order were the altar, the Bible, the Declaration of Independence, the Constitution of the United States, the flag of the Union, censer, sword, gavel, ballot box, sickle, shuttle, anvil, and other emblems of industry. He was told to the accompaniment of clanking chains and groans that the objects of the order were to preserve liberty, to perpetuate the Union, to maintain the laws and the Constitution, to secure the ascendancy of American institutions, to protect, defend, and strengthen all loyal men and members of the Union League in all rights of person and property, to demand the elevation of labor, to aid in the education of laboring men, and to teach the duties of American citizenship.

This enumeration of the objects of the League sounded well and was impressive. At this point the negro was always willing to take an oath of secrecy, after which he was asked to swear with a solemn oath to support the principles of the Declaration of Independence, to pledge himself to resist all attempts to overthrow the United States, to strive for the maintenance of liberty, the elevation of labor, the education of all people in the duties of citizenship, to practice friendship and charity to all of the order, and to support for election or appointment to office only such men as were supporters of these principles and measures.

The council then sang *Hail, Columbia!* and *The Star Spangled Banner*, after which an official lectured the candidates, saying that though the designs of traitors had been thwarted, there were yet to be secured legislative triumphs and the complete ascendancy of the true principles of popular government, equal liberty, education and elevation of the workmen, and the overthrow at the ballot box of the old oligarchy of political leaders. After prayer by the chaplain, the room was darkened, alcohol on salt flared up with a ghastly light as the "fire of liberty," and the members joined hands in a circle around the candidate, who was made to place one hand on the flag and, with the other raised, swear again to support the government and to elect true Union men to office. Then placing his hand on a Bible, for the third time he swore to keep his oath, and repeated after the president "the Freedmen's Pledge": "To defend and perpetuate freedom and the Union, I pledge my life, my fortune, and my sacred honor. So help me God!" *John Brown's Body* was then sung, the president charged the members in a long speech concerning the principles of the order, and the marshal instructed the neophyte in the signs. To pass one's self as a Leaguer, the "Four L's" had to be given: (1) with right hand raised to heaven, thumb and third finger touching ends over palm, pronounce "Liberty"; (2) bring the hand down over the shoulder and say "Lincoln"; (3) drop the hand open at the side and say "Loyal"; (4) catch the thumb in the vest or in the waistband and pronounce "League." This ceremony of initiation proved a most effective means of impressing and controlling the negro....

In each populous precinct there was at least one council of the League, and always one for blacks. In each town or city there were two councils, one for the whites, and another, with white officers, for the blacks. The council met once a week, sometimes oftener, nearly always at night, and in a negro church or school-house. Guards, armed with rifles and shotguns, were stationed about the place of meeting in order to keep away intruders. Members of some councils made it a practice to attend the meet-ings armed as if for battle. In these meetings the negroes listened to inflammatory speeches by the would-be statesmen of the new regime; here they were drilled in a passionate conviction that their interests and those of the Southern whites were eternally at war.

White men who joined the order before the negroes were admitted and who left when the latter became members asserted that the negroes were taught in these meetings that the only way to have peace and plenty, to get "the forty acres and a mule," was to kill some of the leading whites in each community as a warn-ing to others. In North Carolina twenty-eight barns were burned in one county by negroes who believed that Governor Holden, the head of the State League, had ordered it. The council in Tus-cumbia, Alabama, received advice from Memphis to use the torch because the blacks were at war with the white race. The advice was taken. Three men went in front of the council as an advance guard, three followed with coal oil and fire, and others guarded the rear. The plan was to burn the whole town, but first one negro and then another insisted on having some white man's house spared because "he is a good man." In the end no residences were burned, and a happy compromise was effected by burn-ing the Female Academy. Three of the leaders were afterwards lynched.... But on the whole, there was very little actual violence, though the whites were much alarmed at times. That outrages were comparatively few was due, not to any sensible teachings of the leaders, but to the fundamental good nature of the blacks, who were generally content with mere impudence.

The relations between the races, indeed, continued on the whole to be friendly until 1867-68…. With the organization of the League, the negroes grew more reserved, and finally became openly unfriendly to the whites. The League alone, however, was not responsible for this change. The League and the [Freedmen's] Bureau had to some extent the same personnel, and it is frequently impossible to distinguish clearly between the influence of the two. In many ways the League was simply the political side of the Bureau. The preaching and teaching missionaries were also at work. And apart from the organized influences at work, the poor whites never laid aside their hostility towards the blacks, bond or free.

When the campaigns grew exciting, the discipline of the order was used to prevent the negroes from attending Democratic meetings and hearing Democratic speakers. The leaders even went farther and forbade the attendance of the blacks at political meetings where the speakers were not endorsed by the League…. As soon as a candidate was nominated by the League, it was the duty of every member to support him actively. Failure to do so resulted in a fine or other more severe punishment, and members who had been expelled were still considered under the control of the officials. The League was, in fact, the machine of the radical party, and all candidates had to be governed by its edicts….

Every negro was *ex colore* a member or under the control of the League. In the opinion of the League, white Democrats were bad enough, but black Democrats were not to be tolerated…. It was possible in some cases for a negro to refrain from taking an active part in political affairs. He might even fail to vote. But it was actually dangerous for a black to be a Democrat; that is, to try to follow his old master in politics. The whites in many cases were forced to advise their few faithful black friends to vote the radical ticket in order to escape mistreatment….

Some of the methods of the Loyal League were similar to those of the later Ku Klux Klan. Anonymous warnings were sent to obnoxious individuals, houses were burned, notices were posted at night in public places and on the houses of persons who had incurred the hostility of the order. In order to destroy the influence of the whites where kindly relations still existed, an "exodus order" issued through the League directed all members to leave their old homes and obtain work elsewhere. Some of the blacks were loath to comply with this order, but to remonstrances from the whites the usual reply was: "De word done sent to de League. We got to go"....

The few whites who were in control were unwilling to admit more white members to share in the division of the spoils; terms of admission became more stringent, and, especially after the passage of the reconstruction acts in March, 1867, many white applicants were rejected. The alien element from the North was in control and as a result, where the blacks were numerous, the largest plums fell to the carpetbaggers. The negro leaders – the politicians, preachers, and teachers – trained in the League acted as subordinates to the whites and were sent out to drum up the country negroes when elections drew near. The negroes were given minor positions when offices were more plentiful than carpetbaggers. Later, after some complaint, a larger share of the offices fell to them....

Booker T. Washington, from *Up from Slavery*: (5)

I saw coloured men who were members of the state legislatures, and county officers, who, in some cases, could not read or write, and whose morals were as weak as their education. Not long ago, when passing through the streets of a certain city in the South, I heard some brick-masons calling out, from the top of a two-story brick building on which they were working, for the "Governor" to "hurry up and bring up some more bricks." Several times I heard the command, "Hurry up, Governor!" "Hurry up, Governor!" My curiosity was aroused to such an extent that I made inquiry as to who the "Governor" was, and soon found that he was a coulored man who at one time had held the position of Lieutenant-Governor of his state....

Edmund Burke, from his *Reflections on the Revolution in France*: (6)

You will smile here at the consistency of those democratists, who, when they are not on their guard, treat the humbler part of the community with the greatest contempt, whilst, at the same time, they pretend to make them the depositories of all power....

Thomas Carlyle, from his *Latter-Day Pamphlets:* (7)

Like owls they say, "Barabbas will do; ... the Right Honorable Minimus is well enough; he shall be our Maximus, under him it will be handy to catch mice, and Owldom shall continue a flourishing empire."

Walter Lynwood Fleming, from *The Sequel of Appomattox*: (8)

The Southern States reconstructed by Congress were subject for periods of varying length to governments designed by radical Northerners and imposed by elements thrown to the surface in the upheaval of Southern society. Georgia, Virginia, and North Carolina each had a brief experience with these governments; other States escaped after four or five years, while Louisiana, South Carolina, and Florida were not delivered from this domination until 1876. The States which contained large numbers of negroes had, on the whole, the worst experience. Here the officials were ignorant or corrupt, frauds upon the public were the rule, not the exception, and all of the reconstruction governments were so conducted that they could secure no support from the respectable elements of the electorate....

Of the carpetbaggers half were personally honest, but all were unscrupulous in politics. Some were flagrantly dishonest. Governor Moses of South Carolina was several times bribed and at one time, according to his own statement, received $15,000 for his vote as speaker of the House of Representatives. Governor Stearns of Florida was charged with stealing government supplies from the negroes; and it was notorious that Warmoth and Kelogg of Louisiana, each of whom served only one term, retired with large fortunes. Warmoth, indeed, went so far as to declare: "Corruption is the fashion. I do not pretend to be honest, but only as honest as anybody in politics."

The judiciary was no better than the executive. The chief justice of Louisiana was convicted of fraud. A supreme court judge of South Carolina offered his decision for sale, and Whipper and Moses, both notorious thieves, were elected judges by the South Carolina Legislature. In Alabama there were many illiterate magistrates, among them the city judge of Selma, who in April, 1865, was still living as a slave. Governor Chamberlain, a radical, asserted that there were two hundred trial judges in South Carolina who could not read.

Other officers were of the same stripe. Leslie, a South Carolina carpetbagger, declared that "South Carolina has no right to be a State unless she can support her statesmen," and he proceeded to live up to this principle. The manager of the state railroad of Georgia, when asked how he had been able to accumulate twenty or thirty thousand dollars on a two or three thousand dollar salary, replied, "By the exercise of the most rigid economy...."

The effect of dishonest government was soon seen in extravagant expenditures, heavier taxes, increase of the bonded debt, and depression of property values. It was to be expected that after the ruin wrought by war and the admission of the negro to civil rights, the expenses of government would be greater. But only lack of honesty will account for the extraordinary expenses of the reconstruction governments.... A part of the money raised by taxes and by bond sales was used for legitimate expenses and the rest went to pay forged warrants, excess warrants, and swollen mileage accounts, and to fill the pockets of embezzlers and thieves from one end of the South to the other....

The foundation of radical power in the South lay in the alienation of the races which had been accomplished between 1865 and 1868. To maintain this unhappy distrust, the radical leaders found an effective means in the negro militia.... The radical structure, however, was still powerfully supported from without.... The enforcement legislation gave the color of law to any interference which was deemed necessary. Federal troops served other ends than the mere preservation of order and the support of the radical state governments. They were used on occasion to decide between opposing factions and to oust conservatives who had forced their way into office. The army officers purged the Legislature of Georgia in 1870, that of Alabama in 1872, and that of Louisiana in 1875. In 1875 the city government of Vicksburg and the state government of Louisiana were overturned by the whites, but General [Phillip] Sheridan at once intervened to put back the negroes and carpetbaggers. He suggested to President Grant that the conservatives be declared "banditti" and he would make himself responsible for the rest.... Besides the army there was in every State a powerful group of Federal officials who formed a "ring" for the direction of all good radicals. These marshals, deputies, postmasters, district attorneys, and customhouse officials were in close touch with Washington and frequently dictated nominations and platforms....

Such was the machinery used to sustain a party which, with the gradual defection of the whites, became throughout the South almost uniformly black.... It would not be correct to say that the negro race was malicious or on evil bent. Unless deliberately stirred up by white leaders, few negroes showed signs of mean spirit. Few even made exorbitant demands. They wanted "something" – schools and freedom and "something else," they knew not what. Deprived of the leadership of the best whites, they could not possibly act with the scalawags – their traditional enemies. Nothing was left for them but to follow the carpetbagger....

And did the Countenance Divine
Shine forth upon our clouded hills?
And was Jerusalem builded here,
Among these dark Satanic Mills?....
                    - William Blake, *preface to* "Milton": (9)

Edmund Burke, from *Reflections on the Revolution in France*: (10)

When all the frauds, impostures, violences, rapines, burnings, murders, confiscations, compulsory paper currencies, and every description of tyranny and cruelty employed to bring about and uphold this Revolution, have their natural effect, that is, to shock the moral sentiments of all virtuous and sober minds, the abettors of this philosophic system immediately strain their throats in a declamation against the old ... government.... When they have rendered that deposed power sufficiently black, they then proceed in argument, as if all those who disapprove of their new abuses must of course be partisans of the old; that those who reprobate their crude and violent schemes of liberty ought to be treated as advocates for servitude.... Have these gentlemen never heard, in the whole circle of the worlds of theory and practice, of anything between the despotism of the monarch and the despotism of the multitude? ...

Until now, we have seen no examples of considerable democracies. The ancients were better acquainted with them. Not being wholly unread in the authors, who had seen the most of those constitutions, and who best understood them, I cannot help concurring with their opinion, that an absolute democracy, no more than absolute monarchy, is to be reckoned among the legitimate forms of government. They think it rather the corruption and degeneracy, than the sound constitution of a republic. If I recollect rightly, Aristotle observes, that a democracy has many striking points of resemblance with a tyranny:

"The ethical character is the same; both exercise despotism over the better class of citizens; and decrees are in the one, what ordinances and arrets are in the other: the demagogue too, and the court favorite, are not infrequently the the same identical men, and always bear a close analogy; and these have the principal power, each in their respective forms of government, favorites with the absolute monarch, and demagogues with a people such as I have described." (Arist. Politic. lib. iv. cap. 4.)....

You might change the names. The things in some shape must remain. A certain *quantum* of power must always exist in the community, in some hands, and under some appellation. Wise men will apply their remedies to vices, not to names; and to the causes of evil which are permanent, not the occasional organs by which they act, and the transitory modes in which they appear. Otherwise you will be wise historically, a fool in practice. Seldom have two ages the same fashion in their pretexts and the same mode of mischief. Wickedness is a little more inventive. Whilst you are discussing fashion, the fashion is gone by. The very same vice assumes a new body. The spirit transmigrates; and, far from losing its principle of life by the change of its appearance, it is renovated in its new organs with a fresh vigor of a juvenile activity. It walks abroad, it continues its ravages, whilst you are gibbeting the carcass, or demolishing the tomb. You are terrifying yourselves with ghosts and apparitions, whilst your house is the haunt of robbers. It is thus with all those, who, attending only to the shell and husk of history, think they are waging war with intolerance, pride, and cruelty, whilst, under color of abhorring the ill principles of antiquated parties, they are authorizing and feeding the same odious vices in different factions, and perhaps in worse....

Andrew Nelson Lytle, from *"The Hind Tit"*: (11)

Since 1865 an agrarian Union has been changed into an industrial empire bent on conquest of the earth's goods and ports to sell them in. This means warfare, a struggle over markets, leading, in the end, to actual military conflict between nations. But, in the meantime, the terrific effort to manufacture ammunition – that is, wealth – so that imperialism may prevail, has brought upon the social body a more deadly conflict, one which promises to deprive it, not of life, but of living; take the concept of liberty from the political consciousness; and turn the pursuit of happiness into a nervous running-around which is without the logic, even, of a dog chasing its tail.

This conflict is between the unnatural progeny of inventive genius and men. It is a war to the death between technology and the ordinary human functions of living. The rights to these human functions are the natural rights of man, and they are threatened now, in the twentieth, not in the eighteenth, century for the first time. Unless man asserts and defends them he is doomed, to use a chemical analogy, to hop about like sodium on water, burning up in his own energy.

But since a power machine is ultimately dependent upon human control, the issue presents an awful spectacle: men, run mad by their inventions, supplanting themselves with inanimate objects. This is, to follow the matter to its conclusion, a moral and spiritual suicide, foretelling an actual physical destruction....

Jose Ortega y Gasset, from *The Revolt of the Masses*: (12)

In our days the State has come to be a formidable machine which works in marvelous fashion; of wonderful efficiency by reason of the quantity and precision of its means. Once it is set up in the midst of society, it is enough to touch a button for its enormous levers to start working and exercise their overwhelming power on any portion whatever of the social framework.... And it is an interesting revelation when one takes note of the attitude that mass-man adopts before it.... When the mass suffers any ill-fortune or simply feels some strong appetite, its great temptation is that permanent, sure possibility of obtaining everything – without effort, struggle, doubt, or risk – merely by touching a button and setting the mighty machine in motion.... The result of this tendency will be fatal. Spontaneous social action will be broken up over and over again by State intervention; no new seed will be able to fructify. Society will have to live *for* the State, man *for* the governmental machine....

Such was the lamentable fate of ancient civilization. No doubt the imperial State created by the Julii and the Claudii was an admirable machine, incomparably superior as a mere structure to the old republican State of the patrician families. But, by a curios coincidence, hardly had it reached full development when the social body began to decay.... Society begins to be enslaved, to be unable to live except *in the service of the State*. The whole of life is bureaucratized. What results? The bureaucratization of life brings about its absolute decay in all orders....

BOOK V – CHAPTER FIVE

The City upon a Hill

"Whether this is Jerusalem or Babylon we know not.
"All is confusion. All is tumult, & we alone are escaped."
　　　　　 - William Blake, "Vala, or the Four Zoas –
　　　　　 Night the Third" (1)

Rev. J. William Jones, from *Personal Reminiscences of General Robert E. Lee*: (2)

General Lee was conspicuous for a want of bitterness toward the United States authorities and the people of the North. He certainly had much which others would have taken as an occasion of bitterness, if not absolute hatred. While he was suffering privation and hardship, and meeting danger in opposing what he honestly believed to be the armed hosts of oppression and wrong, his home was seized (and held) by the Government, and his property destroyed. When at the close of the war he faithfully and scrupulously sought to carry out his parole, avoided the popular applause that his people were everywhere ready to give him, and sought a quiet retreat where he could labor for the good of the young men of the South, his motives were impugned, his actions were misrepresented, and certain of the Northern journals teemed with bitter slanders against him, while a United States grand-jury (in violation of the terms of his parole, as General Grant himself maintained) found against him an indictment for "treason and rebellion." And yet amid all these provocations he uttered no word of bitterness, and always raised his voice for moderation and charity....

Soon after the grand-jury found its indictment against General Lee, at a time when President Andrew Johnson was showing a purpose to carry out his threat to "Make treason odious by hanging the chief of the rebel leaders," and when ultra men at the North were clamoring for vengeance for what they claimed as "the complicity of the South" in the assassination of Mr. Lincoln, a party of friends were spending an evening at his house in Richmond, and the conversation naturally turned on these matters. Rev. Dr. _____ led the conversation in expressing, in terms of decided bitterness, the indignation of the South at the indictment of General Lee. The general pleasantly remarked, "Well! it matters little what they may do to me; I am old, and have but a short time to live anyhow," and very soon turned the conversation into other channels. Presently Dr. _____ got up to go, and General Lee followed him out to the door and said to him very earnestly: "Doctor, there is a good old book which I read, and you preach from, which says, 'Love your enemies, bless them that curse you, and do good to them that hate you, and pray for them which despitefully use you and persecute you.' Do you think your remarks this evening were quite in the spirit of that teaching?"

Dr. _____ made some apology for the bitterness which he felt and expressed, and General Lee added, with that peculiar sweetness of tone and manner that we remember so well: "I have fought against the people of the North because I believed they were seeking to wrest from the South dearest rights. But I have never cherished toward them bitter or vindictive feelings, and have never seen the day when I did not pray for them."

If the world's history affords a sublimer spectacle than that of this stern warrior teaching a minister of the gospel of peace the duty of love to enemies, the present writer has failed to note it.

It is related that one day during the war, as they were reconnoitering the countless hosts opposed to them, one of his subordinates exclaimed in bitter tones, "I wish those people were all dead!" General Lee, with that inimitable grace of manner peculiar to him, promptly rejoined:

"How can you say so, General? Now, I wish that they were all at home attending to their own business, and leaving us to do the same."

One day in the autumn of 1869, I saw General Lee standing at his gate, talking to a humbly-clad man, who turned off, evidently delighted with his interview, just as I came up. After exchanging salutations, the general pleasantly said, pointing to the retreating form, "That is one of our old soldiers who is in necessitous circumstances." I took it for granted that it was some veteran Confederate, and asked to what command he belonged, when the General quietly and pleasantly added, *"He fought on the other side, but we must not remember that against him now."*

The man afterward came to my house and said to me, in speaking of his interview with General Lee: "Sir, he is the noblest man that ever lived. He not only had a kind word for an old soldier who fought against him, but he gave me some money to help me on my way."

What a beautiful illustration of the teaching of the apostle: *"If thine enemy hunger, feed him; if he thirst, give him drink!"*

Upon the occasion of the delivery of an address at Washington College by a certain distinguished orator, General Lee came to the writer and said: "I saw you taking notes during the address. It was in the main very fine; but, if you propose publishing any report of it, I would suggest that you leave out all the bitter expressions against the North and the United States Government. They will do us no good under our present circumstances, and I think all such expressions undignified and unbecoming."

Soon after the passage of some of the most objectionable of the so-called *Reconstruction Acts*, two of the professors of the college were conversing with him, when one of them expressed himself in very bitter terms concerning the dominant party and their treatment of the people of the South. General Lee quietly turned to his table, and, picking up a MS (which afterward proved to be a memoir of his father), read the following lines:

'Learn from yon Orient shell to love thy foe,
And store with pearls the hand that brings thee woe:
Free like yon rock, from base, vindictive pride,
Emblaze with gems the wrist that rends thy side;
Mark where yon tree rewards the stony shower
With fruit nectareous, or the balmy flower,
All nature cries aloud: shall man do less
Than heal the smiter, and the railer bless?'

He then said that these lines were written "in [Persia] and by a Mussulman, the poet of Shiraz – the immortal Hafiz," and quietly asked, "Ought not we who profess to be governed by the principles of Christianity to rise at least to the standard of this Mohammedan poet, and learn to forgive our enemies?" ....

It was my sad privilege, not long after General Lee's death, to look over some papers found in his army-satchel, together with his parole, and other things which had not been disturbed since his return from Appomattox Court-House. On loose sheets he had written – evidently to amuse a leisure hour in camp – a great many maxims, proverbs, quotations from the Psalms, selections from standard authors, and reflections of his own. On one sheet was found, in his well-known handwriting, the following:

"The warmest instincts of every man's soul declare the glory of the soldier's death. It is more appropriate to the Christian than to the Greek to sing:
'Glorious his fate, and envied is his lot,
Who for his country fights and for it dies.'
There is a true glory and a true honor: the glory of duty done – the honor of the integrity of principle"....

[S]o great bards of him will sing
Hereafter; and dark sayings from of old
Ranging and ringing thro' the minds of men,
And echo'd by old folk beside their fires
For comfort after their wage-work is done,
Speak of the King; and Merlin in our time
Hath spoken also, not in jest, and sworn
Tho' men may wound him that he will not die,
But pass, again to come, and then or now
Utterly smite the heathen underfoot,
Till these and all men hail him for their king....

- Tennyson, *Idylls of the King* (3)

*The sun also ariseth, and the sun goeth down, and
hasteth to his place where he arose.
The wind goeth toward the south, and turneth about
unto the north; it whirleth about continually, and
the wind returneth again according to his circuits.
All the rivers run into the sea; yet the sea is not full;
unto the place from whence the rivers come, thither
they return again.*

- Ecclesiastes 1:5-7

Then from the dawn it seem'd there came, but faint
As from beyond the limit of the world,
Like the last echo born of a great cry,
Sounds, as if some fair city were one voice
Around a king returning from his wars....

- Tennyson, *Idylls of the King* (4)

END NOTES

FRONT COVER ILLUSTRATION

Image: *View in the "Burnt District," Richmond, Virginia, April 1865* – Library of Congress, Prints & Photographs Division, Civil War Photographs, Reproduction No. LC-USZC4-4593.

TITLE SECTION

1. Alexis de Tocqueville, Democracy in America, 2 vols. Trans. Henry Reeve (New York: D. Appleton, 1904) 2: 425.

FRONT PLATE

Image: *Gen. Robert E. Lee in 1863* - Minnis & Cowell (Photographer – Richmond, Virginia) Virginia Historical Society collection – Accession No. 2001.2.107. (Altered to three-quarter image)

MAP

Image: *Map of Virginia Campaign* - from Robert Underwood Johnson and Clarence Clough Buel, eds. *Battles and Leaders of the Civil War*. 4 vols. The Century War Series. New York: Century, 1887-8. 4:164. Virginia Historical Society collection – E470 .B333 pg. 164, edited by Ned Bradford.

PLATE FOLLOWING MAP

Image: *Prior to Antietam. Rebels Crossing the Potomac. Union Scouts in the Foreground* - Drawing by Alfred R. Waud. Library of Congress, Prints & Photographs Division, Civil War Photographs, Reproduction No. LC-DIG-ppmsca-21427.

EDITOR'S NOTE

1. On "Great Men" and the role of the individual as an "Agent of the World-Spirit," see Georg Wilhelm Friedrich Hegel, "Introduction to the Logic of History" in *The European Philosophers from Descartes to Nietzsche*, ed. Monroe C. Beardsley, Modern Library Edition (New York: Modern Library – Random House, 1992) 564. See also Leslie A. White's chapters on "Genius: Its Causes and Incidence," and "Ikhnaton," in *The Science of Culture: A Study of Man and Civilization* (New York: Grove – Farrar, Straus and Cudahy, 1949) particularly 227-30 and 278-81. On History vs. Evolution see White 229-30. Also note Bismarck quoted in Paul Kennedy, *The Rise and Fall of the Great Powers: Economic Change and Military Conflict from 1500 to 2000.* First Vintage Books Edition (New York: Vintage – Random House, 1989) 540.

2. Alfred, Lord Tennyson, *Idylls of the King*, in *The Works of Alfred Lord Tennyson* (1892; London: MacMillan & Co., 1911) 309.

INTRODUCTION

1. The foundation of this work is based principally upon Leslie A. White's essay entitled "Energy and the Evolution of Culture," in *The Science of Culture:* 363-93, and is bolstered by Kennedy's chapter on "Industrialization and the Shifting Global Balances, 1815-1885" in *The Rise and Fall of the Great Powers* 143-93. See particularly the sub-headings entitled "The United States and the Civil War," 178-82, and "Conclusions," 191-3.

2. Harry E. Vanden and Gary Prevost, *The Politics of Latin America: The Power Game* (Oxford: Oxford UP, 2002) 153-4, 156-60.

3. William Cabell Bruce, *John Randolph of Roanoke 1773 – 1833*, 2 vols. (New York & London: G. P. Putnam's Sons – The Knickerbocker P, 1922) 1: 435-6; 431-3.

4. Thomas Jefferson to William Branch Giles, December 26, 1825, in *The Writings of Thomas Jefferson*, 10 vols. Ed. Paul Leicester Ford (New York: G. P. Putnam's Sons – The Knickerbocker P, 1892-1899) 10: 354-6.

5. Thomas Prentice Kettell, *Southern Wealth and Northern Profits*. (New York: George W. & John A. Wood, 1860) 3-5.

6. White 127-9. See also Alexis de Tocqueville's Chapter Eighteen on "The Three Races in the United States," in *Democracy in America*, 2 vols. Trans. Henry Reeve. (New York: D. Appleton, 1904) particularly 1: 387-8, and Adam Smith, *An Inquiry into the Nature and Causes of the Wealth of Nations*, Ed. C. J. Bullock, Ph D, in Charles W. Eliot, *The Harvard Classics*, 50 vols. (New York: P. F. Collier & Son, 1909) 10: 85.

7. Aldous Huxley, *Brave New World*, First Perennial Classics Edition (1932; New York: HarperPerennial – HarperCollins, 1998) *foreword*, xiii-xvii. For the rise of the egalitarian "mass man" and the atomized society upon which totalitarianism rests, see Hannah Arendt's Chapter Ten: "A Classless Society," in *The Origins of Totalitarianism*, Second Enlarged Edition (1951; Cleveland: Meridian – World, 1958,) particularly 315-7. For examples of egalitarianism in overtly collectivist States see "The New Soviet Person" in David L. Hoffman, *Stalinist Values: The Cultural Norms of Soviet Modernity, 1917-1941* (Ithaca: Cornell UP, 2003) 45-56. For egalitarianism in democracies, through the promotion of radical individualism and the assaults on civil society, see Robert H. Bork, *Slouching Towards Gomorrah: Modern Liberalism and American Decline*, First Paperback Edition (1996; New York: ReganBooks – HarperCollins, 1997) 325-30. For an in-depth examination of some methods of social engineering used by the State to achieve social control in both col-

lectivist and democratic societies, see Aldous Huxley, *Brave New World Revisited*, First Harper Perennial Modern Classics Edition (1958; New York: HarperPerennial – HarperCollins, 2006) *passim*. For the rise in power of the State – both actual and relative to society – see Jose Ortega y Gasset, *The Revolt of the Masses*, Trans. Anon. (1930; New York: W. W. Norton & Co., 1993) 118-22. For the king demanded by the people of Israel, see I Samuel, Chapter 8. See also Ecclesiastes 1: 9 and 5:16.

BOOK I – (1861)

Book I - Title Section

1. Louis Untermeyer, ed. *Modern American Poetry: An Introduction* (New York: Harcourt, Brace and Howe, 1919) 154.

Image: Gov. Henry A. Wise - Library of Congress, Prints & Photographs Division, Civil War Photographs, Reproduction No. LC-DIG-cwpb-06502.

Book I – Chapter One

Chapter Title from Matthew Arnold, "Dover Beach," in *Poetical Works of Matthew Arnold* (1890; London: MacMillan & Co., 1913) 227.

1. J. Alexander Patten, "Scenes in the Old Dominion. Number Two – A Tobacco Market," New York *Mercury* 21 (November 5, 1859): 8: Microfilm. Library of Congress collection.

2. Tennyson 448.

Book I – Chapter Two

Chapter Title from Thomas Jefferson's letter to John Holmes, April 22, 1820, in Jefferson 10: 157.

1. John S. Wise, *The End of an Era* (New York: Houghton, Mifflin & Co., 1899) 118-30.

2. "'Tis Done," editorial, *Daily Richmond Enquirer*, December 3, 1859. Microfilm no. 23, Reel no. 21; July 1, 1859 – Dec. 31,

1859 (Richmond: Library of Virginia collection) 2, column 1.

Book I – Chapter Three

Chapter Title from Jefferson's letter to John Holmes, April 22, 1820, in Jefferson, 10: 157.

1. William Drayton, *The South Vindicated from the Treason and Fanaticism of the Northern Abolitionists* (Philadelphia: H. Manly, 1836) 157-8.

2. George Fitzhugh, *Cannibals All! or Slaves Without Masters* (Richmond: 1857) 141-4.

3. William J. Grayson, *The Hireling and the Slave, Chicora, and Other Poems* (Charleston: 1856) 23-4, 26-8.

4. Wendell Phillips, speech, November 1, 1859, in James Redpath, ed., *Echoes of Harper's Ferry* (Boston: Thayer & Eldridge, 1860) 51.

5. Tennyson 385.

6. "The Slave-Trade in New York," editorial, *Continental Monthly*, January 1862, 87, in W. E. B. DuBois, *The Suppression of the African Slave-Trade to the United States of America 1638-1870* (New York: Longmans, Green, & Co., 1896) 179.

7. Grayson 37-41.

8. Fitzhugh, introduction, xvi-xix.

Book I – Chapter Four

Chapter Title from MacBeth, act iv, sc. i.

1. Bruce 1: 418.

2. Chancellor Henry William Desaussure, "A Series of Numbers Addressed to the Public, on the Subject of the Slaves and the Free People of Colour…." (Columbia: State Gazette Office, 1822) 18-9. (Columbia: Courtesy of South Caroliniana Library collection.) 18-9.

3. Thomas R. Dew, *Review of the Debates in the Virginia Legislature of 1831 and 1832* (Richmond: 1832) 2, 8-9.

4. Ibid. 9-10, 106.

5. Desaussure 21-2, 17.

6. Tocqueville 1: 385, 387-8, 391-2, 416 note 39, 394-9, 417 note 45.

7. Dew 80.

8. Tocqueville 1: 404-5, 408.

9. Jefferson 10: 157-8.

Book I – Chapter Five

Chapter Title from St. Luke, 12:1.

1. Mrs. Roger A. Pryor, *Reminiscences of Peace and War*. Revised and enlarged ed. (New York: The MacMillan Co., 1905) 93-7.

2. William H. Seward, speech, Rochester, New York, October 25, 1858, in *The Works of William H. Seward*, 5 vols. Ed. George E. Baker (Boston: Houghton, Mifflin & Co., 1853-84) 4: 289, 291-2.

3. Kettell 138-40, 156-8.

4. Wise 134-5.

5. "The Presidential Election," editorial, Richmond *Dispatch*, November 9, 1860. Microfilm. July thru December 1860 Main Film 20, c2. (Richmond: Library of Virginia collection) 2, column 1.

Book I – Chapter Six

Chapter Title from speech by William H. Seward at Rochester, New York, October 25, 1858, in Seward, 4: 292.

1. "Coercive Policy of the Inaugural," editorial, Richmond *Whig*, March 6, 1861. Microfilm no. 144a, Jan. 1861 thru Jun. 1861 (Richmond: Library of Virginia collection) 2, column 1.

2. Tennyson, Idylls, 449.

3. "The War Begins," editorial, Richmond *Dispatch*, April 13, 1861. Microfilm. January thru June 1861. Main Film 20, c2. (Richmond: Library of Virginia collection) 2, column 1.

4. Edward A. Pollard, *Southern History of the War*, 2 vols. (New York: Charles B. Richardson, 1866) I: 55-6, 58-9, 61.

5. Abraham Lincoln, letter to Captain G. V. Fox, May 1, 1861, in Samuel Wylie Crawford, *The Genesis of the Civil War: The Story of Sumter 1860-1861* (New York: Charles L. Webster & Co., 1887) 420.

6. Pollard 1: 61-3.

7. Kettell 19, 24, 42, 52, 75-6.

8. "The Difference," editorial, New Orleans *Daily Crescent*, January 21, 1861. Microfilm no. 1699, Reel no. 18, New Orleans *Daily Crescent*, New Orleans, Louisiana. 1/1/1861 – 6/29/1861. Courtesy of Special Collections, LSU Libraries, Louisiana State University, Baton Rouge, Louisiana.

9. Tocqueville 2: 425-6.

10. "A Government of Force," editorial, Richmond *Whig*, April 10, 1861. Microfilm no. 144a. Jan. 1861 thru Jun. 1861. (Richmond: Library of Virginia collection) 2, column 1.

11. Gov. John Letcher, letter to Sec. Simon Cameron, April 16, 1861, in Richmond *Enquirer*, April 18, 1861, 2, col. 1. Microfilm. The Daily Richmond *Enquirer*, Jan. 1, 1861-June 29, 1861. Film 23, reel 24 (Richmond: Library of Virginia collection.)

12. Eliot 43: 160-1.

13. Virginia Ordinance of Secession, April 17, 1861. Papers, Convention of 1861. Access no. 40586 (Richmond: Library of Virginia).

BOOK II – (1862)

Book II – Title Section

1. Eliot, 41: 768.

Image: Lt. Gen. Thomas J. "Stonewall" Jackson – Library of Congress, Prints & Photographs Division, Civil War Photographs, Reproduction No. LC-DIG-stereo-1s02859.

Book II – Chapter One

1. Lt. Gen. Jubal A. Early, "Lee Memorial Address," January 19, 1872, in Rev. J. William Jones, *Personal Reminiscences of General Robert E. Lee* (New York: D. Appleton & Co., 1875) 1-2.

2. Lt. Col. Walter H. Taylor, *Four Years with General Lee* (New York: D. Appleton & Co., 1877) 13-4.

3. Pryor 146-59.

4. Wise 169-70, 172.

Book II – Chapter Two

Chapter Title from Tennyson, "The Lady of Shallott," in *Works* 28.

1. John M. Daniel, editorial, Richmond *Examiner*, January 16, 1862, in Frederick S. Daniel, ed., *The Richmond Examiner During the War* (New York: 1868) 34-5.

2. Maj. Jed Hotchkiss, *Virginia*, vol. 3 of *Confederate Military History*, 12 vols. Ed. Gen. Clement A. Evans (Atlanta: Confederate Publishing Co., 1899) 269, 274-5.

3. Robert Underwood Johnson and Clarence Clough Buel, eds. *Battles and Leaders of the Civil War, being for the most part contributions by Union and Confederate officers.* Based upon "The Century War Series." 4 vols. (New York: Century, 1887-8) 2: 442-6.

Book II – Chapter Three

Chapter Title from Tennyson, *Idylls*, 303.

1. Walter Taylor 40.

2. Hotchkiss 282.

3. Maj. Heros Von Borcke, *Memoirs of the Confederate War for Independence*, 2 vols. (Edinburgh: W. Blackwood, 1866) 1: 37-43.

4. Hotchkiss 282.

5. Walter Taylor 40.

6. Maj. Robert Stiles, *Four Years under Marse Robert* (New York: Neal, 1903) 94, 97-9, 101-9.

Book II – Chapter Four

Chapter Title from Tennyson, *Idylls,* 292.

1. Walter Taylor 57-8.

2. Hotchkiss 315, 317-20, 323-4.

3. Von Borcke 1: 136-40.

4. Jones 10-1.

5. Stiles 120, 122-4.

6. Walter Taylor 58-9.

Book II – Chapter Five

1. Von Borcke 1: 181-5.

2. Hotchkiss 336.

3. Walter Taylor 66-8.

4. Johnson and Buel 2: 686-90.

5. George M. Neese, *Three Years in the Confederate Horse Artillery* (New York: Neale, 1911) 124-5.

6. Von Borcke 1: 231-3.

7. Walter Taylor 69-70, 73.

8. Lt. Gen. John B. Gordon, *Reminiscences of the Civil War* (New York: Charles Scribner's Sons, 1904) 88.

9. Walter Taylor 74-5.

BOOK III – (1863)

Book III – Title Section

1. Eliot 41: 768.

Image: Maj. Gen. James Ewell Brown "Jeb" Stuart – Library of Congress, Prints & Photographs Division, Civil War Photographs, Reproduction No. LC-DIG-cwpb-07546.

Book III – Chapter One

1. Von Borcke 1: 258, 268-72, 289, 292-5.

2. Hotchkiss 360-3.

Book III – Chapter Two

Chapter Title from Von Borcke 2: 100.

1. Von Borcke 2: 74-6, 79, 94, 98-100.

2. Stiles 132-3.

3. Von Borcke 2: 100-1.

4. Stiles 128.

5. Von Borcke 2: 101-2.

6. Stiles 130-1.

7. Von Borcke 2: 123-4, 127-8, 131-2.

8. Stiles 131.

Book III – Chapter Three

Chapter Title from Abraham Lincoln to Joseph Medill, in Ida M. Tarbell, *The Life of Abraham Lincoln*, 4 vols. (New York: Lincoln Historical society, 1902) 3: 149.

1. Abraham Lincoln, Preliminary Emancipation Proclamation of September 22, 1862, in James D. Richardson, ed., *A Compilation of the Messages and Papers of the Presidents*, 9 vols. (Washington: Government Printing Office, 1897) 6: 96-8.

2. John M. Daniel, editorial, Richmond *Examiner*, September 29, 1862, in Frederick S. Daniel 60-1.

3. "Another Proclamation from Abraham," editorial, Richmond *Enquirer*, September 29, 1862, 1, column 6. Microfilm. Daily Richmond *Enquirer*, July 1, 1862 – Dec 31, 1862; Film 23, Reel 27 (Richmond: Library of Virginia collection.)

4. "Proclamation the Second," editorial, Richmond *Enquirer*, September 30, 1862, 2(?), column 3. Microfilm. Daily Richmond *Enquirer*, July 1, 1862 – Dec 31, 1862; Film 23, Reel 27 (Richmond: Library of Virginia collection.)

5. John M. Daniel, editorial, Richmond *Examiner*, February 9, 1863, in Frederick S. Daniel 72-3.

6. Tarbell 3: 147-9.

Book III – Chapter Four

Chapter Title from Col. John S. Mosby, "A Bit of Partisan Service," in Johnson and Buel 3: 149.

1. Hotchkiss 373.

2. Stiles 139-43.

3. Johnson and Buel 3:148-9.

4. Walter Taylor 83-4.

5. Maj. Hunter McGuire and Hon. George L. Christian, *The Confederate Cause and Conduct in the War Between the States* (Richmond: L. H. Jenkins, 1907) 214.

6. Johnson and Buel 3: 207-8.

7. Von Borcke 2: 226.

8. Johnson and Buel 3: 211-3.

9. Walter Taylor 85-6.

10. McGuire and Christian 227-9.

Book III – Chapter Five

Chapter Title from "Stonewall" Jackson's last words, in McGuire and Christian 229.

1. Walter Taylor 90-2.

2. Stiles 199-200, 202-5.

3. Jones 187-90.

4. Jones 30.

5. Frank Moore, ed., *The Rebellion Record*. 11 vols. (New York: G. P. Putnam, 1861-63; D. Van Nostrand, 1864-68) 7: 108, 111-14.

6. Brig. Gen. A. L .Long, *Memoirs of Robert E. Lee* (New York: J. M. Stoddart & Co., 1886) 289-90.

Book III – Chapter Six

Chapter Title from Arnold, "Dover Beach," 226.

1. Arnold, "Dover Beach," 226.

2. Johnson and Buel 3: 420-4.

3. Pryor 248-9.

4. Constance Cary Harrison (Mrs. Burton Harrison), *Recol-*

lections, Grave and Gay (New York: Charles Scribner's Sons, 1911) 141-6, 150-2.

5. Von Borcke 2: 304-5.

6. Stiles 227-9.

7. Arnold, "Dover Beach," 227.

BOOK IV – (1864)

Book IV – Title Section

1. Eliot 41: 768.

Image: Lt. Gen. Jubal A. Early – Library of Congress, Prints & Photographs Division, Civil War Photographs, Reproduction No. LC-DIG-cwpb-07033.

Book IV – Chapter One

1. Harrison 166.

2. Pollard 2: 140-2.

3. Jones 36-8.

4. Von Borcke 2: 308-14.

Book IV – Chapter Two

1. Walter Taylor 131-6.

2. Pryor 279-80.

3. Walter Taylor 138.

4. Wise 346, 351-2, 355-7, 359-61, 363-6, 368-71.

Book IV – Chapter Three

1. Sen. John Warwick Daniel, *Speeches and Orations of John Warwick Daniel.* Ed. Edward M. Daniel (Lynchburg: J. P. Bell, 1911) 537-44, 546-7.

2. Lt. Gen. Jubal A. Early, *Memoir of the Last Year of the War for Independence in the Confederate States of America* (Lynchburg: Charles W. Button, 1867) 48 (note), 50 (note), 66-7, 67 (note), 67-8, 70, 70 (note).

3. Sen. John Warwick Daniel 548.

4. Gordon 317.

5. Hotchkiss 496-7.

6. Gordon 326-7,332.

7. Neese 317-21.

8. Hotchkiss 502-9.

9. Gordon 348.

Book IV – Chapter Four

1. Rev. J. B. Traywick, "Prison Life at Point Lookout," in R. A. Brock, ed., *Southern Historical Society Papers*, 52 vols. (Richmond: Southern Historical Society, 1890) 18: 431-5.

2. Neese 344-7.

3. Jones 194-5.

4. John M. Daniel, editorial, Richmond *Examiner*, November 25, 1863, in Frederick S. Daniel 142-3.

5. Abraham Lincoln, Fourth Annual Message to Congress, December 6, 1864, in James D. Richardson, ed., *A Compilation of the Messages and Papers of the Presidents*, 9 vols. (Washington: Government Printing Office, 1897) 6: 251-4.

6. Maj. John Scott, *Partisan Life with Col. John S. Mosby* (New York: Harper & Brothers, 1867) 375-8.

Book IV – Chapter Five

Chapter title from Tennyson, Idylls, 464.

1. Wise 392-6.

2. Jones 41-2.

3. Johnson and Buel 4: 725-6.

BOOK V – (1865)

Book V – Title Section

1. Eliot 41: 768.

Image: Gen. Robert E. Lee, C.S.A. - Library of Congress, Prints & Photographs Division, Civil War Photographs, Reproduction No. LC-DIG-cwpb-06237.

Book V – Chapter One

1. Wise 412-36.

Book V – Chapter Two

Chapter Title from Tennyson, Idylls, 458.

1. Eliot 40: 471.

2. Jones 299.

3. Col. Charles Marshall, "Address on the Observance of the Birthday of General R. E. Lee." Delivered at Baltimore, Maryland, January 19, 1894. *Southern Historical Society Papers*, 52 vols. Ed. R. A. Brock. Richmond: Southern Historical Society, 1890 -. 21: 354-6.

4. Jones 143.

5. Eliot 43: 449.

6. Tennyson, Idylls, 464.

Book V – Chapter Three

1. Lt. E. M. Boykin, *The Falling Flag* (New York: E. J. Hale & Son, 1874) 64-7.

2. Joseph A. Waddell, *Annals of Augusta County, Virginia, from 1726 to 1871*, 2nd ed. (Staunton: C. Russell Caldwell, 1902) 507-8.

3. William Gilmore Simms, *History of South Carolina*. South Carolina edition. Revised by Mrs. Mary C. Simms Oliphant (Columbia, 1917) 310-1.

4. Walter Lynwood Fleming, *The Sequel of Appomattox: A Chronicle of the Reunion of the States*. Textbook ed. The Chronicles of America Series. Ed. Allen Johnson. Gerhard R. Lomer and Charles W. Jefferys, assistant editors (New Haven: Yale UP, 1919) 27, 29, 31-2.

5. Waddell 515.

6. Thaddeus Stevens, "The Conquered Provinces," Congressional Globe, 18 December 1865, 72, in Walter L. Fleming, ed., *Documentary History of Reconstruction: Political, Military, Social, Religious, Educational and Industrial, 1865 to 1906*, 2 vols. (Cleveland: The Arthur H. Clark Co., 1906) 1: 148.

7. Acts and Resolutions, 39 Cong., 2 Sess., 60, in Fleming, *Documentary History*, 1: 401-3.

8. William A. Dunning, PhD, *Essays on the Civil War and Reconstruction: and Related Topics* (New York: The MacMillan Co., 1898) 247-52.

9. Robert Somers, *The Southern States since the War 1870-1* (London and New York: MacMillan and Co., 1871) 153-4.

10. Fleming, *Sequel*, 263-4.

11. Dunning 252.

Book V – Chapter Four

1. Booker T. Washington, *Up from Slavery: An Autobiography* (New York: A. L. Burt Co., 1900) 19-22.

2. Lt. Gen. Richard Taylor, *Destruction and Reconstruction* (New York: D. Appleton, 1879) 210, 236, 269.

3. Washington 84.

4. Fleming, *Sequel*, 174-8, 180-93.

5. Washington 85.

6. Eliot 24: 204.

7. Thomas Carlyle, "Latter-Day Pamphlets No. IV - The New Downing Street" in *The Works of Thomas Carlyle*, 12 vols., Library ed. (New York: John B. Alden, 1885) 8: 133-4.

8. Fleming, *Sequel*, 221, 224-5, 230-1, 233, 236, 239-42.

9. Blake, preface to "Milton," in *Poetical Works* 351.

10. Eliot 24: 271-3, 289-90.

11. Ransome, John Crowe, et al. *I'll Take My Stand: The South and the Agrarian Tradition.* Library of Southern Civilization Series. Ed. Lewis P. Simpson. Louisiana Paperback Edition (1930; Baton Rouge: Louisiana State UP, 1977) 202-3. Courtesy of Louisiana State UP.

12. Ortega y Gasset 119-21.

Book V - Chapter Five

Chapter title from John Winthrop, "A Modell of Christian Charity," in *The Memorial History of Boston, Including Suffolk County, Massachusetts*, 1630-1880. 4 vols. Ed. Justin Winsor (Boston: Ticknor & Co., 1880) 1:111.

1. Blake, William, *The Writings of William Blake*, 3 vols. Ed. Geoffrey Keynes (London: The Nonesuch P, 1925) 2: 40.

2. Jones 186, 195-8. 145.

3. Tennyson, *Idylls*, 309.

4. *Ibid.* 465.

WORKS CITED

Arendt, Hannah. *The Origins of Totalitarianism.* (1951). Second Enlarged Edition. Cleveland: Meridian - World, 1958.

Arnold, Matthew. *Poetical Works of Matthew Arnold.* (1890). London: MacMillan, 1913.

Blake, William. *The Poetical Works of William Blake.* Ed. John Sampson. Oxford: Clarendon P, 1905.

---. *The Writings of William Blake,* 3 vols., Ed. Geoffrey Keynes. London: Nonesuch P, 1925. Vol. 2.

Bork, Robert H. *Slouching Towards Gomorrah: Modern Liberalism and American Decline.* (1996). First Paperback Edition. New York: ReganBooks – HarperCollins, 1997.

Boykin, Lt. E. M. *The Falling Flag.* New York: E. J. Hale & Son, 1874.

Bruce, William Cabell. *John Randolph of Roanoke.* 2 vols. New York: G. P. Putnam's Sons, 1922. Vol. 1.

Carlyle, Thomas. *The Works of Thomas Carlyle.* 12 vols. Library Edition. New York: John B. Alden, 1885. Vol. 8.

Crawford, Samuel Wylie. *The Genesis of the Civil War: The Story of Sumter 1860 – 1861.* New York: Charles L. Webster & Co., 1887.

Daniel, John M. *The Richmond Examiner During the War: or, The Writings of John M. Daniel.* Ed. Frederick S. Daniel. New York: 1868.

Daniel, Sen. John W. *Speeches and Orations of John Warwick Daniel.* Ed. Edward M. Daniel. Lynchburg: J. P. Bell, 1911.

Desaussure, Chancellor Henry William ("A Columbian"). "A Series of Numbers Addressed to the Public, on the Subject of the

Slaves and the Free People of Colour; First Published in the South Carolina State Gazette, in the Months of September and October, 1822." Columbia: State Gazette Office, 1822.

Dew, Thomas R. *Review of the Debates in the Virginia Legislature of 1831 and 1832*. Richmond: T. W. White, 1832.

Drayton, William. *The South Vindicated from the Treason and Fanaticism of the Northern Abolitionists*. Philadelphia: H. Manly, 1836.

DuBois, W. E. B. *The Suppression of the African Slave-Trade to the United States of America 1638-1870*. New York: Longmans, Green, & Co., 1896.

Dunning, William Archibald, PhD. *Essays on the Civil War and Reconstruction: and Other Related Topics*. New York: MacMillan, 1898.

Early, Lt. Gen. Jubal A. *Memoir of the Last Year of the War for Independence in the Confederate States of America*. Lynchburg: Charles W. Button, 1867.

Eliot, Charles W., LLD, ed. *The Harvard Classics*. 50 vols. Vol. 6, *The Poems and Songs of Robert Burns*; Vol. 10, Adam Smith, *The Wealth of Nations*; Vol. 24, Edmund Burke, *Reflections on the Revolution in France*; Vol. 40, *English Poetry* 1; Vol. 41, *English Poetry* 2; Vol. 43, *American Historical Documents*. New York: P. F. Collier & Son, 1910.

Fitzhugh, George. *Cannibals All! or Slaves Without Masters*. Richmond: 1857.

Fleming, Walter Lynwood, ed. *Documentary History of Reconstruction: Political, Military, Social, Religious, Educational and Industrial, 1865 to 1906*. 2 vols. Cleveland: Arthur H. Clark Co., 1906.

---. *The Sequel of Appomattox: A Chronicle of the Reunion of the*

States. Textbook Edition. The Chronicles of America Series. Ed. Allen Johnson. Gerhard R. Lomer and Charles W. Jefferys, assistant editors. New Haven: Yale UP, 1919.

Gordon, Gen. John B. *Reminiscences of the Civil War*. New York: Charles Scribner's Sons, 1904.

Grayson, William J. *The Hireling and the Slave, Chicora, and Other Poems*. Charleston: McCarter & Co., 1856.

Harrison, Constance Cary (Mrs. Burton Harrison). *Recollections, Grave and Gay*. New York: Charles Scribner's Sons, 1911.

Hegel, Georg Wilhelm Friedrich. "Introduction to the Logic of History." *The European Philosophers from Descartes to Nietzsche*. Ed. Monroe C. Beardsley. Modern Library Edition. New York: Modern Library – Random House, 1992.

Hoffman, David L. *Stalinist Values: The Cultural Norms of Soviet Modernity, 1917-1941*. Ithaca: Cornell UP, 2003.

Hotchkiss, Maj. Jedediah. *Virginia*. Vol. 3 of *Confederate Military History*, 12 vols. Ed. Gen. Clement A. Evans. Atlanta: Confederate Publishing Co., 1899.

Huxley, Aldous. *Brave New World*. (1932). First Perennial Classics Edition. New York: HarperPerennial – HarperCollins, 1998.

---. *Brave New World Revisited*. (1958). First Harper Perennial Modern Classic Edition. New York: Harper Perennial – HarperCollins, 2006.

Jefferson, Thomas. *The Writings of Thomas Jefferson*. 10 vols. Ed. Paul Leicester Ford. New York: G. P. Putnam's Sons – The Knickerbocker P, 1892-1899. Vol. 10.

Johnson, Robert Underwood and Clarence Clough Buel, eds. *Battles and Leaders of the Civil War*. 4 vols. New York: Century, 1887-8.

Jones, Rev. J. William. *Personal Reminiscences of General Robert E. Lee.* New York: D. Appleton & Co., 1875.

Kennedy, Paul. *The Rise and Fall of the Great Powers: Economic Change and Military Conflict from 1500 to 2000.* First Vintage Books Edition. New York: Vintage – Random House, 1989.

Kettell, Thomas Prentice. *Southern Wealth and Northern Profits.* New York: George W. & John A. Wood, 1860.

Long, Brig. Gen. A. L. *Memoirs of Robert E. Lee.* New York: J. M. Stoddart, 1886.

Malthus, Thomas Robert. *On Population.* (1798). The Modern Library Edition. Reprint of First Edition. Ed. Gertrude Himmelfarb. New York: Random House, 1960.

Marshall, Col. Charles. "Address on the Observance of the Birthday of General R. E. Lee." Delivered at Baltimore, Maryland, 19 Jan 1894. *Southern Historical Society Papers*, 52 vols. Ed. R. A. Brock. Richmond: Southern Historical Society, 1890 -. Vol. 21.

McGuire, Dr. Hunter, and Hon. George L. Christian. *The Confederate Cause and Conduct in the War Between the States.* Richmond: L. H. Jenkins, 1907.

Moore, Frank, ed. *The Rebellion Record; A Diary of American Events, with Documents, Narratives, Illustrative Incidents, poetry, etc.* 11 vols., New York: G. P. Putnam, 1861-63; D. Van Nostrand, 1864-68. Vol. 7.

Neese, George M. *Three Years in the Confederate Horse Artillery.* New York: Neale, 1911.

New Orleans Daily Crescent, Jan. 1, 1861 – June 29, 1861.

Ortega y Gasset, Jose. *Revolt of the Masses.* (1930). Trans. Anon. New York: W. W. Norton & Co., 1993.

Patten, J. Alexander. "Scenes in the Old Dominion. Number Two
– A Tobacco Market." New York *Mercury* 21 (November 5,
1859.) Microfilm. Library of Congress collection.

Pollard, Edward A. *Southern History of the War.* 2 vols. New York:
Charles B. Richardson, 1866.

Pryor, Mrs. Roger A. *Reminiscences of Peace and War.* Revised and
Enlarged Edition. New York: MacMillan, 1905.

Ransome, John Crowe, et al. *I'll Take My Stand: The South and the
Agrarian Tradition.* (1930). Library of Southern Civilization
Series. Ed. Lewis P. Simpson. Baton Rouge: Louisiana State
UP, 1977.

Redpath, James, ed. *Echoes of Harper's Ferry.* Boston: Thayer &
Eldridge, 1860.

Richardson, James D., ed. *A Compilation of the Messages and Papers of the Presidents.* 9 vols. Washington:
Government Printing Office, 1897. Vol. 6.

Richmond Dispatch, July 1860 – Jun 1861.

Richmond Enquirer, July 1, 1859 – Dec. 31, 1859; Jan 1, 1861 – June
29, 1861; July 1, 1862 – Dec 31, 1863.

Richmond Whig, Jan. 1861 – June 1861.

Scott, Maj. John. *Partisan Life with Col. John S. Mosby.* New York:
Harper & Bros., 1867.

Seward, William H. *The Works of William H. Seward.* 5 vols. Ed.
George E Baker. Boston: Houghton, Mifflin & Co., 1853-
1884. Vol. 4.

Simms, William Gilmore. *History of South Carolina.* South
Carolina Edition. Revised by Mrs. Mary C. Simms Oliphant.
Columbia, 1917.

Somers, Robert. *The Southern States since the War 1870-1.* London
and New York: MacMillan and Co., 1871.

Stiles, Maj. Robert. *Four Years Under Marse Robert.* New York: Neale, 1903.

Tarbell, Ida M. *The Life of Abraham Lincoln.* 4 vols. New York: Lincoln History Society, 1902. Vol. 3.

Taylor, Lt. Gen. Richard. *Destruction and Reconstruction: Personal Experiences of the Late War.* New York: D. Appleton & Co., 1879.

Taylor, Lt. Col. Walter H. *Four Years with General Lee.* New York: D. Appleton & Co., 1877.

Tennyson, Alfred, Lord. *The Works of Alfred Lord Tennyson.* (1892). New York and London: MacMillan & Co., 1911.

Tocqueville, Alexis de. *Democracy in America.* 2 vols. (1835). Trans. Henry Reeve. New York: D. Appleton & Co., 1904. Vol. 1.

Traywick, Rev. J. B. "Prison Life at Point Lookout." *Southern Historical Society Papers*, 52 vols. Ed. R. A. Brock. Richmond: Southern Historical Society, 1890 -. Vol. 18.

Vanden, Harry E. and Gary Prevost. *The Politics of Latin America: The Power Game.* Oxford: Oxford UP, 2002.

The Virginia Ordinance of Secession, 17 April 1861. Richmond: Library of Virginia. Papers, Convention of 1861. Access no. 40586.

Von Borcke, Maj. Heros. *Memoirs of the Confederate War for Independence.* 2 vols. Edinburgh: W. Blackwood, 1866.

Waddell, Joseph A. *Annals of Augusta County, Virginia, from 1726 to 1871.* Second Edition. Staunton: C. Russell Caldwell, 1902.

Washington, Booker T. *Up from Slavery: An Autobiography.* New York: A. L. Burt Co., 1900.

White, Leslie A. *The Science of Culture: A Study of Man and*

Civilization. New York: Grove – Farrar, Straus and Cudahy, 1949.

Winsor, Justin, ed. *The Memorial History of Boston, Including Suffolk County, Massachusetts, 1630-1880.* 4 vols. Boston: Ticknor & Co., 1880. Vol. 1.

Wise, John S. *The End of an Era.* New York: Houghton, Mifflin & Co., 1899.

*

ILLUSTRATIONS

View in the "Burnt District," Richmond, Virginia, April 1865 – Library of Congress, Prints & Photographs Division, Civil War Photographs, Reproduction No. LC-USZC4-4593.

Gen. Robert E. Lee in 1863 - Minnis & Cowell (Photographer – Richmond, Virginia) Virginia Historical Society collection – Accession No. 2001.2.107.

Map of Virginia Campaign - from Robert Underwood Johnson and Clarence Clough Buel, eds. *Battles and Leaders of the Civil War.* 4 vols. The Century War Series. New York: Century, 1887-8. 4:164. Virginia Historical Society collection – E470. B333 pg. 164, edited by Ned Bradford.

Prior to Antietam. Rebels Crossing the Potomac. Union Scouts in the Foreground. Drawing by Alfred R. Waud. Library of Congress, Prints & Photographs Division, Civil War Photographs,

Reproduction No. LC-DIG-ppmsca-21427.

Henry A. Wise. Library of Congress, Prints & Photographs Division, Civil War Photographs, Reproduction No. LC-DIG-cw-pb-06502.

Lt. Gen. Thomas J. "Stonewall" Jackson – Library of Congress, Prints & Photographs Division, Civil War Photographs, Reproduction No. LC-DIG-stereo-1s02859.

Maj. Gen. James Ewell Brown "Jeb" Stuart – Library of Congress, Prints & Photographs Division, Civil War Photographs, Reproduction No. LC-DIG-cwpb-07546.

Lt. Gen. Jubal A. Early – Library of Congress, Prints & Photographs Division, Civil War Photographs, Reproduction No. LC-DIG-cwpb-07033.

Gen. Robert E. Lee, C.S.A. - Library of Congress, Prints & Photographs Division, Civil War Photographs, Reproduction No. LC-DIG-cwpb-06237.

EDITOR'S BIOGRAPHY

Author graduated from the Virginia Military Institute in 1967 with a degree in Civil Engineering and a Regular Commission in the US Army. His service included command of an Engineer company in Vietnam, where he received the Bronze Star. After his return, he "wandered in search of the Truth," and ended by making a career as a tugboat captain. During this time he was able to earn a Master of Liberal Arts from the University of Richmond, with an international focus on war and cultural revolution. He currently lives in Richmond, where he studies history and cultural anthropology, and occasionally commutes to Norfolk to serve as a tugboat pilot.